CREATIVITY, IMAGINATION, LOGIC

A

CURRENT TOPICS OF CONTEMPORARY THOUGHT

A series devoted to the publication of original and thought-evoking works on general topics of vital interest to philosophy, science and the humanities

Edited by **Rubin Gotesky** and **Ervin Laszlo**

Volume 1 SYSTEM, STRUCTURE, AND EXPERIENCE. Toward a Scientific Theory of Mind
Ervin Laszlo

Volume 2 VALUE THEORY IN PHILOSOPHY AND SOCIAL SCIENCE. Proceedings of the First and Second Conferences on Value Inquiry
Edited by **Ervin Laszlo** and **James B. Wilbur**

Volume 3 INTEGRATIVE PRINCIPLES OF MODERN THOUGHT
Edited by **Henry Margenau**

Volume 4 HUMAN VALUES AND NATURAL SCIENCE.
Proceedings of the Third Conference on Value Inquiry
Edited by **Ervin Laszlo** and **James B. Wilbur**

Volume 5 HUMAN DIGNITY: THIS CENTURY AND THE NEXT
Edited by **Rubin Gotesky** and **Ervin Laszlo**

Volume 6 HUMAN VALUES AND THE MIND OF MAN.
Proceedings of the Fourth Conference on Value Inquiry
Edited by **Ervin Laszlo** and **James B. Wilbur**

Volume 7 EVOLUTION–REVOLUTION
Edited by **Rubin Gotesky** and **Ervin Laszlo**

Volume 8 FULL CIRCLE: THE MORAL FORCE OF UNIFIED SCIENCE
Edited by **Edward Haskell**

Volume 9 UNITY THROUGH DIVERSITY (in 2 parts)
Edited by **William Gray** and **Nicholas D. Rizzo**

Volume 10 COMMUNICATION: ETHICAL AND MORAL ISSUES
Edited by **Lee Thayer**

Volume 11 SHAPING THE FUTURE—Gaston Berger and the Concept of Prospective
Edited by **Andre Cournand** and **Maurice Levy**

Volume 12 CREATIVITY, IMAGINATION, LOGIC
By Horace M. Kallen

CREATIVITY, IMAGINATION, LOGIC

Meditations for the Eleventh Hour

by

HORACE M. KALLEN

GORDON AND BREACH

New York   London   Paris

39798

Dedication
To ALFRED J. MARROW

Cherished Friend and Fellow-Worker of Many Years
Whose Imagination and Logic Have Brought into Existence
New Forms of Cooperative Liberty
In the Relations between Managements and Men
In Industry, Government and Education,

these meditations are affectionately dedicated

Foreword as Afterthought

LOOKING BACK on this book now that I have finished it and read the whole of what I have written, I find an unexpected continuity. The meditations came discontinuously. Writing them down had been a succession of utterances; to my feeling indeed, happenings at different times in different places at different hours of the day and night during some three years. They did not come as events of a self-disclosing unity now at last seen clearly and seen whole. Together, they had at first sight looked to me as Goethe is reported to have said his *Faust* looked to him; it begins and it ends and has no unity. But looking again, I do experience a unity, not the structured unity built up by the logic of a systematic treatise but the unity of intermittent unification generated by the confluence, next to next, of waves of consciousness. In this, what comes next does not come out of what has gone before, but comes into it out of elsewhere or out of nothing. The future enters the past, becomes a part of it and so changes it. We might rightly say that the present is the past being changed by the future.

And the wholeness of this book seems to me such a specific and singular presence. The meditations which it discloses were transactions—amid the changes and chances of mankind's unceasing struggles, generation by generation, to stay alive and not die—between my alteringly philosophic faith and their multiple reimagings of Homo sapiens, his nature, his powers as he defends his identity in a milieu into which he happens generation by generation to be born, and out of which they willy nilly die. Die no less surely after they have remade their milieu into forms most suited to confirm their hopes and allay their fears. In this man-made world of civilization and culture no less than the world they happen in, their existence and destiny are, in common with all else that lives, to struggle, to keep on struggling not to die. Their imagings are portrayals in sapient Homo's singular medium, the Word, which his unusual powers of creativity, imagination and logic (reason as wordings) produce as creeds and codes wherewith death shall be overcome—if not with an Afterlife in an Afterworld, then with the sapiency which accepts and expects it, but lives on heedless of it.

The newer philosophic portraits may, indeed do, in some respects repeat the older ones. But they diverge from them as the discoveries, the inven-

vii

tions, the creations we call modern, post-modern, even futurist, diverge from the works and ways of the earlier generations. The divergents go by different names. Prevailing among them are what has come to be generalized as scientism with its positiveness and logicality, phenomenology, existentialism, communism and nazism, and humanism. Each has had or still has its prophets, some its priests, to preach and teach its doctrine and discipline as alone the whole truth about man, his world and his destiny of immortal life or immortal death. Each has been or is a vision of living man's future as the best possible or the worst possible. Each has been taught as a counsel about how to realize the first and make the best of the last.

Much in my meditations came as commentary and appraisal of one or another of those philosophic images of man, his world and the give-and-take between them, and of the portraitists who created them, now or in earlier ages. When, finally I read them beginning to end, I felt I was reading a last confession of my own philosophic faith confronting alternatives new and old, and in serenity without illusion cheerfully struggling to keep on struggling.

The word with which to end this *Afterthought* cannot but be a word of thanks from the heart for the careful reading and checking of my mostly illegible script, to my cousin, the late Phyllis Grossberg; to my friendly critic the sometime Editor of *Dimensions*, Myrna Pollak, now in Israel; to that ever present help with troublesome copy problems, Dr. Alfred Marrow's secretary, Bea Pelzer. I salute them for their patience, their art and their workmanship. To my friends and fellow workers, Milton Konvitz and J. M. Kaplan, and to Leighton Rosenthal and Charlotte Kramer, son and daughter of my cherished comrade the late Samuel Rosenthal, I am indebted for unfailing interest, encouragement, support and understanding. I bid them *l'chayim, b'herut, b'simcha ub'shalom.*

HORACE M. KALLEN

Contents

Foreword as Afterthought vii

Book I

Section

1 Ex Nihilo 1
2 Mythologies, Other Interpretations and Rationalizations 9
3 Creativity, Evolution and Creative Man . . . 24
4 Creativity, Death, Nothingness 47
5 The Genius and His Inspiration 60
6 Imagination and Image-Making 78
7 Imagination, *Mimesis*, in the Struggle for Survival . . 82
8 Existence as Value: Culture 93
9 Original and Image: Truth 96
10 Figures and Configurations in Philosophic Images . . 101
11 The Image as Dream 109
12 Image, Learning, Myth as Survival-Values . . . 114
13 Back to the Word and the Name 122
14 The Logos of Language 129
15 Pursuit of Precision, Hunger for Certainty . . . 139
16 Precision, Certainty, and the Rhetoric Art . . . 150
17 The Rhetoric of Science 155

Book II

REPRISE: CREATIVITY, IMAGINATION, LOGIC
AND THE SOCIETY OF FREE MEN

18 The Time of Our Lives as We Live Them Out . . . 163
19 Power, Authority and the Price of Peace . . . 166
20 How Intelligence and Intellect Serve Survival, and Fail to 174
21 Some Philosophic Images of the Free Man . . . 183
22 The Free Man's Free Society 189

23　　Survival as Immortality, Immortality as Experience　　.　　197
24　　Philosophic Images of Value and Existence as Optimism,
　　　Pessimism, Meliorism　　.　　　.　　　.　　　.　　　.　　　.　　204

BOOK I

Ex Nihilo

FRIENDS MEETING soon or late ask each other, "What's new?"—Strangers, being strangers, don't. They are instant news to one another, attractive or repellant. Our hunger for news is as original as our hunger for food or love. and as demanding. Boredom is starvation. It starts going uncountable deviations from established ways of personal habit and interpersonal folkways and mores. To escape it the individual sets off in new directions, toward different and unknown goals. Curiosity about first beginnings and subsequent mutations keeps infiltrating and subverting a nature over-whelmingly repetitive and reproductive, alike as man's arts and crafts and sciences and techniques. The *first* editions, the unrepeatable and un-reproduceable, the original and unique *firstnesses* which alone can be one and only one, gain a scarcity-value which establishes them so incomparably more precious than the repetitions of their identities, by whatever means. Those to whom the firsts of any kind are believed to be due are esteemed as creators, as inventors, as discoverers. They are believed to be specially endowed, to be originators, first causes, innovators who bring news into the same old world ever repeating itself. They are seen as a different kind from the producers, the manufacturers and all other makers—the kind whose *ne plus ultra* the theologians would tell us is God.

So television companies make a distinction in the "credits" they give for a play or a spectacle. They announce that it was "created by" so-and-so, and "produced" by such and such. If they describe a show as a "pro-duction" the difference gets blurred. At some point in preparing a "creation" for the public performance it gets absorbed by the "production." If no replica of the original survives, then to discover what it had been before it was absorbed, to discover how production changed it and to make clear its identity within the producer's product, becomes tantamount to an adventure in detection. In Academia this is called research, be it authentic or inauthentic. The creator's creation has been taken by the producer for a stuff to remold, to use, to use up. In the process of pro-duction, it has served as his matter and means, not as his design and mold. And his use of it may, on occasion, qualify him as more truly a creator than its creator. Nevertheless, "created by" is an honorable mention, "produced by" is not. Our culture holds "creator" and "creation"

1

in higher regard than "producer" and "production" or "product". Even at its most sophisticated—with all the disillusion of psychoanalysis and the other new psychologies to draw on—the critical spirit is disposed to esteem the "creator" an inspired man of genius, one of nature's originals, whom an elder generation might count like unto God, and the true, the necessary cause of the producer's productions. At best productions can be imitations only, distorting reproductions of the creator's creations. The latter are the design to which the former gives body, the spirit which it merely incarnates, making it flesh and setting it to walk upon the stage. At best, production is only materialization.

Not uncommonly, materializations disclose themselves to be, instead of a fitting of the matter to the spirit, a fitting of the spirit to the matter—a fitting which changes the spirit's intent and remolds its form. But this does not detract from the esteem in which the creator is held. On occasion, such an inversion may even enlarge and heighten esteem—the more so, perhaps, since the creator identified by "created by" is not the director, nor the actor, nor the scene painter, nor the photographers, nor any other of the assembly of engineers, craftsmen and practitioners of diverse arts who together participate in the making of the television. "Created by" refers only to thinkers and writers. Since the Renaissance the practice has spread of including practitioners of the graphic, the plastic and the musical arts among the creators, and the trend is growing to join men of science to men of art. But the first to be assigned this likeness to the gods were the poets—the men who make with words, words they chant, words they speak, words they write. *In the beginning was the Word*: and it was with the power of the word that the poet could bring news—visions of things without precedent, things which, regardless of what relations they might have to things already there, could not be attributed to those as effects of which these are the cause. The poet's words disclose ineffable newcomers among the old things. The primary cause of the words is the poet himself. His material is the creation of his own psyche; he creates it *ex nihilo*.

It was, I believe, the eighteenth century poet and critic, John Dryden, who made fashionable the notion that an authentic poet's ways with words were the ways of a creator, that he create poetry *ex nihilo*. There had been suggestions of the same sort before Dryden's day, and they have come in various contexts since. But until Dryden, and for many generations after his, the poetic art was conceived as the Greek *paidea* had conceived it— not purely creation, not creation *ex nihilo*, but re-creation, that is, *mimesis*, primary and original insofar as man *re*-presents nature, but derivative, only secondary, when he imitates the words and works of man. Pure creativity, the power to originate utterly, to create matter and medium as

well as form, to create *ex nihilo*, was a notion that had become alien to
Greek life and thought even as the notion of power belonging to God
alone had become alien to their thinking. Aeschylos happens to ascribe
such power to Zeus in *The Suppliants*: "He speaks and it is done. He
hastens to execute whatever his counselling mind conceives." But the
ascription is only poetry to classical antiquity. All art, all thought was
mimesis: art and thought imitate either the creator's uncreated self by the
creation of his not-self; by the creation of the moving things which he, the
forever unmoved mover, moves; or they imitate the creature of the
creator, *re*-presenting or *re*-producing other creatures.

The god who can command that there be news even in heaven is no god
in the Graeco-Roman pantheon. Nor is he, at first, the one and only God,
the Jehovah of the Israelites. The divine makers of the Hellenic cosmos
and the Hebraic universe are first, alike workers on a material without
beginning and without end. The Hebrew words for it are *Tehom, Tohu-
Bohu*. They signify formless void, darkness, waters over which, Genesis
tells, the breath of the Lord blows or his spirit hovers and speaks the words
with which he causes the world we know as nature to exist.[1]* God says,
and light pierces the darkness, the formless shapes into the forms we
experience and explore, the void is changed into a diversified fullness.
Then God says: let us make man in our image, after our likeness. He
molds Adam, a figure of earth, breathes his own spirit into his handiwork
and gives it dominion over the earth and all that dwell thereon including
Eve, the female shaped from Adam's rib. It is not clear that for Jehovah,
the creator in Genesis, chaos is not the coeval Other, no less eternal than
himself. But it is clear that the Word is not coeval, that it comes into
existence only when and as God speaks it, that it is the mold and instrument with which he informs the uncreated formlessness and creates the
world which the Old Testament purports to account for. And Adam,
being a man like God, bestows upon the animal inhabitants of Eden, with
words of his own that name them, the identities which transform their
anonymity.

The Word would seem to have had similar importance among the
Greeks, although the word's role in creation seems a much later attribution.
The tale is Hesiod's. Of the nine daughters of the Titan Mnemosyne
(Memory): one is the Muse of eloquence, three preside over poetry, one
over tragedy, one over comedy, one over history, one over the dance, and
one over astronomy. The nine signalize the religio-cultural configuration
of the Hellenic heritage. Perhaps there is no Muse of music because music
accompanies the verbal arts and comes broadly as the diversified form of

*Numbered notes are collected at the end of each section.

verbal utterance. Songs without words appear late in the history of music, as do songs without actions.

It is not easy to decide which came first—the idea that the word is function of the act or the thing, or that thing and act are functions of the word. Deaf-mutes also make sounds as they carry on the struggles to keep on struggling which is man's existence. Hearing and speaking mankind regularly take the sounds they make, of which speech is but a part, for both power *over* and signs and symbols *of* the succession of experience in which they figure—for revelations of the struggle, of its events, its occasions and its conditions. Like the animals, we make them the meanings of one another unaware that we do so. When writing happens to supplement chanting and speaking and preserves their meanings in less perishable forms, its shapes and modes figure in their turn as events and things and occasions, to be in their turn signified with still other signs and symbols that thus serve us as the meanings of the meanings—as meanings thereby thrice removed from the struggles which initiated them. Next, we find ourselves requiring meanings for those meanings, then for the meanings of the meanings; and we set them up, meaning after meaning after meaning. We keep assembling dictionaries of meanings until the feeling which Aristotle called *ananké steinai* stops us for the nonce. We call the stoppages universals, that is, meanings of meanings of meanings always and everywhere the same. Then, soon or late, we resume again, dictionary after dictionary, multiplying and diversifying meanings. [2]

But there is no principle which ordains when or whereat we should experience this will-to-stop which arrests the unlimited formation of meanings, arrests it as the struggler's decisions regarding the survival-value of the process in struggling. For the long run, the stops figure as only way-stations, not terminals. The record of the ways of our minds with meanings is one of ongoing passage from a meaning to a meaning of a meaning of a meaning, each more spiritual, more sheerly the Word. We not only contain experience with language; we thin experience with language. And then we thin language with grammar, grammar with logic, logic with mathematics, mathematics with symbolic logic. Like Pythagoras, like Plato, we labor to prove that the last is the creative in the first. But from first to last, there works the Word. And the more we envisage the Word as power and as substance the more its relevance to the immediate and concrete gets thinned into signifying, like *mana*, everything in general and nothing in particular. This ultimate abstraction is felt to guarantee the success of our struggles to keep on struggling; it insures the survival of our values as the value of our survival. It lifts the Word to omnipotence.

We articulate the omnipotence as the unchanging laws of nature which the scientists are purported to seek and the eternal revelations of God which theologians are used to proclaim. As items of the successions of meanings they figure as arrests of activity and movement, as compenetrative identifications of centrifugal heterogeneities. Some words for the arrests are Being, Eternity, Unity, Universality, Absolute—all signalizing, each in its mode, a collapse of manifold concrete heterogeneous processes into a single, unaltering instancy. This collapse is presented as the consummation of meaning, the meaning *ne plus ultra*, at which we stop because to us there no longer is, there cannot be, any meaning "beyond." As the terminal meaning it is the only one imperishably "real"; thus the meaning is the meaning which all other meanings willy-nilly mean. In the light of it, our existence of struggle and the changes and chances which engender our meanings are merely appearances. Those of us who have won to this ultimacy are thereby freed to live on like our terminal meaning, unchangingly at peace, always and everywhere the same.

Alas, that mankind's histories do not record one and only one ultimate meaning of meaning! Alas, that the record is of a multitude of ultimates; that it tells how the true believers of each ultimate creed struggle with one another over which alone shall be taken for the true one, while still others come up with new ones. The record discloses no meaning that comes to ultimacy, unless it happens that men's struggles to keep on struggling, which created the meanings men struggle over, are their own ultimates. Ultimacy is no less a temporary stop in the succession of meanings than any other. It differs from the others; it differs in that the minds, which attribute their stopping at this ultimacy not to themselves but to it, crave to prolong their stop. They would cling to the Word which they feel is their salvation and resist separating from it. Straining to preserve it unchanged, they change its function in their struggles for survival; they would keep it the instrument it naturally is, but they make of it an idol as well. They apothesize their instrument. Like Bertrand Russell avowing his Pythagoreanism, they join the generations of Platonizers who keep remaking the words of struggling man into the laws of an unchanging nature or the Word of an unstruggling God—usually the last Word is said to have been "in the beginning," to have been with God, and to have become flesh and to be walking on earth.

The survival-value of the Word is its relation to beginning; that is to the coming or making of the *new*. The human function of the Always-and-Everywhere-Same is to provide safety and certainty regarding the comings and goings and enjoyment of the Different. The values of actually ultimate concerns are the new and the means to bring the new.

Unlike the Hebrews, the Greeks did not begin their tales of creation with this commitment to the Word as power. Although their philosophers were the first to propose the idea, to develop and elaborate it by abstracting grammar from language, logic from grammar and by reifying logic's functions as "laws of thought," they were later than the Hebrews in identifying the Word with creativity and still later in conceiving creativity as absolute, as the sheer act of peopling non-being with all sorts and conditions of beings. Plato maybe hints at some such miracle in the *Timaeus*; but even his aficionados among the cognoscenti are unsure that this is what he meant. So far as I am aware *creatio ex nihilo* as a philosophic conception is a residue from Judean Philo's endeavor to reconcile Plato and the Hebrew prophets. Much later, Aristotlelianizing theologians like Thomas Aquinas held that the God-Creator could be only a revelation to faith; as Paul averred in his Epistle to the Hebrews: "that the worlds have been created by the Word of God so that what is seen hath not been made out of things which do appear." For the God-eternal, reason required an equally uncreated Universe.

The poets who have left us the earliest Greek stories of creation no more intend sheer creativity than the Hebrew ones. They describe creation as a making over of a material already at hand—if without form, creation informs it; if with form, creation transforms it, much as Jehovah transformed the dust of the earth when he created Adam. It is believed that Hesiod's *Theogony* identified for the Greeks their own equivalent of the Hebrews' *Tohu-Bohu*—that which John Milton elaborated as "vast immeasurable abyss, all dark and waste and wild and outrageous as the sea." The Greek word for it is *Chaos*. Within Chaos—Aristophanes tells this—Love, hatched from a "wind-born" egg, without rhyme or reason created Light and the day which is a function of Light. Love also caused Earth and Heaven to be—Earth, the goddess Gaea; Heaven, the god Ouranos. Gaea and Ouranos become the parents of the Titans, among them Chronos and Rhea, brother and sister. Zeus, the sixth son of Chronos and Rhea, rebels and with the help of another Titan, Prometheus, overcomes his father. But Zeus in his turn must face Titanic rebellion after Titanic rebellion. With his thunderbolts he conquers even Typhon, even the Giants. And now the undisputed reign of Zeus begins—undisputed but not everlasting. For Zeus, too, is doomed to overthrow. Prometheus knows when and by whom, but refuses to tell. He had been the heavenly father's ally and champion. But with the aid of his brother Epimethus he had brought his creature a torch alight with the living fire of the sun of heaven, and launched it on its career of Homo *sap*.[3]

Or, alternatively, the Olympians themselves made man, molding his figure in various metals, from gold to bronze, and so establishing the sorts and conditions of their creations. But not the female of the species. It was Zeus alone who created her—and not, like Jehovah, from a concern for the male's loneliness, but from anger at Prometheus' care for man. Jove's creation was that evil loveliness, Pandora. The Olympians presented her with a locked box and warned her that it was not to be opened. But like Eve she was eager to know. As Eve's disobedience brought "death into the world and all our woe," Pandora's brought God's punishment for disobedience. Pandora opened the forbidden box and let loose all the ills that flesh is heir to. Like Eve, she brought news, bad news, newly liberated, not newly created.

NOTES

1. In the Brahmin-Vedic tradition, matter, void or chaos do not seem to figure. The consequential center seems to be the experiences of breathing—the breath rather than the blood is the life, and its exercise and control, ultimately *Yoga*, is the rite and rote leading to ultimate insight, the identification with Brahma. In the mythology, the triune godhead consists of Brahma, the creator, Vishnu the preserver, Siva the destroyer, the three personifications of the phases of Becoming which pervade all our existence. Significantly, Sanskrit philologists suggest that Brahma is a variation on the root *brih, bahr*, which is translatable as *mighty, great, thick*, and also *breath*. The ultimate Brahma is the controller of breath—the *jnana yogin* who has come to shape his breath in mantrams. Mantrams are vocalizations of breath which serve the true believer as tools. Their purest, simplest/formation is the sacred syllable *Om, Aum or Hum*—the passing information of the breath whose own still creativity gives and takes the life of all things and is different from everything.

2. A man's voice is at once the accompaniment and expression of his experience, and as definitive of his identity as his thumb-print. It utters the ups and downs of his days and nights—bespeaks his health, his sickness, his depressions, his exaltations, his hopes, his fears, his certainties, his agressions, his submissions. A man's voice tells all his changes of mood and stance in his life-long struggle with the world around him. The changes generate or evoke the words which impattern the voice's altering pitch and tempo, and the words endow the man's experience with the meanings which the dictionaries preserve. Giving voice, the man discloses a condition an attitude and an action which we signify by such sounds as *shout, whisper, whine, scream, murmur, mutter, sing, hum, coo, sigh, sob, shrill, cry, laugh*, and so on. Sounds, alike as sheer noise and as word-forms, endow sights with a real presence, an inward dynamic they otherwise lack; they add force to the word-forms. As shaped into words, as language, sounds incarnate most of what the word "spirit" denotes: They signify the human difference, the humanity of mankind. All animals produce sounds as long as they live; birds even possess a voice-organ singular to their kind, the syrinx, which men lack. The animal function of the human "vocal chords" is simply to let air in and out and to keep dust and other matter from getting into the lungs. Their human function is not primarily physiological; it is, to help shape sounds into words, to make

language. For man as man, it is literally true that in the beginning was the Word. It could not but follow that the Word was also in the beginning of man's world, that the Word was God, or that it was with God and became flesh and dwelt on earth.

3. Significantly, all the Olympians have parents. No sexual genesis is attributed to Jehovah and his heavenly hosts.

Mythologies, Other Interpretations and Rationalizations

HISTORIANS OF culture, anthropologists concerned with faiths and works of more "primitive" people than their own, have assembled many parallels to the Hebrew and Greek tales of creation. Each of the tales features its own variations within the impressive repetition of identicals. This had led speculators like Carl Jung to treat them as individuations of an identical insight, the same for every family of mankind. We are told they concern the origins of things, the weathers of existence—concern their beginnings, their behaviors and the means and ends of their management by humans, collectively and individually. Sometimes we are also told that such managements are forms of the human struggle to live on and never die. Their manifold styles seem to give shapes to what John Ruskin once called "the pathetic fallacy," what in Martin Buber's idiom would be the "thouing" of an *It's* circumambience—that is, treating all in our experience which is not human as if it were human. Thereby existence is rendered a drama or epic in which the heavenly bodies, the earth, its land and waters, its plants and animals are all embodied spirits, divine and non-divine, whose passions and purposes, like the passions and purposes of men and women and children, shape the course of events even as fate and fortune shape it.

We call most such portrayals of existence mythologies—literally words that are spoken, tales that are told. Carrying a tradition which starts with the earliest philosophers and which, after Plato, the Stoics, and Philo Judaeus, has dominated the religious outlook of the western world, we take the mythologies for allegories of the forces and forms of nature and the hopes and fears of men. We interpret their passions and plots as transvaluings of an alien and unfriendly world into a homelike dwelling place. We tend to believe that this is done by means of a natural, spontaneous self-deception, a childlike make-believe which, truly believed and acted on, must needs endanger survival and work destruction. Mythologies are declared pathetic fallacies or vital lies invested with survival-values which they cannot effect unless freed from their masks of fallacy and lie, unless the truth within the make-believe is disclosed. So we have come to

9

call any undisguised fiction used to clarify or illuminate some issue of value or existence and presented as such, a fable like Aesop's or a parable like Jesus', but we call fictions presented as truths disguised, myths.

This is a new use of myth, one which the original myth-makers could not have accepted even if they had grasped it. To them, their myths were no more fictions than their dreams, and their dreams than their waking realities. Their world was a world of persons human and non-human and their struggle to continue alive in it was an ongoing drama. Creation was an every day event; miracle and magic were recurrent modes of it, human and divine. The natural and the supernatural were functions of one another, distinguished by their visibility more than by their behavior. That existence was an expression of value, was value embodied, seemed self-evident. Even such divinities as were not the inward powers of natural processes—for example, Athena or Ares or Hermes who were said to be wisdom, war and communication personified—figured as real individuals with human passions and purposes and powers heightened and more instant and more insistently arbitrary. Not less so was the sun-god, Phoebus Apollo, leader of the Muses and genius of music; the moon-goddess Artemis, huntress and patron of chastity, and so on. In the gods, natural powers and human propensities are confluent and somewhat resonant of each other; in the cant of our times, none is an *It*, each is a *Thou* of the other's *I*. For the first mythmakers, man could not but be the measure of all things, of those that are, that they are; of those that are not, that they are not. The tales of the gods and the words of their roles in man's survival were made according to this measure, the scale of which was instinctively graded to hope of life and fear of death as in fact life was changefully lived and death suffered. Poets—say Homer, Hesiod and Pindar—perhaps chanted the changing myths in the more or less fixed forms we now read and know.

To posterity, the written chants first became sacred books to be handed on by generation to generation. Then they became subject to doubt, and to disbelief that the tales could be true tales, telling it "like it was." A time comes when the epigons cease to take the whole man for the measure of all things; when they separate existence from value and value from value. It is the time when the generations become concerned over the nature and power of words, over meaning and the meaning of meaning. It is the time of the philosophers; of Heracleitus, of Cratylus, of Socrates, of Protagoras and of Plato—outstandingly of Plato. The philosophers become more and more suspicious of existence and charge it with deception. They exalt certain values as the truly good. They degrade certain others as the truly evil. They charge gods with the evils they condemn—long after,

Nietzsche reversed this reversal. Finally, we find the philosophers demonstrating a dual world—a real one, where existence is value and value existence, and an unreal one which is but a passing shadow, a changeful distorting reflection of the real one, to which it owes whatever meaning it can intend. The world we struggle to live in from birth to death is this unreal world of change and images and distortions and reflections. It is the world that the misleading, the deceiving, mythmakers describe and explain. At best it can be but an unhappy, an unsuccessful imitation of an imitation of the real one, can be but a sign and symbol of the real one. At best, our world of the dying can be but a meaning of the undying reality which so stirs the soul as to turn her struggle not to die into a quest after the perfect world of the Eternal Ideas, the world which is always and everywhere the same. This world is the Logos, that ineffable hierarchy of perfections whose togetherness is the Idea of the Good. It is the world-soul which inspirits the shadowy passing world of our sojourn with whatever substantial reality it has.

First the Pythagoreans, and after them Plato, most of all Plato, spurn the web of meanings out of which the daily experience of creation gets refined into an idea of creativity and the mythus of the people get translated from matter-of-fact drama of the beginning of things into symbols and allegories of the hidden Logos from which the world that we live our lives in depends. Those whose quest attains to it envision that World Soul. They contemplate an arithmetico-geometrical hierarchy, a system wherein creativity nevertheless has a place and a role—has both regardless whether it comes into them like the modern astronomer's Big Bang, *ex-nihilo*, or like an explication of an implication, or like a reproduction or representation of some unoriginated original form, or like absolute origination. The fiction, the fable, the parable, the allegory, the myth—whether disguised or undisguised deceptions or revelations—are creations. Each, as it happens, evokes a challenge. What is *new* about it? And is novelty, if any, merely a change of place or of relations, or is it an insurgence of an unprecedented and unpredictable *quale*, a consequence not to be accounted for by any antecedent, an authentic creation whether by God or man— *ex nihilo*?

Plato met the challenge, for the last time, in the Timaeus. There is the usual debate among the cognoscenti as to what the old philosopher meant —was he, indeed, a Platonist? And whether he meant what he said or was only having fun with meanings. But this debate does not affect the decision about the nature and origin of newness. The question had tittivated Plato most of the long, less than serene, semi-itinerant enterprise that was his life; the Timaeus is said to have come toward the end of it. Plato knew first and last what he wanted. He wanted a snug harbor of certainty and safety into which he could pilot the ship of state. He had early discovered that the world he had been born into and was making his life in, did not and could not provide such a harbor. He early learned that surviving in this world required the vigilance of courage and the skills of wisdom. He came to persuade himself, and to believe, that these could best be achieved and nourished by the vision of an Otherworld that is both the ground and the goal of this ever-changing, ever-dangerous Here-and-Now. He came to believe that so utterly faithful a world could be neither in space nor in time, but it must needs be one actively but unchangingly universal and eternal Good, supporting the identities of the archetypal forms that it holds together in harmony. If Being *is*, this is *what* and *how* Being is.

Yet neither as this *what* and *how* can Being, by itself alone, account for the stream of our day-to-day existence. To do that it requires encounter with an Other, an opposite as changeful as Being itself is unchanging, a mobility that it can somehow arrest and contain and mold via the Ideas, informing it in accord with these eternal forms. Plato calls this Other, Non-being; he also calls it by more concrete names: matter, place, mother, foster-mother, nurse. As matter, he endows it with the elemental "forms" of earth, water, air and fire, and models them together in a "receptacle," a limited place within the eternal boundlessness of Non-being. It is the place of creation, where the ever formless Otherness is penetrated and informed by the always Same, by the eternal Forms or Ideas.

Now, creation could be the forms only by themselves eternally containing the formless in forms. Or else it could be the eternal outflow of the good God's eternal spirit, and thus be the Logos framing the Cosmos within the Chaos. Whatever the role assigned the Ideas—that of originals, eternal, universal and sovereign, or that of God's spirit or Logos—they are, as God is, uncreated Being. The forms whose configuration is the Cosmos which God or Being informs Non-being with, cannot be sovereign: they must be dependent; they cannot be always and everywhere the same, they must be different, at least, by their times and places. Since they are not creators but creations, they cannot be originals. All of them have beginnings—they were not, and then they were. And most of them have ends; sooner or later they will not be. Also, the souls of men are creations, they have a beginning, even though they have been created immortal and have no end. When men are said to create, they only imitate other creations which themselves are but imitations, never originals.

And this is the case if also the eternal Logos should somehow not serve as both the object of God's eternal contemplation and the power-pattern of his always-and-everywhere Sameness. This is also the case if the Logos should exist separately, a Demiurge everlastingly fulfilling the Eternal's providence. The Demiurge (this Greek word first signified "one who works with people"; the English for it might be interchangeably *chief craftsman, artisan, artificer*) is the intelligence which fashions anarchic matter into our better-ordered cosmos. He is the arch-imitator, the image-maker, imaging in primordially imageless and unimageable matter the perfect structure of the uncreated original, imaging the eternal and universal archetypes, whether or not God-given. The image—this cosmos which we enter at birth and leave at death—is image, because it is *made* existence, derivative and secondary, a mere creation; because, logically, it is an entity with a beginning even though without an end, immortal but not eternal, since the eternal neither starts nor stops but ever is, a total present.

There are those who argue, plausibly enough, that Demiurge and God must be interchangeable terms. Their being such would not affect the judgment that "to create" is merely to repeat, to image an original, or to change the places or relations of otherwise unchanged originals, or simply to cause originals, the absolutely new, to exist. Creativity could distinguish each such act. All of them make news, even if the novelty of an original, or of a different place or different relations for originals, or of an image of an original, or of an image of an image, is experienced as an incommensurably singular novelty. Nor need the belief that God and Demiurge are two names for one identity mean a significant divergence among answers to the concurrently terminal question: *Why creation at all, of any kind?* Or, for the fun of it, *Why not?* The answer to both is an ineffable *Because*; that is, the ultimacy of both is transient, it is a happening without rhyme or reason.

In Plato's configuration of man and nature and destiny, the world of transient appearances amid which he wove his mortal history could be original in no respect. He imagined it a most imperfect copy of a world divinely perfect, or else a weak, a hopeless, reflection of a divinely perfect vision he aspired to win to for himself. But his aspiration was almost all reach without grasp. Some vestige whereby it could be a poor likeness of the original, a poor likeness, yet a likeness which passes on the whole but in fragmented detail like the succession of the seasons, like the cycles of life and death, like the motions of the stars—from form to form, yet attains consummation in none. For at consummation, existence would leave time for eternity, image would consume itself in reality, change die into changelessness. Time is but eternity's creature, its moving image; time is eternity's compenetration with elusiveness, with fragmented mobility, into a distortion of the timeless originals which together are the immortal life of time. If the mythologies speak more intimately the human sense of the world that mankind strains and strives to keep on straining and striving in, they speak less truly than their interpreters. Even so, an image mostly blemish is, in God's sight, better than no image at all.

That uncreated, utterly unjealous Goodness which is God-universal-and-eternal, multiplies itself. By impressing its image, it represents itself, reflects itself on the elusive blankness of the sheer matter which is as uncreated and as universal as the God divine. It is of God's essence, of the *Goodness's* goodness, to mirror himself in the unformed mobility of matter, to fill it, and by filling, contain it in the multitudinous reflections of the divine goodness. The reflections are all momentary, all distorted and deceptive, yet all informing the formless with intelligible forms, as the sunlight informs the black emptiness of night and the patterned plenteousness of day and renders darkness visible. Creation is God, creation is likewise God's idea, reflecting itself on the Void, thereby instituting time, delineating boundaries however transient, shaping the plastic receptacle in unbounded and unboundable space. Creation is God's self-representation. Creation is the everlasting self-mimesis of Grace eternal. God is the eternal and universal Narcissus enjoying his own reflection in all things. What other cause or ground or goal of creation can there be? What else save the overflowing generosity of Goodness would fashion upon the co-eternal flux a Cosmos in its own image? And if the human father be not the prototype of the Father divine, why else did Timaeus identify this flux by such words as *mother, foster-mother, nurse?* The analogy of creation to begetting strikes one in the face. God-above is the male, the active, the dominating power. His eternal ideas are his patterning seed, *Eidoi spermatikoi.* The receptacle shaped by the Ideas of Ether, Air, Water, and Earth into a place bound in space is the plastic female and the Cosmos is the image of God which she receives.

However, creation, so conceived and imaged would, no more than any other of Plato's versions of it, comes *ex nihilo.* If Plato suggests any such a free event, it is because Being's ingress into Non-being, Eternity's overcoming of change, Form's bounding of unbound formlessness, is an event ineffable. It happens, and we accept the happening. We take it without reflection for the ground on which we may then more or less successfully construct our explanations of all following events, but which is itself groundless. We sometimes call the groundless event First Cause, a synonym for God; other times we call it miracle, chance coming, contingency. But whatever we call it, we perceive it as an alien force intruding an established order, defying the order's laws and breaking their rule. Or else we perceive it as in itself creation, a unique event without precedent, a creation *ex nihilo,* turning existence in new directions, towards new forms with new consequences. We might say it is perceived as the irrational origination of originality.

By and large, the Hellenic paidea averted from irrationality. The diverse interpretations of value and existence that it comprehends—even the Heracleitan—only define, defend and vindicate the rational and ex-communicate the irrational. They crown the rational with both earthly and heavenly glory. They enthrone it as the highest excellence of *genus humanum,* that whereby we are unlike the animals and like the truly divine. Not so the culture of the Hebrews. Charmed and converted by Hellenism as were those Judeans who came to know its paidea, they did not underestimate the irrational, nor ever take rationalism without reservations. Rationalism never quite offset their awareness of the power of evil, their remembrance of how perilous, how ominously recurrent were irruptions of alien and arbitrary force into their own lives, into the lives of their neighbors, into the whole or creation. Greek rationalism provided no workable counter to experience of disruption and overturn at home and abroad. It only discounted them by declaring them appearance, not reality. The destruction and re-creation of order and rule, so causing old things to perish and new things to exist (except for stirring hopes for a new earth and a new heaven at last, where men might live on at peace and free) are appearances.

Vision of man, his world and his destiny was, in this context, rather a creation of fear and hope than an attainment of understanding. Man, as the Book of Job declares, was born unto trouble as the sparks fly upward; to man, only the fear of the Lord is wisdom and to depart from evil is understanding. True wisdom is God's alone, beyond man's attainment, it is the pattern in which he created the world: "He established it (wisdom) yea, and searched it out." He revealed it to Moses that it might be a rule of life, especially for the children of Israel with whom he chose to make a covenant, binding them forever to believe in it and to obey the rule, promising them in return a land where they could live a life free, safe and more abundant. The epical drama of the people of Israel is the drama of their struggle with God over the intent of their covenant. In the course of it, prophecy figures much less as a prediction than as a monitory response to the fear of the Lord's unpredictable intervention: *Thus saith the Lord,* and the oracle was always: "Depart from present evil, believe in my promise of *future* good." The words of the Lord nowhere assured everlasting Otherworldly salvation from Thisworldly drama of struggle to keep on struggling. The Word but encourages perseverance, but plays on fear and hope to offset knowledge with.

Even without Plato, there was that in the Hellenic vision of man, the world, and man's destiny which could not fail deeply to appeal to the Judeans, as to all peoples who became aware of it. Jews, from their first contact with Greek ways of life and thought became, in varying degrees, Hellenizers. But in Plato's philosophic vision, especially the vision of his maturity and old age, there were utterances which could, without too much modification, be interpreted as renderings or allegories of the Torah of Moses, and vice versa. The consequence was the trend toward identifying the logic of identity of Plato's system of eternal and universal Ideas with the epical drama of the Hebraic revelation. To achieve the identification, a changeable cryptography of meanings was assumed. The saving truths of revelation were taken, even as revelations, still to be *hidden* truths. Every human soul might, like the native of Plato's cave, be too weak to look upon the revealed truth in its effulgent nakedness. For human sight this must first come veiled and dimmed. The Revealer, in his loving-kindness, may not be saying nakedly what he means, or meaning what he says. He delivers himself rather in oracles and allegories which initiates will be able to translate into their meaning for man. God's Word, first spoken, then written, that we call Scripture, is such a deliverance. His Torah is the Logos; the persons, the powers, and the events which Torah tells of, the doctrines it sets forth and the disciplines it institutes are cryptograms for the perfection, for the principles and the forms which the Logos consummates, and through which God ultimately channels his creative powers.

Thus, in sum and first and last, was Hellenic reason used to rationalize and reinforce the ultimately irrational Hebraic revelation. Foremost among the practitioners of the allegorist's art of translating rather unsophisticated Hebraic experientialism into Hellenic rationalism was Philo the Jew of Alexandria. He flourished during the first century of the Christian era. A native of the Jewish community of that Hellenized Egyptian megalopolis, Philo seems to have been educated in the Greek paidea far more profoundly than in the Hebrew Torah, which he learned in Septuagint Greek rather than in the sacred Henrew tongue. Some doubt that he could speak or read Hebrew, or that he had ever seen Jerusalem. But there is no doubt of his commitment to the Torah, or of his utter faith that it was God's authentic Word, spoken to the Jews, not for them alone, but for the salvation and perfection of all mankind. There is no doubt of his deep concern to vindicate the philosophic significance of God's testament against all detractors, all critics, be they polytheist, atheist, agnostic or skeptic. And it happened that one or another of Plato's *Dialogues* could help him most happily to gain this end, inasmuch as they, as well as Scripture itself, could be invoked against all sorts and conditions of critics and dissenters.

Especially, the *Timaeus.* By means of the Timaeus, one could identify what is "The Word of the Lord" in the epical drama of Israel with that which is the Logos in Plato's dialectic. But the Word of the Lord is not the same as the being of the Lord; it is not what God is, but what he creates as speaking; it is not the Timean hierarchy of ideal values, each universal, each the existence which is the value, the value which is the existence, each an eternal moral identity with place and functions due to that value of values—that Idea of the Good which is the ground and goal of them all. Timaeus assigned this Otherworld of essences and principles a locus in relation to the eternally boundless and unboundable Void. Philo contended that there is no such void nor any secondary space or "receptacle" which the Ideas subsist in. He contended that the Word of God, the Logos, is its own space, self-containing and self-contained; that it compenetrates without altering the everlasting diversities of the divine Ideas.

Only, the Word is not God's peer, eternal and universal like him; the Word is only God's first creation, the first-begotten of the Father of all things, the one original and perfectly generic among all God's creatures, the Idea of Ideas. The Word is the "place" which God's creativity has filled with those incorporeal spermatic powers, the Ideas; filled in the same way as a whole may be said to be filled with the parts that together are its wholeness—Word, Idea of Ideas, Demiurge, yet the creature which alone is, next to God, the truly real, since it is not only the thought that God thinks but also the act of thinking which causes it to be. Nevertheless, it is neither an absolutely original, like the act itself, nor an image of the act, but a new being, genuinely Other. For the act of the Eternal, as without end or beginnings, made the Word as a beginning, and can put an end to it, even though it was begun to endure forever. But enduring forever, enduring briefly, beginning, ending, happens as God wills.

Although Adam's rib was the material which God formed into Eve, the *nekevah* or passive receptacle,[1] it is debated whether Philo also believed that the formless *tohu bohu* which the Word informs likewise was an original created by an Act of God. If so, the divine goodness would have created the Non-being so utterly the opposite of the lesser real Being which is the Logos, and thus, God's goodness would have been compromised by Philo as by some of the prophets, through whom God avows himself the creator of evil as well as good. On the face of it Philo seems to have preferred Plato to the prophets. And indeed, could the material used by God-Creator be an eternal Otherness, as absolutely Other than the created world as God himself is absolutely Other? It may be that Philo—and for that matter, Plato—assimilated creation to the experience of the beginning of new life, human and animal. The female figure is receptacle. The male does ultimately mount her and pierce her; to him, she is a passive void, submitting to be filled. Little was known of her true share in the procreative action, as of the male's. On the face of it, she contributes nothing; the known giver is the male, the known receiver, the female. What come to birth is what has been given; it is what the female gives back. And even if its body is a reproduction of the parent body, it is a new soul, with a singularity all its own. It birth brings news to earth and heaven, and is welcomed and celebrated as such; *Unto us a child is born*. As for the Eternal Feminine—her who received it as seed and returned it as an image of God—she but serves the newborn as *mother*, *foster-mother*, *nurse*—the attributes are Plato's which Philo repeats. That God is in almost all cultures also the *Father*, possessed of all the ever-multiplying powers and privileges with which human need and theological imagination endows the All-Father, is a commonplace among the families of mankind.

Verbalizing the relationship as experienced and as perceived brings on a dialectical sequence of meanings. None of these establishes the notion that either the passive receptacle within which the creative act starts the new creature into being, or the unformed material which the act informs, is unbegun and eternal. There is no authentic formlessness. The same act which creates form creates the room which form establishes and encloses. Bodies and the space they fill are created together. Their extension, their form, and their substance are one. Indeed, is not the Almighty *Makom?*

The Hebraic intent would seem to be that the first act of creation creates *ex nihilo*, from no matter in no medium. The Lord *said*, let there be, and there was and is. The act is unconditional; a free act of the divine will *choosing* that the first new being shall be the image-making Word, shall be the universal and everlasting—not eternal—Logos which is to render itself the living law of the living nature it is to create. This must be so if it be true—and it must be—that the good God is also God omnipotent; that there is nothing he cannot do. The designs for a cosmos which he could will into being are beyond counting—each a Logos he can if he chooses actualize into a cosmos. They are, in Leibnitz' language, *compossible*. The one which God has chosen to render actual, the world man lives in, is the one which follows from his absolute and perfect goodness. It is the best of all the possible worlds. What different ground can there be for God's action? Lacking this ground, it makes as little sense that our cosmos should exist as that any alternative to it should not exist. It leaves creation without a ground and without a goal. It transvalues existence into an absurd dark, contingent and futile. That the good God should freely choose saves the value of existence and the existence of value from this abyss of nothingness. His choice is not a limiting of his will but an expression of it—the creation before recorded creation. Of that original, recorded creations could well be imagings, repetitions in a medium distorted by the medium into the imperfect likeness of perfection wherein we struggle to live on and not die. The work of the Word is to function first as the original, the model, of the images; again, as the plan or design of them; and yet again as their architect and instrument—all serving to create the images. Such are the diverse functions of the Logos. It is thus alike the soul of our cosmos, its inward life and rule, and the outer pattern of transcendent perfection which generates this life and which this life should strive to attain in vision and in act, even though it cannot by itself alone.

That it cannot and why it cannot, is evinced by the human condition. Man thinks, even encounters, God, by an analogy with himself, either as a member of a communion or in his utter singularity. The analogy is experienced, usually, in an intuition less than vital. How, indeed, ask Philo and the *periti* of every later cult, can a finite and perishing earthly creature perceive and understand his eternal, his infinite, his omnipotent Creator? We would have to become God in order to understand God, the absolutely free, the perfectly good, the infinitely creative, whose creativity never ceases. God is *absconditus*, ever transcendent, beyond all prediction. For prediction is limitation, and how can the being who is the limitation of everything else, great and small, be itself under limitation? All that our Creator has of his grace revealed to us, is *that* he is, not *what* he is. Whatever else beyond we do become aware of, is not God but the Word of God, the Word which in its essence, in its intrinsic nature, is outside all creation, yet is by God's will also in all created things, endowing them with their identities and containing them. But still, so God has willed, the Word remains in all respects the Logos, within the Father and only in him.

Now, man, God's image, is a microcosm, the sole figure of earth which God made to be like unto himself. If man's mind within is the Thisworldly likeness of the World-mind-without-and-above—of the Logos, that is—man's soul, which is the life of his body, is the push and pull of God's adamic earth, with all its impulsions toward the disorder and irrationality native to its earthliness. As Timaeus tells it and Philo maybe retells it, Everyman's existence is a struggle between his rational soul and his irrational psyche. His rational soul is alien where his irrational psyche is native. In the struggle, the soul's victory is goodness, virtue, wisdom, righteousness; its defeat is signified as impiety, wickedness, sin. Which, victory or defeat, does not follow from the nature of things as, after the

Flood, God had covenanted to maintain the nature of things: "Jehovah said in his heart, I will not again curse the ground any more for man's sake, for that the imagination of man's heart is evil from his youth; neither will I again strike any living thing as I have done. While the earth remaineth, seedtime and harvest, and cold and heat, and summer and winter, and day and night shall not cease" (Gen. VIII, 21, 22). Victory or defeat follows from still another differentia of man-the-unique-image-of-God; victory or defeat follows from man's self-governing will which is free, and as independent of unreason and reason as the executive branch of government in a free society is presumed to be independent of the legislative and judiciary branches. They may advise the executive but may not coerce its actions: as Harry Truman had stencilled on a plaque he kept on his White House desk, "The buck stops here." The will is the place of no return, the spring of decision to speak the Word which renders reason or unreason the shape of events to come. The will is that in man which can choose *not* to obey the laws of nature and of nature's God, and thereby be alone answerable for the consequences. Man's free will is the more truly original part of him, the more Godlike part.

Of God's free will Philo says somewhere that it is his "most peculiar possession and most worthy of his majesty" and that God's providential exercise of this most peculiar and worthy divine attribute is his grace (one could replace "grace" by "luck") which miracles manifest, as also do the various other wondrous helps wherewith man's essentially insufficient will sometimes attains even more than sufficiency. Indeed, grace is manifest in all changes that do not follow from the laws of nature which God chose to establish after the Flood. Nature is God's handiwork and, as Plato held, always and everywhere the same. But nature *can* be changed; nature *is* changed; nature can *also* be destroyed. Not destroyed, however, because of any built-in fatality, not by inner necessity, but by the will of God. The will which freely established nature to endure eternally, can also shatter Nature if it so decide.

Why? What for? Why not? We cannot know. We can only believe. God-Creator is the utterly Other, the ineffably Other, the one and only uncreated Being whom no attribution can qualify, no classification contain, no name identify. What he is, what he does, why he does it our reason cannot reach to. As Franciscan Duns Scotus avers, speaking the Philonic faith: "There is no cause why God's will is willed unless it be that his will is his will." We can only accept what he reveals to us: that he IS, and does what he chooses. The revelation is vouchsafed to us because he made us in his image, and in a remote, a mysterious, a shadowy way, also our will images God's—its freedom, and its creativity, perhaps even *ex nihilo*.

For, miracle of miracles, every man, however other than the utterly Other, is a man like God. We are but images, true, but alone among God's creatures, unique images who are also image-makers, somehow aware, as we live out our live day by day, of the images we make and why and how we make them. Some of them we become aware of with surprise, with feelings of suddenness and awe, perhaps with fear. We can think of no original to compare them with. They are somehow different; new, auto-nomous, originals in themselves. As we grow older they become rarer, but they abound in the experiences of childhood, and they continue to influence our struggles to keep on struggling. They are the critical moments in perhaps the earliest, the most naive and childlike of our experience of creativity. They suggest a trajectory in which events follow not *from* each other, but freely, next-to-next, and each with its own newness, its own surprise—as happens so often in our dreams. The events come, as it were, out of grace, neither effects nor causes. Each evinces its own singularity, its essential *haecceitas* and its own phonal and lingual reverberation. Until the Word is achieved to bring the singularities to union. The Word orchestrates their diversity into an identity taking on and homogenizing their many survival-functions. By orchestrating, it subordinates the diversities into connotative background for the Word's unifying function which, in the most satisfactory use of words, it so often performs.

But for the most part, as we grow up and grow older, the Word is signalized as the meaning of the image or the image as the meaning of the Word. Our appreciation of any as effect or as cause is a function of its role in our immediate experience. We feel drawn to it or averted from it, or first the one and again the other, and vice versa; we are moved to get ever closer to it, to take it into ourselves, or to get farther and farther away from it, to cut it off or shut it out of our sensibility. Whatever enables us to attain either end we appreciate as a survival-value for our struggles to live on and not die. We predicate the happening as this cause of that effect. And from the first day of life the sounds we keep making figure thus as causes. When, in due course, the sounds have happened into words and our words into the Word, we attribute to the Word the causal efficacy of averting Evil and attaining Good; we think it as the direct cause of both. Is there a culture anywhere whose institutions, be they religious, political, economic, esthetic or scientific, do not have a tap-root in the begetting and bearing of children, and do not branch out in rites and rotes wherein the preponderant power is the Word reverenced, indeed idolized, for the good it assures and the evil it saves from? With the Word, attitudes are expressed, values are confirmed or denied, and beliefs are challenged. With the Word, action is initiated, its course mapped, channeling present energies toward a future which their goal defines and informs and which the Word names. Alternative terms for Word have been Image, Form, Idea, Ideal, Logos.

So critical a means are the Word's diversifications in our struggles to keep up the struggling which are our survival, that it holds the foreground of our minds, and appraises the survival itself only background and atmosphere. Means replaces end as end, and the mature experience which has generated and modified the means has been superseded by the innocence of childhood in the cult of means. Without Plato, Philo would simply have developed the tradition which Scripture and the myths embody; with Plato, he modifies them in the direction of necessary providence but retains in God the qualities of the naive experience of young children because, in this, creativity and novelty stand out.[2] The cultural exaltation of the Word first makes God in the image of man, then inverts the intent of the creative act and makes man in the image of God. For both, the making is the differentia, and for both the image, the idea, the Logos must be created first, to be materialized or established afterwards; and for both that first creation is *ex nihilo*.

Alternatively, the event need not be original at all, only sempiternal. Logic, although not experience, requires it to be one or the other. And if it is an original, then it is a surd in experience—at once a good craved and a power feared. To establish it as wholly the first, we devise and try out all sorts of instruments of analysis and reconstruction—grammars, logics, computers, system of signs, graphs and figures. But, on the record, that which our instruments bring to light is not anything whereof the surd is seen as the necessary consequence. They render visible opportunities and occasions of its coming, but no causes. Its serendipity eludes the coercions it is assigned to; it come to, with, but not *from* them, it comes and adds itself to them or perishes. Hence, in leaving our urgent hunger for rationality instilled, the surd impels our strivings to rationalize it—that is, to fit it so into an established order as to assuage the uneasiness and fear which its singularity arouses. For rationality makes a snug harbor of our world. By enclosing existence in a foreordination, whether providential or mechanical or both, it deprives the original, the new, the strange, the unique of their autonomy. It contains and binds them, perhaps less proximately than ultimately, in a system of ineluctable and repetitive fittings which follow from one sole power always and everywhere and the same. Rationalist systems define this power as a unique and uncaused cause which reduces the originals which we experience to items of the necessary continuum that we trust its effects to make. Their rationalization renders their comings in experience *non-sequiturs* of logic, absurdities of nature. Nevertheless, the sciences do willy-nilly provide a place for them as chance or contingency while the religions cherish them most ardently as miracles or *gratia dei*. In so doing both enterprises avert from the rule of reason to the realities of experience. Only the arts—the theatre, painting, poetry, sculpture, philosophy—have, although not unambiguously, occupied themselves with "the absurd."

NOTES

1. Usage gives *nekevah* (female)—akin to *Kever*, grave, perhaps cave or cavity—a sharply sexual meaning. The *nekevah* is quite literally, the pierced one, the receptacle which receives the seed. Calling any person a *nekevah* is an insult. The socially correct terms is *Ishah*, the feminine of *Ish*, man.

2. James Joyce, being read to during his blindness, commented to one reader: "about the sound of words and the sound one word makes on another, and the sound of the silences between the words . . . the word is creative. The divine creativity of the word."

Creativity, Evolution and the Creative Man

LET WHO will read irony in the event that it was philosophers of science and art who became most fearful of the discontinuities of freedom, novelty and uniqueness which "the absurd" aggregates. In their systems, those figure as the foes which reason must overcome if it was still to provide the spirit of man with the security that it yearns for. From Plato on, the recorded philosophic enterprise was a Sisyphean labor by means of logic to empty the brute events of experienced novelty of their reality and so to fill mind and soul with peace that passeth understanding. To put the brute event in its place, philosophers have postulated a void which is likewise a flux—an utter nothing which nevertheless reflects and by reflecting distorts, dilutes, yet in no way alters the eternal Original which eternally multiplies itself in images upon this fluid nothingness, producing in the shadowland the hapless diversities that ghost-write its aboriginal ultimacy. In the unphilosophical man's experience the appearances of the appearance of the philosophical man's substances are the realities. The unphilosophical man must accept them (since all he encounters is the conflicting impacts of those broken), as moving images of the unmoving, eternal and universal Original Whole that reflects itself so generously yet so secretly to give content to the contentless, flowing, misleading Void.

After Darwin, however, Western philosophers filled up their Void. They endowed its mobility with Being and made its flood a plenum of substance and power, something like the Long Body, the *lingua sharira*, of the Vedantists, to several of whom time was the fourth dimension of space, the dimension of the succession of somatic changes for which "growth" is the substance of the eventuation: past, present, future. It is the single singular, one and unchanging change, the change which changes not while all things change. It is temporality, but not what we mean by "Time." We mean our immediate experience of the compenetration of past, present and future that is "growth" to us. Any present moment of it is first and last like a cinematographic still—a cross-section of an unending yet self-contained movement whereof the past is a now unperceived presence in its perceived present which its future joins. It is this seamless self-diversification of growth which the Hindus named "The Long Body." A man's total life story, from conception and before, to death, is but an instant cross-section of the total stretch, at once sequential and simultaneous.

But the Western portrait of "The Long Body" came with a quantification of Body which gave the image a different import. The mathematical physics of Galileo, Kepler and Newton had already devised geometric and mathematical containers for Body, binding it up in eternal and universal laws of nature and of nature's God. Spinoza had demonstrated it as the changeless change of *causa sui*. After Darwin's *Origin of Species*[1] the containers were first strained, then cracked, then broken, and generations to date have been laboring to mend them. With every measure, from the infinitesimal to the infinite, philosophers and scientists keep striving to reduce "spontaneous variations" to "necessary connexions." The urge, as paradoxical as it is inveterate, impels scientists, poets and philosophers to imagine process and passage, alteration and innovation as self-contained structure of ever self-confirming activity. Our will-to-believe bets that soon or late the practices which we call science and the speculations we call philosophy must attain to and display the Long Body's inalterable substance of alteration and its indubitably eternal and universal laws. Charles Peirce, who believed "that our knowledge is never absolute, but always swims, as it were, in a continuum of uncertainty and of indeterminancy," spoke for all such searchers and seekers when he defined truth as "the opinion which is fated to be agreed upon by all who investigate," and its object as "the real." Beside the opinion and object thus "fated," all else called "truth" and "real" must needs be false and unreal.

Yet Peirce had been deeply affected by Darwin's postulates, although his philosophic faith drew more from deliverances of German Schelling than the examinations of British Darwin. For the import of Darwinism was a rejection of philosophical realism—even of the Scotian variety which Peirce espoused—first, to supplement, then to replace the nominalism which Darwin's observation that species originate reinforced. He conceived "natural selection" as a transaction between the environment and organism whose give-and-take works from without inward, from alterations of organic form to alterations of its genes. And since no convincing evidence beyond reasonable doubt was produced—not during Darwin's lifetime nor since—that acquired characteristics are heritable—that is, become potentials of the genes—Darwin postulated ongoing "Pangenesis" to provide for the variations that nature selects. Variations do appear— some are called "sports," others "mutants"—and they survive or perish as they fit or fail to fit the circumambience amid which they struggle for survival. Biologically, the fittings and failings are genetic, not personal. The variations they follow upon are spontaneous; they are independent formations, and evolution is an ongoing epigenesis. The individual, the person, is only a witness, not a force in the evolution so signalized. There, the force is his genes. It is in the evolution of culture that he is a force, and he is one in virtue of his discoveries, his inventions, his creations; in virtue of the novelties he imagines and produces, of their impact on the repetitions of heredity and habit and the re-ordering of set ways and fixed styles that follows.

Darwin's postulates not only stirred many to consequential efforts either at reconciling them with both providential and mechanical necessity (such as produced the evolutionary philosophies of the Enlightenment), or at rendering them the meaning of such necessity. They also freed men of science and philosophers to break through the barriers of necessitarianism, to relax the inhibitions of their logic and to look at the course of events from new standpoints in new relations. "Spontaneous variation," "natural selection," "survival of the fittest," came to be used, aware and unaware, as working hypotheses in the formation of alternative interpretations of man, the universe and man's career in it. Each such interpretation devised its own image of *genus homo* and its relations; each worked out its own style of conception and experience. But all gave "origin" a new import, as did the revolutionary *Origin of Species* with its negation of the invariancy and mutual exclusiveness of forms, its evidence that forms vary and pass over into one another. "Origin," now used to indicate spontaneity, could no longer serve to suggest "First Cause," "Special Creation," "Source," "Ground." Its intent was shaped by a new awareness of the perduring impress that every beginning is somehow a "first," that all successions are real and not merely instant and permanent effects of one eternal cause or inevitable conclusions from one universal premise. "Origin" came to represent taking the experience of chance, and of time passing, as experience of reality, not of appearance; "origin" could now mean images of "laws of nature and of nature's God" as processes of change, as growths from chance beginnings, first into cosmic habits, then, with the aeons, into "natural laws," all of them aging, changing, each of them at a tempo singular to itself, until it dies out into the nothing in and from which it started, or else is consummated in the immortal ultimacy which Peirce foresaw. "Origin" could mean Nature's God himself beginning, growing and dying, or else entering into that immortal Peircian ultimacy in comradship with Nature's lesser lives.

What "origin" could not connote is the ever-changing Long Body's unchangeable changing—the eternity and universality of change, the identity of the ongoing nullifications of identity which logic and discourse require. Nevertheless, some of the newer post-Darwinian philosophies attempted this very thing, evoking from Darwin's postulates images of a universal evolution as a closed, unaltering activity. Others envisioned it as an open, self-altering activity; still others, when they came down to cases, claimed for their images the self-evidence of intuition; cannier ones proceeded by means of postulation. Motives seem to have been mixed. All, perhaps, wanted to show that "Changelessness," "Structure," "Being," had only been mistaken for ultimate realities; that the real ultimates are the never-ultimate "Becoming," "Process," "Change," and that they may no longer be mistaken for unreality and illusion. Nature cannot be "original"; indeed Nature cannot be unless it be the ongoing self-alteration which "Becoming" names. In the newer image of man, going-on displaced goals-to-go-to, Man's originality, his creativity, like Nature's is his changing himself, his growing. Man's substance is process, his career as man is to be accounted for as movement at once the inner diversification and outer consummation which the words "progress," "development" are used to name. *To be* was stripped of the invariancy it usually connoted and invested with the variations of *to become*. *To become* was made into something of a synonym for *creativity, origination*. How else, indeed, could "process" be known "like it is," if not as experienced creativity and origination? How otherwise than by ongoing differentation could even simple succession of identicals or simple change disclose itself? What else do we ever know it as, if not the sequence of formations altering as they form in an eventuation that forms goals which it leaves behind while forming them?

For the common word to name this sense of passage, usage took "evolution" with "process" for an alternative. The meanings triggered the launching of centrifugal elaborations in various new philosophies of Nature and of Man, their key concepts serving rather as stations to depart from than destinations to stop at. When taken for stoppage, the new systems which were worked out from the concepts formed only more variants upon the *philosophia perennis*. Origination figures in them yet again as a repetition of identicals. Reading evolutionist philosophers (they are now very many and I can discuss only those among the better known ones who have seemed to me the more significant producers of new meanings for origination and creativity: C. S. Peirce say, Henri Bergson, Alfred North Whitehead, Herbert Spencer or Samuel Alexander or Julian Huxley or Teilhardt de Chardin). A reading of those philosophers, I would say, raises doubts concerning some of the new interpretations of ultimacy. Which of them does, which does not, I wonder, against oust

"Becoming" in order to enthrone "Being" in its image of an ultimate "Becoming" that is nevertheless *causa sui*, nevertheless at once cause and effect of itself, ever one and the same energy busily maintaining its changelessly active unchanging self? Could such a Being in fact or in logic originate anything new or different, anything not somehow ever present? Existentialists—more conspicuously Martin Heidegger and Jean Paul Sartre—bring one to a like doubt from quite another direction. In each new system, what challenges query is the *what*, the *how*, the *whatfor* (if any) of originality and creativity. Somehow, Darwinism had been fitted into the *philosophia perennis* or the latter into Darwinism, but with both fittings imparting to Darwinism a non-Darwinian intent. They subdue it into a reinforcement of the traditional creed if not its code. The discourse of reason could bring the mind *up* to the rationalist ultimate but not *into* it. Before this ultimate the understanding remains profane; it passeth the understanding; only tuition or faith can enter into it. The understanding must assume the ultimate, must take it for the foregone conclusion which impels the labor to demonstrate it and the struggles to defend the demonstrations against companies of doubters or inquirers or analyzers or agnostics, also employing the Darwinian postulates. For believers and challengers alike, the point of no return would be a decision regarding the *what*, the *how*, the *whatfor* (if any) of creativity and origination as events in our experience of our world and ourselves.

Here is Charles Peirce postulating a foreordained—his word, we recall, was 'fated'—*terminus ad quem* of truth and reality that his perduring "continuum of uncertainty and indeterminacy," which environs every actual opinion, prevents all from attaining. Nevertheless, it was his faith that the obstructions would be overcome and human fallibility consummated by infallibility. He set forth this faith in Darwinian terms. He imaged reality coming to be from an aggregation, not of beings, but of dynamic *might-be's*. He imagined the might-be's becoming actual unrelated entities—monads?—entering into relations. He imagined the relations developing into habits of togetherness and the habits in due course working as the laws which are believed to direct the sequences of change and chance in material nature. Somewhere, Peirce called matter "effete mind." The expression suggests that he imagined the ultimate process as an ongoing uninterruptable commingling and interweaving of chance movements in a single direction, toward a single goal—the *fated* Real and True. If so, the commingling and interweaving work to unify the aboriginal diversity, and the working is a manifestation of an ultimate creative impulse. It begins at a Darwinian "total absence of regularity,"[2] and must terminate in a "total absence of spontaneity," Its formations and reformations ensue as spontaneities intrude upon regularities and are by them absorbed and naturalized—with unforseen and unforeseeable consequences. This phase of the process Peirce calls "anacastic." The third phase of the evolution Peirce conceives in somewhat Lamarckian terms. His sure model of growth is the growth of science, for science diversifies as it "does its thing" or sets its inquiries on a certain gradient toward a chosen goal simply because this goal is "the idea itself whose nature is divined before the mind processes it, by the power of sympathy, that is, by the continuity of mind." Intelligent discourses do not count. The feel of the Idea irradiates sympathetic individuals in a group without regard to their intellection, or it comes to one or another when alone, as St. Paul's Christianism came to him on the road to Damascus. Or it takes a person absolutely by inspiration. The sequences of Evolution start by chance and develop as "habit-taking"—an eventuation which grows from "an infinitesimal chance tendency toward an activity of generalization" which consummates in generality. Peirce's key words for the ongoing sequence of creation are *Chance, Love, Continuity*; as *isms*, they are *Tychism, Agapism* and *Synechism*.[3]

Although William James adopted these key words of Peirce's as well as the word "pragmatism," he used them with very different meanings. The legend that he misunderstood Peirce was an invention of philophasters who would take differences of meaning for nothing but the errors of understanding. As the record shows, James understood Peirce correctly enough; but "tychism," "synechism," "pragmatism" named the conspectus of a very different philosophy from Peirce's. James became a nominalist and remained one fully aware of Peirce's Scotian realism. He never gave "love" the metaphysical role that Peirce set it in. His pragmatism and his nominalism were functions of one another, and his account of truth may be said to grow from them. Peirce rejected the idea James had newly worked out and signified by "pragmatism." To project the difference of his own philosophy from James's, he invented the word "pragmaticism," and made both his Scotist realism and his semantic, almost Pythagorean scientism aspects of its intent. This rendered him not an authentic but a pseudo-Darwinian. James's Darwinism was authentic; its postulates are in play in all his beliefs about man and his world, his ways and his destiny, and in his "overbeliefs" as well. To both thinkers, reality is process, becoming, evolution. To Peirce, however, its tychistic *terminus a quo* was measureless prelude to its "fated" synechistic *terminus ad quem*. His universe is self-contained and closed. James's universe has no ultimate terminus; no part of it is fated; parts come, parts go, each with its own whence and whither, or none; events begin and stop, gather up and scatter;

they come to no conclusions. "What has concluded," his last question asked, "that we should conclude about it?" To Peirce, creativity is genuine; but, for all its multitudinous branch roads, its way is progress on a highroad to an ineluctable conclusion. For James, creativity is genuine and pervasive, highways and branch-roads receive their classifications not from what they are but from how they forward the creative work, whether human, transhuman, or nonhuman.

James's interest in creativity began early in his career. It had been an ultimate concern of his father, the elder Henry James, in whose Swedenborg-derived philosophy it was a permanent article of faith. James the father kept shaping and reshaping this philosophy all his long and pain-ridden life. He had begun it with a working-over of Swedenborgianism. Crippled as a young boy, pain-ridden and anxious the rest of his life, brought up and more or less schooled in the Calvinist doctrine and discipline, these kept failing James the father in emergencies of mood and action from which he needed either release or that assurance of personal independence and dignity which would compensate his deficiencies, enable him to face existence and, if not master, to endure it in serenity and hope. A while, he thought he did find this release and assurance in Swedenborg's portrayal of the universe and of God's place, and man's, in it. But its imaginative ratiocination also failed to compensate the actualities of evil which men suffer and inflict, so entirely an inversion of the good they envision. Father Henry James found it, however, a congenial material that he could reshape into a truly reliable philosophic image of reality.

On the foreground of this image was the relation of the creature to the Creator. Father and son argued it in an exchange of letters during the late sixties of the last century. According to the father, the relation is an internal relation, which means that the creature's identity is a function of the Creator's creativity, that its *haecceitas* expresses its interdependence with all God's other creatures and its dependence on Creator-God's total creativity. Nevertheless, the creature's being itself and no other, its having a logical identity, a sense of itself as an autonomous and not a created existence, must be acknowledged as the effect and image which it is, of the divine cause. "Let it go at present into your memory." father wrote son in September of 1867, "if no further—that in the true order of thought individuality is primary, and universality and community altogether derivative. That is, that the only universal existence is individual existence. In other words, there is but one created or universal species. Man and all the genera or kinds of existence are only implications of that individual form."

To the son, this was as paradoxical as it was not to Peirce. The son reminded his father of life's being a process going on, in terms at least of the commonplace diversification of forms from mineral through vegetable, animal, to human. He wrote that the relation of the sequence to its consummation is held to be constant, and so likewise is that of the chain of creatures to the Creator. But the relation need not be thus implicative. As given, the differences are different. They all "unite in philanthropy," son William wrote from Berlin in October 1867, ". . . . atheists too, more than any, for sympathy is now so developed in the human breast that misery and undevelopedness would all the more powerfully call for correction; when coupled with the thought that from nowhere else than from us could correction possibly come—that we ourselves must be our own providence."

In action, what could being "our own providence" point to other than creativity as self-alteration? James's tychism expressed his realization that "spontaneity cannot be eradicated"; that it is a given of our experience and not to be left out by our philosophies. As hap or chance, it pervades every order, fringing with indeterminancy every determination, intruding contingency upon every necessity. It is what in his research of the *Origin of Species*, Darwin identified as "spontaneous variation"—differences coming fortuitously, coming without rhyme or reason, persisting, fading out or quickly vanishing piecemeal or by multitudes, in a drama of conflict and cooperation with the order they enter; a drama which their struggle for survival at once improvises and acts out. The action links the actors up—some altogether externally, next to next, with no inner change from their juxtaposition; others more dynamically, binding some actors together reciprocally, others asymmetrically. Their ways with one another may become habits, as diverse as the intruders and the orders they relate. Obstruction, aggression, mutual acceptance, progress, development, dependence, independence may all become habitual relations between an old self-repeating order and a new event; the novel may be recurrence of the old with such a difference that it can be neither predesigned nor foretold: "What comes is determined only when it comes." In the experience of the observer, the Different seems to come *with* and *to* the repeating Same, yet *from* nothing. Ask, *what* from, *whence?* And the answer comes: *Ex Nihilo*. The future seems, so to speak, grafted onto the past, fusing with it, enlarging it. So to the radical empiricist William James, the universe was an open-ended growing. Bit by bit, drop by drop, event by event, the universe becomes. Reality, say James, refuses to be pent in; reality is "an action, and it takes two or more to produce an action." Of course, any number more than two can and do count among the makers and their makings.[4] It is this radically pluralistic give-and-take (synechistic pluralism) which distinguishes the actions we call nature from the activity

B *

which their plurality redirects and alters. In one place James called it that production of novelty in fresh activity situations which is "causality at work" and the same as free will. In such situations the unique cause is effect, unique following the unique. There is no question of repeating consequences. When there is, we call the relationship causal. The traditional words for activity are, more or less, *causa sui* and *emanation*. No more need be said than that so signified, activity is the ultimate of the closed universe clear and sure to the philosophic tradition—a *totum simul* either sempiternal or an ineffable happening for which the astronomer's parallel is, as already said, the Big Bang—like the one and only explosion of fireworks into a diversified succession of explosions which Bergson favored—all color, noise and stench, that add nothing to and substract nothing from the sole, self-contained creative act, and are nothing apart from its ever-lasting instancy.

James's notion, more harmonious with Darwin's postulates, seems, regardless of his perhaps panpsychic overbelief, closer to what recent physics has denoted as "the steady state"—that is, the spontaneous coming and going of "quanta" of matter, energy, hulé, substance, psyche, or what else you choose to call it, each a particle in a sense like a Democritan atom, but each with an entropy of its own, and with the aggregate processes of the coming of all out of nowhere and their disappearance into nowhere definable as a statistically "steady state"—that is, an overall pattern of habits which we specify as the "laws of Nature."

The human is one such a quantum compounded of lesser quanta, a very late and immensely complicated one among the variations of this "state," a happening with its own built-in measure of time between birth and death. It is a measure which the struggle with the world around for survival may shorten but cannot lengthen. In the newborn, this world comes as a *blooming, buzzing, confusion*, perhaps because the human itself starts as a like confusion. "Man's chief difference from the brutes," William James told an audience of Unitarian clergymen in 1881, "lies in the exuberant excess of his subjective propensities—his pre-eminence over them simply and solely in the number and in the fantastic and unnecessary character of his wants, physical, moral, aesthetic and intellectual. Had his whole life not been a quest for the superfluous, he would never have established himself as inexpugnably as he has done in the necessary. Prune down his extravagances, sober him, and you undo him."

But in the human nature of things, the extravagances prune themselves. Like the rest of nature, human nature exceeds, finding nothing it values ever enough, save when it has too much. So with the inner events of our struggle to keep on struggling, with its intentions and willings. They arise, spontaneous variations among our constitutive urges, our instincts and our habits. But unless we act them out, they disappear, simply perish as do most spontaneous variations. Were they present images anticipating a future which never came, a happening of possibilities that passed away unactualized? How then, can anything be an image which has no original? How can a possibility happen into existence and not be an actuality? However we rationalize these variations, they keep coming and passing. Their flux is intrinsic to our experience—of anything—of talking, say. We feel our meanings in their singularity before we utter them—"premonitory perspective views of schemes of thought, not yet articulated." Unless spoken, we lose them. They come on and pass out, ineffable.

Yet, survival being a process of selection, a fitting either *to* or *of* some other existence *is* a running down. It is a containment of spontaneity in habit, and James quotes the Duke of Wellington against Pascal: "Habit, second nature! Habit is ten times second nature." It is the relation with thoughts, things and other people which thins spontaneity down to repetition, replaces the anxious paralysis of indecision and the strains and stresses of taking thought by the confident promptness of decision. Habit is thus security, and security which frees attention from its bondage of concern about the habituated to give itself to the insecure exploration of the new and the different; that it, habit frees our propensity for the initiation of new habits and for the effort to enable them to go on with least effort, while still other habits are in the making. The diversification and orchestration of habits is our ongoing self-creation; it is growth into the life more abundant. At bottom, humans are "merely walking bundles of habits," spinning their own fates—"permanent drunkards by so many separate drinks," or permanent saints, sinners, or anything else "by so many separate acts and hours of doing one's own chosen thing."

The vital center of this doing, its differentation, is mind as a, perhaps *the*, power of survival distinguishing the hairless from the hairy ape. Reality comes to us actually as a chaos of fragmentary impressions interrupting each other. Via the sciences, reason shapes it into an "abstract system of hypothetical laws." Thus we transform what comes "into a totally different world as a mode of our struggle to survive and a means and process of survival, each uniquely according to its volitional nature." Events happen in the brain which "set *new* (emphasis mine) internal forces free to exert their effects in turn."

Whatever attracts our attention from outside, the life of the mind inside goes on as a jungle-like stream of ideas, "a native wealth of inner forms," says James, "whose origin is shrouded in mystery." Relations of time and space seem "imprinted," as patterns of them shape up and pass, and we initiate responses to them which solidify into habits. But together with habituation come inward spontaneous combinations that arouse moods . . . they render us curious and expectant, or sceptical, or condemning. We may question or deny them, hesitate to take a stand toward them, use them for means of exploration or reject them utterly, in our strivings for certainty about their *haecceitas*, about whether they are or represent realities, whether they are genuine possibilities or sheer fantasies. But however diverse, they are autonomous. James signalizes them as "ideal and inward relations among the objects of our thought which can in no intelligible way whatever be interpreted as reproductions of the order of outer experience. . . ." Relations of difference and resemblance, relations in and between time and space, the rational result of comparison, the sequential linkage of any succession, do not depend on observed existence. "We may disregard the intermediates yet not be obliged to alter anything in what remains written." We can not only skip intermediates, we can render differents identical which as existences continue in their different identities. Our identification is a functional equalization. By using differents as sames, we are able to skip intermediates, to substitute any for any other—of course, for our own good, and at our own risk. Of course, we can also be brought up short; we don't love another whom our beloved loves; nor, if we kill a killer are we killers of his victim. If we contradict an opponent we don't thereby contradict any other opponent of his. Equalization, identification, are survival-values for us, which, although differently, we elaborate and employ in all our sciences, as in our philosophies and religions. This repetition of identicals is the first principle of reasoning, and it works until we experience the consequences of such an identification as creates the Index Numbers of economic science—say, the familiar ones ironically reviewed as *Horses* and *Apples*. The differences continue inexpugnable. James writes: "The most characteristically and peculiarly moral judgments that a man is ever called upon to make are in unprecedented cases and lonely emergencies, while no popular rhetorical maxims can avail and the hidden oracle alone can speak, and speaks often in favor of conduct quite unusual, and suicidal as far as gaining popular approbation goes."

In sum, there is a spring of spontaneity in each human, as in every item of the universe, wherein he struggles to keep on struggling, there is an urge which declines to be fitted, but chooses either to preserve its identity, to fit the world to itself, or to perish preserving its selfhood. The Book of Job of the Old Testament is a *locus classicus*. So is Aeschylus *Prometheus Bound*.

Henri Bergson's *Creative Evolution* probably made the philosophic identification of creativity with evolution customary. It initiated a trend. But it was a trend away from Darwin's "spontaneous variations" and back to the philosophic tradition regarding creativity. It prolonged the latter while diverging from it, diverging radically. It continued the tradition because it accounted for the diversity of variations as consequences of one single creative act within whose ever-growing span the multitude of changing formations were sequent events. It diverged radically from the tradition precisely because the creative whole was not an instant, unaltering and unalterable activity always and everywhere the same, was not Being but *Devenir Reel*, authentic Becoming. Bergson envisioned it an ever-growing self-diversification into new events, new forms which follow from their antecedents yet are so different from them that they cannot be accepted as necessary effects of given causes or providential attainment of eternal purposes.

This universal creativity is neither determinist nor teleological. It is evolutional—that is, its present is not to be predicted from its past, yet belongs with its past; its future not to be predicted from its present, yet belongs with its present. Present, past and future flow inseparably together; they suffuse one another and are somehow one without ceasing to be many. They are phases of an ongoing act of which the beginning and the middle perdure into the presently ever receding, never-to-be-attained end. Our reason, serving our needs, purports to segregate them. It treats them as juxtaposed instants, each outside the others, whereas they make up aspects of the interpenetrated stretch which is the living of life growing up and growing older. It is the immediate datum of consciousness which we labor to measure and contain in spatial containers we call Time. It is original activity and freedom, bringing to be new possibilities as well as new realities. Bergson has different words for it to suit different contexts. In one, he calls it *real duration*; in another, *spirit*; in another, *God*; in still another, *poussé formidable* (formidable thrust), *élan vital* (push of life), and most influentially, *creative evolution*. All signify "unceasing creation, the uninterrupted upsurge of novelty"—in experience ineffable since conception cannot arrest it, nor language do anything else than conceal the continuity of change by an illusory "permanence of substance." We might signalize these configurations by the astronomer's Big Bang, ever reverberating in itself.

William James, exploring our sense of time passing yet lasting, lasting yet passing, had made his own discovery of what Bergson calls real or pure duration. But his account is descriptively pluralist, empirical rather than metaphysical and his words for it are "the specious present . . . of which we are immediately aware and incessantly sensible." It is "specious" because past and future cannot be segregated from its ongoing immediacy. The phases of time suffuse one another in any instance of our perception of objects. "We cannot," James wrote, "take any one of them so short that it will not in some fashion or other be a thought of the whole object . . . they melt into each other like dissolving views, and no two of them feel the object exactly alike, but each feels the total object in a unitary undivided way." The past lingers while the future enters; the future comes as the present enlargement of the past. The paradoxes tried the pluralistic-minded pragmatist's patience and empiricist logicality. Finally, reinforced by Bergson's own findings in his exploration of time, process and creativity, James "gave up logic" for acquiescence in the experience which logic falsified. Henceforth, this experience was to him more reliable knowledge than logic could provide.

But neither the experience nor its consequences were the same as Bergson's, nor led in the same direction. They remained consistent with the Darwinian postulates. Bergson's never were. Darwinism was little more than a jumping-off place for him. Natural selection of spontaneous variations, struggle for survival, survival of the fittest, Bergson argued in "Creative Evolution," were all too chancy to produce the integrated sequence of variations such as, for example, characterize the divergent evolution of the eye from that of the Pecten Mollusc to that of *Homo sap.* The human eye emerges rather than originates. For there is no reliable evidence that acquired characteristics become heritable, and none of chance convergence of organic forms and functions. Genuine variation might destroy rather than develop organs, limit rather than diversify functions—doesn't it do both?—as the functions of the eye are diversified by its role in locomotion. Only the élan vital's unceasing propulsion can account for the innovations along its trajectory in space. Bergson's "evolution"—Samuel Alexander's is a variant of it—might as rightly be called "emergent" as "creative."

It is our intuition, Bergson believed, which reaches to duré réel as the authentic thing-in-itself, neither all one or all many, neither machine nor purpose. Our intellect can only treat its much-at-once as one by one. Our intellect draws from the total of the living past which we each are such of its contents as it can compact into a dynamic whole directed toward the specific shaping of the future it enacts. Our memory-images are not aroused by association; they are aroused for their task in this specific phase of our struggle for survival. Since, in this struggle, failure to remember or ineptness or irrelevancy of remembering is a creative weakness, creativity must fashion its path as it advances. For creativity is time making itself by passing the future ever presently into the past, feeding the past, enlarging it, as the pure memory, the perduration of Becoming, the memory we are not aware of. The remembrances which our intellect mobilizes to serve our strivings work more like stills of a motion picture than passages of movement. They make for the repetition of identicals, not the creation of differents; and to employ remembrance thus is the role and power of intellection. To think is to realize more and more details of the confluence of diversifications which our attention takes in. Our awareness is not image or sign or symbol. It is direct perception of the ever-changing élan ringing its changes, direct perception of the inner life of things to which the Word is not creative power but the power's tool.

It is our direct perception which for example, takes hold of the authentic nature of the poem we hear its author reading; we "enter his thought . . . relive the simple state he has broken into phrases and words . . . follow his inspiration in a continuous movement which, like the inspiration itself, is an undivided act." The act going on propels past into present and generates the future. "And if I let go, if I relax," says Bergson, "the further I move in this quite negative direction, relaxation, the more extension and complexity I shall create, and the more admirable will be the order which seems to reign undisturbed among its elements."

The apex of this surrender to creativity is mystical. Not art, certainly not science, only religion strives toward the peak. And true religion is the mystic's: "the ultimate end of mysticism," Bergson declares in *Two Sources of Morality* and Religion:

. . . is to establish contact with the creative urge which life itself manifests. This urge is of God himself. The great mystic is to be conceived as an individual being transcending the limitations imposed on the species by its material nature, thus continuing and extending the divine action . . . Religion is to mysticism what popularization is to science . . . mysticism and religion are virtually cause and effect . . . going on. Yet there must have been a beginning. And indeed, at the origin of Christianity, there is Christ.

Bergson does not quite commit himself on the evolutionary status of Christ. Was he as true a Bang as the Big Bang is believed to be or only one of that Bang's mightier reverberations among the succession into which it diversifies itself?

There are resonances from Bergson's insights in Alfred North White-head's portrayal of "reality." But Whitehead's account of creativity seems much closer to the Platonic than to the Philonic, and like Bergson's, heedless of Darwin's postulates. There are echoes of William James in his expression—especially regarding religion—and maybe of other pragmatists. But however much this philosopher's later beliefs diverged from his beginnings, the creed intrinsic to the *Principia Mathematica* which he invented and worked out in collaboration with Bertrand Russell is a very visible influence in his non-mathematical expression. This creed seems to me a kind of Pythagoreanism in semi-modern dress. Its affirmations concern the structure of systems by repetitions of identicals. As logic and mathematics they postulate and combine relations of parts to one another within their wholes, and to the wholes they are parts of. They are formations without content, are their own content, shapes that shape nothing at all, platonic ideas with Pythagorean powers. As Bertrand Russell once remarked about modern physics, "it is mathematics not because we know so much about the physical world, but because we know so little; it is only its mathematical properties that we can discover." And those properties seem so reliable to our searching and seeking after certainty! Defining the future before it happens, they dispense with creativity.

But reliable as they show themselves, these definitions deceive; creativity goes on and must be acknowledged and dealt with. The post-mathematical Whitehead did acknowledge and deal with it. Such works of his as *Process and Reality, Religion in the Making, Adventures in Ideas*, do both. In *Adventures in Ideas*, his acknowledgement of creativity comes like a reverberation from Bergson: "The creativity of the world is the throbbing emotion of the past, hurling itself into a new transcendent fact. It is the flying dart of which Lucretius speaks, hurled beyond the bounds of the world." That world, somehow, is through and through an organism, level by level a whole of wholes from the infinitesimal to the infinite. It is a pattern of universals each with a uniqueness of its own which is so related to the others that thereby it achieves "status" in existence. The relations, it is, which confer existence. The ultimate or initial universal is not an existence; it is only a possibility, related to existence as a strategist's design for a battle is related to the events of battling. Not itself in the battle but, so to speak, above it, the design organizes men and material and directs their encounter. Thus, creativity figures as the actualization of possibility; it draws eternal objects together with "concrete occasions." Because it sustains them, they last. So "I", the perduring identical self, sustains the diversified manifold "me" of my personal history as organic events of my living selfhood.

The "I" of "me" is an ongoing creative act. We are like God who, Whitehead avers, is the "principle of concretion," the formative process respecting which creatures figure like points on the trajectory of ongoing creation. Whitehead suggests in *Religion in the Making* that the order of succession composes an esthetic consistency; that the Godhead by which we measure it is an actual entity, outside of time, determining indeterminate process into determinate freedom, that is, fitting the novelty of the future into the presence of the past, establishing novelty as a value or satisfaction, while new turns, new decisions ensue world without end, to create like concretions to make like fittings. For "unlimited possibility and abstract creativity can procure nothing."

The autonomy and freedom of the creature is assured by the successive tides of the creative act. As process, it is instant one-and-many—a whole of somehow independent-interdependent parts. Because sheer independence, mere juxtaposition, makes no difference; because only internal relations can make any difference in and to the beings they relate. The world teems with wholes so related. Whitehead calls each a "prehension" of all—that is, a center, different from all others, at which the universe is focused while the centers as such remain outside one another—they do not "prehend" each other. It is through this relatedness that each is under "a categorical obligation" of both freedom and determination. There is complete contemporary freedom. It is not true that whatever happens is immediately a condition laid upon everything else. Such a conception of a complete mutual determination is an exaggeration of the community of the universe. The notions of sporadic occurrences and of "mutual irrelevance" have a real application to the nature of things.

This categorical obligation can be condensed into the formula that in each concrescence what is determinable is determined but that there is always room for the decision of the subject-supersubject of that concrescence. This subject-supersubject is the universe in that synthesis, and beyond it there is non-entity.

In brief, Whitehead's divergence from the Platonic tradition is a simplification and inversion with new language and new appreciation of process. For Plato, creativity involves a threesome of God, the eternal ideas and non-being. For Whitehead, the relation is a duo; the ideas are not powers but possibilities; the power is the divine act which solidifies a possibility into an actuality; and the ongoing play of this transforming power is the flow of events—"the historic route of actual occasions" and God appraising the world he is creating. God is creativity. God innovates and intensifies. "We can say that God and the actual world jointly constitute the character of creativity for the initial phase of the novel concrescence. The subject thus constituted is the autonomous master of its own concrescence into subject-supersubject." First and last, God and the world are the poles of ongoing creativity. Creativity is ultimate, is the substance which is *causa sui*, without purpose, without prevision or end-means relation—in effect, although Whitehead doesn't say so—creativity is ineffable. "It is as true to say that God creates the world as that the world creates God."

Does this transaction between God and the world establish creativity, Bergson-wise, as the continuity of becoming, or Peirce-like, the becoming of continuity? How far does the future relate to the past, that which may be and is not yet to that which already was and is no more? Whitehead invokes "the observed immanence of the past in the future." Since concrescence, continuity, becoming, has direction and makes progress, the creator of it must be aware—that is, his attention must span the sequential stretch between the *terminus a quo* (the past wholly present) and the *terminus ad quem* (the ever absent, open-ended shaping of things to come) which is never a terminal but the passage from way station to way station. God's role as "principle of concretion" renders him also the power knowingly feeding on itself and growing by what it feeds on. It is conscious of itself making itself. If the power is Creative Evolution in person, he is non-Bergsonian Creative Evolution. What is actually observed when the immanence of the past is said to be observed in the future—of that which is no more in that which is not yet? Is the future, then, the totality of Leibnitzian compossibles, one of which the Creator chooses to render actual, to grow into a concretely present? Is the past the actual, become possible again, reduced from a state of concretion to a state of dispersion? Or are the possibles Old Fortunatus' purses each ever refilling itself with cash values? If the future be truly the future, if it be an authentic novelty, not some repetition of the past or recurrent concretion of an eternal compossibility, it can contain the past only after it has itself become past; certainly the past cannot contain it in advance, pregnant with its emergence. The creative act may take the past for occasion, but its creation comes into the past *ex nihilo*, comes out of that non-entity of Whitehead's which he sets "beyond" the universe of either subject-supersubject or Little Bang-Big Bang. If the past be soil which the Creator seeds, the creatures he grows in it are at least as alien to it as the seed; if not an emanation from himself, then an intrusion from nothingness.

To pass from creativity as Whitehead imagines it to the image left us by George Herbert Mead is to pass into another style of seeing and thinking. There is nothing Pythagorean in Mead's postulates. Familiar as he was with German transcendentalism and its American modifications, Mead's philosophic vision developed untainted by those colorations. It is bad luck that he translated into the written word very few of his spoken ones. His *Nachlass* is a reconstruction of his spoken ones by others. But their intent is preserved and surprises and persuades. Mead sees anew, thinks anew, and so supplements and enriches the sights and reflections which identify authentic pragmatism. The initiating postulate of schools of it is the reality of change, of the formation and dissipation of events as pulses in an ongoing becoming. This made the nature of time which could be said to feed on itself and grow by what it feeds on an overruling concern, the more vital because its beats are pulses or waves of the stream of a man's consciousness, the patterning of his personal history. We have already noted what ensued from this realization in Henri Bergson's rethinking of the *haecceitas* of time and what developed from William James's direct inspection and description of our experience as the flow into one another of present, past and future, and his working with the Darwinian postulates. To Mead, the *haecceitas* of time was paramount. It was the implicit theme of his *Philosophy of the Present* and his *Philosophy of the Act*. The perception of it as duration suffuses the deliverances of his *Mind, Self* and *Society*. And of course, creativity, originality, novelty, diversity, name nuclear aspects of the implicit theme.

Mead, inspecting our experience, described its actuality as a "temporal present"—that is, a stretch of time whose presence is passage of which the *terminus a quo* is a solidified and solidifying past and the *terminus ad quem* is the unformed and forming future. The first is "determined" and the second is "indeterminate," both being fields, not points, neither being a pole of the other. Our existence as humans is one among the variety of formations disclosing the temporal present. The human condition manifests itself in a sequence of temporal perspectives, of eventuations wherein the present spans both past and future with novelties entering the present and working as alteration of its past. The eventuations are manifold and diverse; each present is the receptacle of a future, singular to itself, of ever new happenings and perspectives, a future which changes the present it enters. Together, the eaches make up the multiplying aggregate of present which are the all of reality. Beyond them is the nothingness of ancient Buddhism or of modern Existentialism. Within them are man-and-his-world-in-the-making. Within them is Creativity. We create ourselves by means of our give-and-take with our human and our unhuman circum-ambience. The give-and-takes, reverberations of sound for sound, gesture for gesture and posture for posture, shape up into roles which we re-act to as we perceive them enacted, and our awareness of our reactions compounds into our image of ourselves, while the multiplicity of our unappropriated images compose into the "generalized Other" for which "Humanity," "Man," may be taken as synonyms.

So we create ourselves and do it in terms of the distinctions we sustain between the "I" and "Me" of the self we struggle to preserve. The struggle is creation. It is our existence, and our existence is the action of the act we perform, as we manipulate and order the tools, the matter and the media of the unceasing alteration of our past which is our future survival.

It is "I" acting on "Me", responding to its own gestures as it to an Other's; it is Self, echoing Others by way of empathy and sympathy, and thereby creatively altering its selfhood, diversifying, growing, becoming Other while remaining Same. This is the process of history as, in this community or that, human beings came to give up magic for craft, craft for technics, technics for automation, and religion for science—first in their exploration and use of nature, then in their study and education of man. On the record, the sequence discloses creativity in act; it renders visible how means displace one another, how they compound and by compounding bring to birth and justify new ends.

The sequence uncovers the inwardness of the process of evolution, which is the ultimate of nature, naked *natura naturans*. It is the action of the infinitely Many uniting into Ones.

The import of the theory of relativity is one instance of this. For how else is relativity postulated, if not by taking an Other's place and comparing that view from that place with the view from one's own? How otherwise does science work? Mead took the doings of science for the action of a free community; reciptocal give-and-take of its members creates their language, their instruments and their skills, with which they progressively make innovations and alterations. To Mead, science is totally social. Where a scientist or any other observer fails in this reciprocity, he isolates himself within his own horizon. Where he practices it, he perceives that neither time nor space nor any stretches of them need be absolute; that any and every perspective, however it eventuates, is a *present* seeing or finding, is the uniquely *present* seat and test of reality. He recognizes that the future which is not yet, nevertheless comes *now*, that novelty enters *now*, that any past which already was, is *now*, and no more absolute than the future. However the two diverge from the present, they are confluent in it and the three together are, as Bergson argued, a seamless lasting, a duration changing through and through as it continues, changing from within— thus creativity which is an emergent evolution. Our reason postulates the past as cause, envisions the future as effect which shall come next, and reluctantly acknowledges that novelties alter both as they come. The ideas of *past*-and-no-other, *future*-and-no-other, *present*-and-no-other cannot be reliably segregated from the *passing* present within which future and past flow together, and which is our actual "test and seat of reality."

Non-reality, as relativity purports to account for it, is, Mead holds, a situation wherein "the object must be contemporaneously in different systems, to be what it is in either."

It has long seemed to me that John Dewey sees "creativity" in man and nature and their relations similarly. Of course, his, like Mead's or anyone's, has its own concrete identity—the "product" of his personal history. The give-and-take-between his temperament and fields of experience nourished its making, and impelled the formation of the style of talking and writing that duly became his signature. But the fields and the faiths of the two philosophers were confluent. They were colleagues and friends, members of the same philosophic brotherhood and teaching in the same academic establishment—that new, brash assemblage of diversely pioneering intellectuals, the University of Chicago. With their brethren they were, each in his way, of course, proponents of pragmatism—the Chicago School of it—and Dewey remained its principal spokesman also after self-respect required him to leave that headwater of Baptist liberalism for Episcopalian-frosted Columbia. The insights of William James has given a new turn to the philosophic judgments of both Chicagoans. Dewey, disillusioned by the pretensions of the spokesmen for *philosophia perennis*—among whom, in terms of his projected ultimacies Charles Peirce was one —like James, also "gave up logic."

But while James turned from the eternal verities of pure reason to the transitive actualities of pure experience and the "sentiment of rationality," Dewey felt impelled to work up a "theory of inquiry" which should do a better job than the logic of the rationalists. He aimed at a mutation of logic which should enable "warranted assertibility." The new logic would rest upon experiment and reflection dynamically relevant to what scientists actually do; it would postulate that the changing events which make up our experience—their mobility, their diversifications from repeating Sames into varied Differents—in sum, that their creativity is genuine, real, and not mere appearance and deception.

Our experience is an altering sequence of our transactions with one or another aspect of the circumambience amid which we struggle to live on and grow. It is no flow of consciousness in a void but an ongoing encounter with events that we afterwards remember and, whether or not aware of it, we assimilate into our selfhoods. Assimilated, they figure in the living past that we presently use to achieve the future survival we are born to struggle for. This survival-function compenetrates inference and reflection—they are the past at work—as well as sense.

Their labor succeeds or fails as it enables us to control our environment, to "neutralize hostile occurrences," to "transform neutral events into cooperative factors or into an efflorescence of new features." Controlling the environment frees us from hindrances and coercions that we otherwise must endure and suffer under. Such hindrances and coercions are instrinsic to the human condition which, from conception to death, we struggle against and strive to overcome, by every test of trial and error which happens or which we can devise. The struggle brings on variations and innovations that more and more successfully fit the environment to us, and thus humanize it. A sequence of successful fittings and refittings is what "progress" signifies in experience. For "experience" exhibits things in their unterminated aspect moving toward "determinate conclusions"; so inquiry is "the controlled or directed transformation of an indeterminate situation into one that is so determinate in its constituent distinctions and relations as to convert the elements of the original situation into a unified whole." Ultimately, such a whole must needs be as changing an event as any other event of experience.

It may be that Dewey was never quite averted from the hegalian eternalism and monism of his youth (as Peirce was not from the Schelling variety), and cherished closure. For a similar sentiment recurs in *Art as Experience*, so that the Dewey esthetics leaves no room for the play of chance or spontaneity in artistic creation: no work of art can be a happening simply. Improvisation is not creation, nor can any work of art left unfinished or of doubtful pattern be counted as an esthetic object. Indeed, art does not create. The artist's work consists of selecting and arranging forms in ways which should "enhance, prolong and purify the perceptual experience." The moderns, going in for formalism may be apt craftsmen, or may indeed invent, innovate and discover and introduce new contents into experience, but always of a stable pattern of ordered relations, lifting the object of experience out of (or sinking it beneath?) the ongoing flux.

Whatever the import here, for Dewey logic consists first and last of a summary of ways (successful or not) of knowing and by means of the knowing, harnessing to future uses the events of present experience. Our pursuit of such ways is impelled by our attitudes, our hopes and our anxieties. Our means for any "successful" invasion of the future is the remembered past as our imagination forms it. Taking it for an instrument or a weapon of our struggle to live on, we deliberate, we extrapolate, anticipating *now* a later shape of things; and we start reshaping them *now* from the formations which had us anxious into the formations we hope for. So doing, we aim deliberately to intrude, into the existing order, variations, novelties, inventions. We are exercising intelligence, not alone practically or effectively, but creatively; we are transvaluing what would otherwise be a blind, random "fateful" intervention in the course of events—as do Democritan atoms or modernist particles, let follow what novelty we will into a providential process—into "an end-in-view" of the shape of things to come. "A pragmatic intelligence is a creative intelligence, not a routine mechanic."

So intelligence, the distinctive organ and function of the human struggle for survival, is imagined as a variation upon the sheer creativity which pervades all becoming. "Every thinker puts some portion of an apparently stable world in peril and no one can wholly predict what will emerge in its place." Providence, foresight, is not more infallible, is only less fallible, than any other instrument or organ of man's struggle for survival. "To catch mind in its connexion with the entrance of the novel into the course of the world," Dewey writes in Creative Intelligence, "is to be on the road to see that intelligence is itself the most promising of all novelties, the revelation of the meaning of the transformation of past into future ('why not future into past'?) which is the reality of every present. To reveal intelligence as the organ for the guidance of this transformation, the sole director of its quality, is to make a declaration of present untold significance for action. To elaborate these convictions of the connexion of intelligence with what men undergo because of their doings and with the emergence and direction of the creative, the novel, in the world, is of itself a program which will keep philosophers busy until something more worthwhile is forced upon them." . . . "Faith in the power of intelligence to imagine a future which is the projection of the desirable in the present, and to invent the instrumentalities of its realization, is our salvation."

NOTES

1. Darwin seems never to have been quite the Darwinian that readers of *Origin of Species* became. He hesitated between the tradition and his own working hypotheses, describing the *Origin* as a "view of life with its several powers, having been breathed by the Creator into new forms or into one; and that while the planet has gone on cycling according to the fixed laws of gravity, from so simple a beginning endless forms most beautiful and most wonderful have been, and are being, evolved."

2. "Reality consists in regularity. Real regularity is active law. Active law is efficient reasonableness, or in other words, is truly reasonable."

3. There are notations in Pierce's *Nachlass* (6.6) which suggest, as does his apparently paradoxical "matter is effete mind," that the activity of the universe is an evolution whereby spirit is forever enfleshing itself, thought forever materializing, essence forever crystallizing itself into existence; there are suggestions that the iffyness of an *if* keeps passing over into the thenness of a *then*—that the relation *if-then* is not a sequence but a providential creative development. What, logically, does this do to Darwin's postulates?

4. Human freedom, free will, must involve that modification of activity which "action signifies." It must—if any actor can rightly be held accountable for his actions—take shape as a redirection and alteration of activity. Otherwise, he is no more

responsible than if his deed were the necessary effect of an ineluctable cause. Free will as utter spontaneity denies responsibility; it renders this relation meaningless. "If a free act," James writes in *Pragmatism*, "be a sheer novelty, that comes not from me, the previous me, but *ex nihilo*, and simply tacks itself onto me, how can I, the previous I, be responsible?" There is, however, the question whether the tacking on is irresistible and imposes itself, or is accepted or resisted; a choice comes which creates the responsibility simply by coming.

Creativity, Death, Nothingness

ONE MIGHT say in brief that creativity might be called the identical twin of freedom and the Siamese twin of insecurity and uncertainty. In our struggle for survival in this world no more made for us than for any other item of it, this world into which we happen and must either fit ourselves to or fit to ourselves if we are to live on and not die, creativity is at work (or, as some prefer, in play), wherever deviation splinters regularity, innovation upsets repetition or differentation appears like a graft into identity.

And this, when we look closely, is everywhere. Everywhere spontaneity challenges necessity—or conversely. The relation is the "metaphysical" import of Darwinism, with its reappraisal of space and time and their comminglings—especially its subordination of space to time, being to becoming, and its abandonement of the logic of identity with its "laws" of contradiction and "excluded middle" for the sake of the perceptual acceptance of middles and its identification of differents within a plenum of becoming whose only boundary is the ever-present yet ever-receding nothingness whence, on the face of it, the real future comes. This import transvalues the determinist postulates of the scientific method of the sciences into working hypotheses of our struggle for survival. It puts in a different perspective our feelings that the future comes with our propulsions to make something into something else or to displace something by something else altogether different. As to the nothingness, it could be Democritus' void or emptiness which his atoms freely make their unceasing declineations in, and wherein some of their chance encounters repeat themselves at last to shape up the circumambience of law and order we call nature, and wherein eventually, we humans similarly bond ourselves into the societies in which we live, move, and make our being until we die.

A void such as this is no occasion for anxiety or dread. On the contrary, it is the not unfriendly passive container of our developing histories, the receiver of the events which make up existence. This void is a means we use, not a power we fight off. It is not death, which so often is itself a welcome termination of misery and unhappiness. Death is also a happening like other happenings, the term—yet no *ad quem*—which all, each in its

47

own tempo, come to. It is Vergil's Syrian dancing girl, whom Justice Oliver Wendell Holmes recalled on his 90th birthday: "Set down the wine and the dice," she sang, "perish who thinks of tomorrow. Here's Death twitching my ear." "Live," says she, "for I am coming." This death is not non-being. This death is also a becoming like others welcome or unwelcome, an event which comes into being as another event's passing out of being; death is the turn at which a becoming, becoming something else, becomes nothing of itself. Death is a temporal event, a complex event in the void.

That void is the simplest of simple beings, and the medium and opportunity for all other varieties of being to have and to hold their true *haecceitas* (like men in "the great open spaces where men are men"). It is anywhere that the past is present and the future takes place. It is not what Bergson means by the nothingness which he accepts. That is not an object which we perceive but an act of aversion and rejection we perform when we encounter a different object than the one we have been expecting, anticipating, hoping for, yearning for, working for. Our disappointment is not in the place but in the object holding the place, the intrusion of an Other instead of the enfleshment of an image. The place itself is the perceptual Original of Whitehead's *non-entity*, of Mead's *Beyond*, indeed of every generalized "Beyond" of the philosophic tradition—indeed, of God, for whom a rabbinic synonym is *Makom* (place or space) and whom Spinoza transvalues into Extension and identifies as the outside of the totally one substance whose inside is thought or reason. And perhaps even more pertinently this Place is the perceptual Original of the space once filled with all the evils flesh is heir to—all men's sorrows and sufferings, all their cares, all their errors and all their illusions—but blown utterly clean of them, windswept back into its own original ineffably wholesome purity known as spirit.

One name for perceived space thus transvalued is *nirvana, nivvana, nibbana*. It signifies that purified, that blessed, nothingness which we may attain, or as some prefer, create, by blowing away the evils which fill up our existence. It is the place *Beyond* the *maya* of suffering and illusion wherein we so struggle for existence, only to suffer its consequences in the successive existences of Karma and Sangsara. Nirvana is the place we come to when we have extinguished, have literally *blown out* (Sanskrit: *nis*, out; *vaina*, blowing from *vati*, it blows) all the desires which drive us to struggle on, and have by this means freed ourselves from the pains and penalties of the struggle not only, but from the Selfhood they form, as well. To experience, the power which blows is Wind (*vati*, again): so, the breath of the Lord, Spirit, Logos, the Word. Job hears it as the voice of the Whirlwind. His ear impatterns it, for by itself it is all force and no form; it is action uncontained—the almighty, creative nothingness. As human, it is our own drive when we "get the wind up," or the urge, the élan, of whatever is coming to be that we "have in the wind." In approval, we "*blow up*" our image of persons and places and thoughts and things; in condemnation, we not only *blow up* people, but *blow down* both people and things. Sometimes again we *blow* people to food and drink and other desirables. We *blow* hot, we *blow* cold: we scare, and *blow* town. And if we merely pretend to the power of the blast, we are *blown up* for *blow-hards*. While if our power has left us in danger of defeat, we have become *blown*; the spirit, however willing, has like the flesh, failed us. The creative élan is the Spirit Beyond and as ever, it bloweth where it listeth. The metaphor—if it be a metaphor—tells its own tale. Call it Nivvana—and it figures as creativity in act, first extinguishing evil, then lighting up, actualizing Good. Buddha is the Enlightened One who can do both. For Nivvana, the Void of self-fulfillment by means of not-desiring, not-caring, not-seeking, as when Cha'n or Zen transvalues aversion from all appearance into the impartial enjoyment of each appearance as it passes into and out of Nivanna, or as when Tao gives forth and takes back all changes, at once the formations and the confluence, diffluence and the passing of formations.

This Nothingness, eternally Void and Plenum, imagined by certain saints or sages of India, and China, and Japan, may have some affinities, as Van Meter Ames argues, with English-American Whitehead's "non-entity" and American Mead's "Beyond." It might even be allied with the plenum of Bergson's "creative evolution." But the Existentialists display, among their other innovations, an image of a terrifying (so they say) Nothingness which has no lawful kin among the earlier pre-Darwin ones. The Existentialist imagination turns the value-systems of the *philosophia perennis* upside down, West and East. If Existentialist nothingness be reality, it is reality as evil, never as good. For some Existentialisms what we call good, indeed, can ultimately be only illusory, not real. Then what is death?

Heidegger answers: The Nothingness of which our life-long vague anxiety or dread is the awareness; for we are born unto death and all our lives fight it off, surviving defeat after defeat only at last to be utterly overcome. Death is the creator of the dread which ever impels us, the object of our awe before its absolute Nothingness, this utter Negativity which shows up our existence for the sequence of absurd and meaningless contingencies it is. He might have called it Macbeth's tale told by an idiot full of sound and fury, signifying nothing.

But if we teach ourselves to live with this universal idiocy, death, we learn also that in the end no good is better or worse than any other, that all are alike simply no good. Their equality reduces all values to no value. Once aware, we cease to care. We are, if not alienated, detached; and we each stand on his own record as the Self he thus makes himself into, at last an ineluctably free and independent power, with the dignity and sufferance which are the attributes of the free and independent. To keep oneself thus, is, however, to isolate oneself, to live on solo in autonomous loneliness, and to carry the guilt of it to the day one dies, freely acquiescing in one's finiteness, willing it and assenting to the all-pervading Nothingness. Creativity would be this anguished passage from Nothingness to Nothingness. It would be a progression of "self-transcendence" into a continually freer Identity. This, as it works, liberates Selfhood, diversifies creativity itself (or the affirmative power of initiation and innovation) and consummates the purposeless autonomy of existence.

Creativity's import, here, seems again defence rather than growth; the events compenetrated as "self-transcendence" are growth started and sustained by successive acts of self-preservation. Only, alas, we don't preserve ourselves. We die, impelled by dread of death, picking from alternatives we dread to pick from, merely to sputter out at last, like a firecracker leaving a burnt-out stench behind. The East goes the other way because the East, confronting death, cultivates the "inauthentic" life.

So Heidegger, so Sartre, as I understand and translate their metaphysical cryptography. The inspiration of Heidegger was the State of Germany after the First World War and before the insurgence and diffusion of the Nazi movement with its exemplification (in doctrine, discipline and organization of society), of the Creator's power of self-transcendence and progression which is the defensive utmost of his struggle against nothingness as Martin Heidegger interpreted it. In due course, this interpreter made a commitment to a creed and a code which should on the face of it have been a demonstration that the interpretation could be relied on. "Not doctrine and ideas be the rules of your being," he told his listeners on being inducted as Rector of the University of Freiburg (November, 1937), "The Fuhrer, himself and alone, is the present and future German reality and its law. Learn ever deeper to know; that from now on, each and every thing demands decision, and every action, responsibility. Heil Hitler." He seems, however, later to have uncommitted himself. He survived Hitler and his chieftains. He altered his cryptography and with it enabled the shaping of a new image of its inventor. The alteration has been signalized as a *kehre*—it might, but ambiguously, mean conversion *from*, if not an inversion *of*, his metaphysic of *Sein und Zeit* to a metaphysic of *Sein und Sinn*—a turn from non-being and meaninglessness to Being and Meaning. He now found the simple, straightforward naive naturalism of the pre-Socratics the reliable pro-paedeutic to that *Unverborgenheit des eins* which is truth disclosed— *aletheia*; now mythology is such a disclosure—and all *Denken* is such a *Dichten*.

So the "later Heidegger," but as yet without a later revelation of creativity.

Jean-Paul (what pregnant given names!) Sartre, the other major apostle of the Existentialist revelation, was Heidegger's pupil. He has a morally other but analogous intellectual history. His vocational *terminus a quo*, following Heidegger's, was the phenomenologism constructed by Edmund Husserl. But he and most of his fellow countrymen were the victims and foes of, not the crusaders for, the principles and practices of Nazism. Sartre became a soldier of the French "resistance" to the Nazi might, exposing himself to its ever-menacing danger, its never-allayed feelings of the imminence of capture, torture and death because of carelessness or bad luck or betrayal, its need of unceasing alertness and mistrust in order to fight on. Jean Paul's experience of this variety of give-and-take amid human relations in his war against the ultimate evil, disclosed to him the indefeasible aloneness and ultimate loneliness of the human person. Even in the most intimate of mutualities, the individual first and last could count solely on the loyalty of himself to himself, and about this, too, he might well be deceiving himself—with Marx's opiate of the people not only, but with every other variety of the *philosophia perennis* that a mind can conjure up or invent.

A personage with an imagination and a literary skill that Heidegger could only dream of, Sartre gave voice to this sentiment in plays and stories as well as such skilfull dialectical performance as *L'Etre et le Neant* and *Critique of Dialectical Reason*. Let me now state his philosophic creed —he does mean it, since he publishes and argues it for a communication, not a soliloquy—in as common (essential) language as I can muster. Repeatedly he postulates—a sentiment as pregnant as it is strange—that we humans are *condemned* (my emphasis) to be free, that we are not free to be free (much like insisting that a triangle is *condemned* to be a triangle and not free to be itself). We happen into a circumambience—"situation" is Sartre's word—which we endow with meaning by our selections from the interacting aggregate which, like it or not, we are confronting. What-ever we make of our lives is a creation: first, of the decisions we make on what to do, whom to deal with, where to go, in our choosings between alternative and alternative; and again, of the strength we gain or lose as we team up with, or segregate ourselves from, our situation. The self that we thus work ourselves up into becomes a transactional whole of which our situation is the other half. Our choosings endow that with meanings and values which vary with each choice between persons, tasks, goals near, goals far, and always, life and death. Creativity thus discloses itself to be a non-stop sequence of choosings and decisions which so ineluctably commits us to the object of our preference (whatever it be) that we become entirely engaged with it, bonded to it, even unto death.

Willy-nilly we are the authors of our being, inescapably free and independent tragical individual selves, masters of our own fates, captains of our own souls, in ourselves and for ourselves "authentic." Indeed, what we call good can ultimately be only illusory, not real. So Sartre's hero, Jean Gênet, whom he canonizes into St. Gênet, earns this consecration by freely choosing, like Milton's Satan, evil to be his good and so achieving authenticity. The authentics of this highly imaginative criminal novelist of evil are the transvaluers of all the traditional values who make their nihilism their career and glory in it. His *ne plus ultra* of counter-heroism is Hitler, who boasts in *Funeral Rites*: "I have killed, pillaged, stolen, betrayed. What glory I've attained! But let no run-of-the-mill murderer, thief, or traitor take advantage of my reasons. I have gone to too great pains with them. They are valid only for me. That justification cannot be used by every Tom, Dick and Harry. I don't like people who have no conscience."

Yet Gênet, like Sartre, was a hero of the Resistance. Beside him, the being of us others is inauthentic, factitious, in bad faith. For it comports, *pour soi*, the emptiness of *en soi*, of their futurity, which is forever always and everywhere the same Nothingness wherewith our singularities, our multitudinous awarenesses, our being *pour soi*, are ever incommensurable. So we struggle on, anguished choice after choice, until we die. Since, in the confrontation, God is dead and everything is permitted, we alone are responsible for our acts, and our sole duty is to sustain the honest consistency which authenticity names. Failing this, we are a sequence of free events, without identity, without character, practitioners of "bad faith." To be in good faith "authentic," we must make a "commitment" to an over-all cause which serves us as a design for living and crystallizes into achieved habit. Else we are each a sequence of fictions we create in our struggle to survive, with which we deceive ourselves. We imagine them in order to offset the basic anxiety of our existence. It has no object but obtains in the stress and strain with which we keep fighting the circumambient Nothingness that ever threatens to engulf us, and sooner or later does, in death. Our unhappy identities, in the making from birth to death, are formations of this struggle of ours, of our ever-repeated acts of self-creation as defenses against that ultimate annulment.

Any style of being other than this is "inauthentic." The other fails in the naked sincerity, the absolute "good faith" which adequate upkeep of our struggle to survive requires. It is an impotence, an inability to take the decisive action which creates values and goals—thus an unfreedom for which determinism, signifying necessary connection, could be the correct name. Decisive action can be only free action, ongoing choices in the transit from what is to what is not yet which is our existence as humans confronting Nothingness, ever impelled by anguish to keep choosing; to keep striving, in order—ultimately without success—to assuage our psyches by creating this, that or something else and thereby ourselves, just simply to cut off and shut out the all-penetrating Nothingness.

A less rationalist and more reasonable Existentialist, Karl Jaspers, observes somewhere that Existentialism derives from extreme experiences, and it is quite likely that an examination of the personal histories of the different spokesmen for this variegated *ism* would support Jaspers' observation.

His own, for example. He grew old—he died at 80—with bad lungs and a bad heart. Virchow had prophesied that invalids like him would die before thirty. His existence was a tightrope of survival. It was truly an ongoing struggle *in extremis* ever aware "of the fragility of being." It was in the cards that his initial occupation should be that of psychiatrist with whatever this disclosed to him of man's nature and man's plight— conspicuously perhaps, the ongoing predicament they compose. In terms of the Germany of Jaspers' mature years and old age, man's plight consisted of a sequence of crises, from the elimination of the Kaiser through the exhalation and dissipation of Hitler. After the latter came to power, the philosopher was deprived of his chair at Heidelberg. He lived from 1937 under police surveillance and threat of a concentration camp until 1945 when, rescued by Allied forces, he was able to resume his teaching at Heidelberg. There he spoke out. He published a book pointing out the guilt of all the Germans (*die Schuld Frage*) and chose to leave Heidelberg for Basle in Switzerland and the chair of philosophy at the University there. He wrote, now wary of conclusions, with a concern for the immediate new formations of the deepening predicament of mankind— the import of the atom bomb, for example—as well as the perennial issues of *philosophia perennis*. His formulations seem open-ended, a series of "possible perspectives," all with a hint of the probable self-destruction of man and his works by his own works, and with the hope of designing ways of insurance against it. He called himself somewhere *der Schwebende Philosoph*, with a sort of humanism for his philosophic perch. Expounding his philosophic faith in *My Philosophy* he wrote: "Philosophy cannot look for Transcendence (read *Essence,* in the idiom of Sartre and Heidegger) in the guarantee of revelation but must approach Being in the self-disclosure of the encompassings that are present in man as man . . . in the history of the language of Transcendence." In that history, Humanism would be, Jaspers indicated in his essay on *Existentialism and Humanism,* a creed for a code still to be enacted, an eventuation still to come as salvation from death, and even more today from mankind's present man-made plight. This, *qua* salvation, is ever beyond, ever Transcendental; a consummation we may create by our working and fighting for it—for this is both ground and goal of all contingent existence, and is implied by the freedom we become aware of "when we fail ourselves and cannot attain it by ourselves alone." True, "Transcendence speaks nowhere directly. It is not there, not tangible (i.e.: is 'nothingness'?) God speaks only through our freedom . . . enhances us and simultaneously enables us to see through ourselves and realize that we are nullities in a circum-ambience ever unfinished, and alone to whose movement Beyond our Existence surrenders itself without reservation." This Beyond seems a kind of *Deus Absconditus*[2] which we existents postulate, helplessly and without reason. Our postulation validates itself consequentially, not logically. The history of the human enterprise is the record of a perduring endeavor "toward a single, great, organized unity of opposites which at the boundaries fail to yield solutions in time, and in failing, bring to awareness the truth of Transcendental Being. Presumably, creativity is another name for this endeavor, which figures as a transaction (Jaspers phrase is "Aufschwung in der Transcendens") of self-aware existence, with a never-disclosed Transcendence—or Nothingness—as plenum rather than void. "To learn to live and to learn how to die," Jaspers wrote in 1953, "are one and the same thing."

Sartre's personal history presents a like or more dramatic confirmation of Jaspers' word regarding the springs of Existential philosophies. Sartre, unlike Heidegger, could not commit himself and become bound up (*engagé* is his word) in any social movement with a creed and a code not orchestrable to his philosophic faith. "From the period when I wrote 'Naussée', he tells us, "I wanted to create a morality. My evolution consists in my no longer dreaming to do so." Instead, he committed himself to Marxism and became *engagé,* more or less, with France's Communist party. Yet he would also have his Existentialism "a humanism"—inasmuch as it neither generates nor maintains rules for the choices which make up the Existentialist conduct of life. Love or Duty? Family or Country? Submission or Extinction? There exist no means of judging. Alternatives are always concrete, singular and unpredictable. Means need always to be invented, and the thing which alone counts is, "to know whether the invention is made in the name of freedom" Sartre does not disclose how the invention called Communism, without a doubt made in the name of freedom, serves it in any "authentic" way whatever. But he does disclose, in images concrete enough, his own concern for "other people." "I suddenly discovered that alienation, the exploitation of man by man, undernourishment, relegated to background metaphysical evil, which is a luxury. Hunger is an evil; period."

It is, however, the luxury that Sartre's plays and tales best betoken—the amoral morality, so to speak, of utter aloneness. Take this novel antinovel, *Nausée*. Its non-hero, Roquentin, gets disgustingly sick at the sight of the most commonplace objects—sick in sickening detail at perceiving a beer glass, a bench, a rock, a blue shirt against a brown wall. His aversion—"alienation" for the *periti*—from the phenomonological detailing of these items—segregates him, turns him as nearly as possible inside out, puking lonely and alone. Or take the much more widely read and viewed play *Huis Clos*, known in its English versions mostly *No Exit*, but also as *In Camera* and *Vicious Circle*: the setting is characteristically middle-class French. The personae belong there. They are a male journalist, a valet, a couple of girls, one lesbian, the other nymphomaniac. Their dialogue composes into a fable or an allegory for the Existentialist clash of mutually blocking freedoms and counter-freedoms engaged in each character's struggle to keep on struggling no matter at whose cost. The climax or consummation is the ineffable Existentialist self-segregating summary on human relations. "Hell is other people." In the *Critique of Dialectical Reason*, Sartre, repeats this variation upon Hobbes' war of all with all. Any Other's freedom is a threat to one's own. We have to enslave or kill the Other. Ultimately we shut them out or cut them off—"praxis the negation of alterity," "violence is self-creation."

Is this *terminus ad quem* of an Existentialist's exhibition of relations between humans, the foregone conclusion he and his fellow libertarians are committed to presented in that utter "good faith" which the true believers demand? Or is it another happening of the dialectician's and dramatist's make-believe? Is it an "authentic" or an "inauthentic" commitment? Sartre provides an answer, in that he chose to forego the luxury of metaphysical evil and bonded himself to the program of the no less metaphysical (Nazi-reprobating and not infrequently emulating) Communist good, including its atheist charges against the inhumanity of the rest of the world's God. Yet, on the record, the creed and code shared by the denominations of Communists are no less authoritarian than those of the traditional cults they righteously condemn in the name of the

c

providential Dialectical Materialism which is their replacement for their demoted providence of God. "If God does not exist," we remember Sartre warning us, "we find no value or commands to turn to which legitimize our conduct. So, in the bright realm of values we have no excuse behind us, nor justification before us. We are alone with no excuses." And what else are we if the Communist creed and code did not "exist?" If our imaginations have created the one, may they not also have created the other, and are not both free choices, taken or not in good faith? Are the theists who fight exploitation, poverty and hunger in their God's name any less concerned than those who fight in their Dialectical Materialism's name, espousing atheism or humanism for its name's sake? "Existentialism is a Humanism," Sartre advises. A humanism for which Hell is other people. Considering the historic situation which started this Humanism off, and with which it became a transaction, we can think it's Hell undoubtedly other people. It's Hell was the Nazi assault on mankind. But the record shows this Hell harmonized to an Existentialism—Heidegger's and, via Jean Gênet, Sartre's—and was acquiesced in by their creators as the authentic practice of the principles of their philosophies. Hell could as well be other people in happenings of cowardice, treachery, cruelty and greed among comrades united in resistance to the Nazi metaphysical evil. But other people could also be—and for the most part were they not, are they not?—examples of the devotion of comrades to one another, of conscience and courage, of loyalty unto death, not only in the war and work of resistance to the obscenely merciless foe. Sartre's Extentialism does take into account these qualities of men and their creative roles as Heidegger's does not. But it derives them from our presumed life-long anguished confrontation with the all-penetrating, ultimately victorious *en soi* of Nothingness.

In so far as this or any other Existentialism thus orchestrates to the Darwinian postulates, it is, with all its nihilistic heroics a pragmatism *manqué*, a timid pragmatism, inhibited from carrying the import of those postulates to the positive meanings that the cultures of mankind progressively embody respecting the relations of man to man and man to nature or value and existence to essence, as the radical-experience-ethic of James, Dewey and Mead sums them up. Beside the consensus of their diverse perspectives of existence and value, Existentialist foetus-pragmatism is also a sick pragmatism. It projects the still crescent defensive sickness of soul which the weather of human relations occasioned in the intervals between the First and Second World Wars. It made into stale, flat and unprofitable betrayals of the aroused hopes of man—a "nausée" not only of the achievements of scientific insight and discovery, of technological inventions and their products, but also of their future promise for the self-ordered freedom, for the health, for the education, for the diversified satisfaction and civility of mankind. The sickness of soul projected images of man wherein the skills of intellect and the creativity of intelligence figured as crippling weaknesses, not creative strengths. The sickness keeps averting the mind from the human past as from intolerable evil. From the Bolsheviks to the Maoists and beyond, the generations of the faithful would cleanse the future from the contamination of the past by proscribing its faiths, razing its institutions and destroying all its works. The wording of this suicidal urge of theirs came in new creeds and manifestos; its fulfilment, in the assemblings of new congregations of the new true faith and in evangels of violence and destruction for the truth's sake among which the Maoist cultural revolution from revolution is the most imposing success.

But the passionate wish fulfilled itself most consequentially in the Existentialist exaltation of "the Absurd,"[3] and the creation of its gospels by diverse practitioners of the literary, theatrical, graphic and plastic arts. These, during the more than half-century since the First World War, exalted the naked, crude creations of an assumed self-conscious infantilism into the excellence of maturity. With masterful dialectics, the revolutionary sick-souled Existentialist philosophy, welcome to the young of the age's generations, enshrined "the Absurd" as the providence which shapes our ends, rough-hew them by reason as we may. The thinker or artist whose works are acknowledged and proclaimed "authentic" is the individual whose propensities of vision or performance produce absurdities—artist Gênet, thinker McLuhan, for example—which somehow render more homelike the anguish-evoking Nothingness. Their means is their formlessness—no-forms of novels, no-forms of plays, of persons and characters, of words and things and paintings and sculptures, all would-be-*now*-creations with neither *terminus a quo* nor *terminus ad quem*, instances all present, with no future and without a past, each a much-at-once bespeaking the ultimacy of the ever-wild chaos of nature before nature was, and the spontaneous variations in man, unharnessed to the laws of the nature that is or the habit and reason of human civility.

Creativity here is as close as maybe to the physicist's "steady state" which is imagined as the *terminus a quo* of creative evolution, à la Darwin. It is creativity as Beyond the Behind, Behind the Beyond. In creator-man, it works *at* the boundaries, not outside them. The nothingness whence creations flow is *within* nature if it be not, indeed, nature itself, *natura naturans*. Not, however, *natura naturans* as the perennial philosophy argues it—one unaltering substance, *causa sui*, self-identical and self-maintaining, the same always and everywhere. Rather *natura naturans* as an open-ended infinitude of spontaneities coming together, going apart, dissipating into nothingness in unimaginable entropic shapes and sizes, from the infinitudes of infinitesimal particles to the infinite multiplicities of galaxies and beyond. It has been the need of *genus humanum* somehow to reduce, contain, arrest, repeat and confine these happenings. Unity is a survival value; unification, whatever its means and method, is an achievement of this value, so that every happening is treated as an effect to be bound to a cause that by necessity serves man's strivings to control and use the effect as he wishes. This has been and largely continues to be the vocation of philosophy, even though the sciences have been doing the same job better in specific fields. But all the fields together, the "universe," —literally, the *turn* toward oneness—continue the domain of philosophy. Yet the two vocations are Sisyphean. Each again and again suffers the frustration of the "infinite regress" and invokes in vain the Aristotle-like relief of *ananké steinia*. Both again and again struggle against the "anxiety" which Aristotle knew as "wonder"; its assuagement is what they seek by means of their formulations of "laws of nature" and their designs and constructions of philosophic systems. Creativity and nothingness continue ever "Beyond."[4]

NOTES

1. Or until those whose philosophic faith this is have died out, and the true believers in another view of intelligence and its role no longer have this alternative to confront. As Max Planck observed in his *Autobiography:* "A new scientific truth does not triumph by convincing its opponents and making them see the light, but rather but because its opponents eventually die, and a new generation grows up that is familiar with it." How much more is this the case with philosophic truth.

2. "As soon as I had realized that God was not yet but was becoming and that his becoming depended on each one of us, a moral sense was restored in me. No impiety or presumption in this thought, for I was convinced at one and the same time that God was achieved only by man and through man, but that if man led to God, creation, in order to lead to man, started from God; so that the divine has its place at both ends, at the start and at the point of arrival, and that the start has been solely in order to arrive at God. This bivalvular thought reassured me and I was unwilling to dissociate one from the other: God creating man in order to be created by him; God the end of man; chaos raised up by God to the level of man and then man raising himself to the level of God. To accept but one of them, what fear, what obligation! To accept the other, what self-satisfaction! It ceased to be a matter of obeying God, but rather of instilling life into him, of falling in love with him, of demanding him oneself through love and of achieving him through virtue."

3. Albert Camus, occasionally called an Existentialist, rejected the denomination, and described the *ism* as a myth which had become popular. Like his mythmakers, he believed in freedom but urged that a man becomes aware of it not in affirming "the Absurd" but in rejecting it, rebelling against it as man's inhumanity to man. The inwardness of the rebel's rebellion is a "natural grace," an *essential* humanity common to all humans whence the rebellion springs. Already in 1945 Camus had proposed that he and Sartre publish a joint statement to the effect that they had nothing in common and would not be responsible for each other's debts. In December 1959, Camus gave an interview in which he said: "Our existentialism ends in a theology without God and a scholasticism which inevitably ends by justifying regimes of inquisition." Bertrand Russell, asked in June 1966 for an estimate of "the existentialist philosophy of Martin Heidegger, Karl Jaspers, J. P. Sartre, replied to the two Jugoslav journalists who asked: "I think the Existentialist philosophy is pure nonsense, based intellectually upon errors of syntax and emotionally upon exasperation." There are psychoanalytically-minded thinkers who read Existentialism as a regression to infantilism—an elaboration without alteration of the animality of infancy, which is as nearly existential-like a physicists's particle—as a living humanoid can be—infancy absurdly propelled by animal drives without any notion regarding their *Whys*, their *Hows*, or their *Whatfors*. To vindicate this animality with an elaborate dialectic is either a consummate, yet naive practice of existentialist-condemned "bad faith" or a fantastic misunderstanding of the human enterprise. In this Jaspers alone seems not guilty.

4. One recalls Taoist LiPo: "We poets struggle with non-being and force it to yield being." Or blind and godless Christian James Joyce saying to a friend reading to him: "about the sound of words and the sound one word makes on another and the sound of the silences between words . . . the word is creative. The divine creativity of the word." Or Auden: "The poet marries the language and out of this marriage the poem is born."

The Genius and His Inspiration

BELIEF IN creation *ex nihilo* seems to be engendered by the perception of a felt and compelling newness in the created thing. Whatever it be, it is, to him who perceives it, a presence somehow unique, somehow unprecedented with no antecedent in the perceiver's past, or in the maker's, and with no authentic like in their present. The newness appears as an ineffable *this*, which for the nonce suffuses the most familiar sights and sounds. If the latter arouse a feeling of *dejà vu*, the newness compenetrates it with a sense of *jamais vu*.

Not uncommonly, artists and thinkers, inventors and discoverers whose works are thus experienced are themselves believed to be unlike other men: their habits of life diverge noticeably from the common ways and values of their neighbors. To the latter they appear unneighborly, they figure as misfits. But as misfits to whom none can be indifferent, whom all will either deride or cherish, exploit or protect, precisely for their roles of misfits in the community life. Their words are heard as nonsense, or as poetry, or as prophecy, or as necromancy. Their actions are seen as the doings of men beside themselves, men possessed by a spirit not their own, causing them to chant or speak they know not what nor how, and to act they know not why. They give voice and move like madmen, and it is often said that the creative spirit does make madmen of those it inspires. But mad or divinely sane, the inspired are held to be chosen instruments of the ineffable creative power, which enters them from without and works its works in them and through them. Some know themselves to be thus elect. Of themselves, all feel powerless to create; they say nothing new, they do nothing new. In creating, they are only receptacles, mediums, carriers or agents. Alone when the spirit has chosen to enter and take possession of their persons do they become truly prophets and poets, bringers of news from heaven—or hell—restorers of the past to present vision, revealers of the future to prevision.

These perhaps favored ones may be born to the role; they may have been apprenticed learners of it, or it may have been suddenly thrust on them. The spirit works in many dark ways its wonders to perform, and the roles of those it takes possession of may be as diverse as that of the female, the wizard, the sybil, the medicine man, the saint, the prophet

60

the poet, the inventor, the discoverer. In every role they may hear voices, see visions, dream dreams, speak with tongues, pronounce oracles foretelling the future or evoking the past. To ready themselves for the divine possession, some fast, some eat sacrificial flesh and drink sacrificial blood, some ingest drugs, some inhale vapors, some beat and tear their own flesh, some dance and shout and chant, some bring themselves into cataleptic rigidity. After the spirit has made its use of its chosen and has left them to return to themselves, they enter into a dull stillness, each less able than the least of his neighbors to think wisely or to act skilfully in coping with the daily tasks of his struggle to live on. Somehow, the neighbors, the community, provide for him—or excommunicate him and starve him, maybe to death.

"Authentic" inspiration or possession is a happening. Both come as intrusions into the massed sequence of a personal history. They come with a kind of suddenness, regardless of expectation. Attempts to conform them to expectation, to reduce them to sure effects of known causes, seem to be endemic in most of mankind's cultures. The rites and rotes of every cult are such attempts, so are the diversely formalized manifold of conditions and occasions under which once and again possession ensued and inspiration gave voice. By and large, repeating and stylizing the conditions of occasions, installing them as a ceremonial art or craft, rarely renders them better fitted to bring on the authentic experience. This cannot be induced or caused by rite or rote, whatever their kind. Their use displaces authenticity by intentional role-playing, for which prostitution is perhaps an analogue. For a person to be possessed and inspired becomes for him to play a part knowingly and on purpose. His voice is not changed by the spirit, but stays his own, his hand does not become the hand of the Lord but stays his own. The possessed is the possessor, the inspired is the inspirer. Pretense plays the part of presence, and make-believe the part of means to create and nourish belief. In due course make-believe and pretense become ceremonial arts practiced and enjoyed for what they are in themselves instead of for their roles of vehicles and media serving the occasion to incarnate the discarnate protean mana which the pantheons of the peoples everywhere inform with the local habitations and the names recounted by their myths and allegories. This holds for all the arts if not the sciences. As Vasari observed in his *Lives of the Painters*: "Many painters achieve in the first sketch of their work, as though guided by a sort of fire of inspiration, a certain measure of boldness; but afterwards, in finishing it, the boldness vanishes." The inspiration may be manifest regardless of artistic mastery. It comes independently.

Authentic inspiration segregates. It evokes public recognition of a private madness; "no excellent soul," Aristotle observes, "is exempt from a mixture of madness," and John Dryden, who was perhaps the first in his time to make explicit that poets are truly innovators who bring new life into old bones, who transmute the familiar into the strange, wrote that "great wits are sure to madness near allied." He may also have been among the first who recognized men of art, mostly wordmen, poets, as men of genius. Republican Rome generally believed that all men were attended by divine beings, tutelary or other, who moved them to good or evil. Renaissance humanists tended to sufflate attendant into attendee, and to regard the genius which possessed the poet as the poet's own soul. In Dryden's phrase, "a happy genius" was a "gift of nature," a capacity for inspiration unique, strange, but not unnatural or supernatural. The enlightened souls of the Age of Reason—because tradition has held inspiration akin to madness—decided it to be a weakness and a menace, in no way the artist's own genius impelling him toward his unique excellence; nor even the common man's by nature uninspired.

But in due course the men of wit and reason became aware of sentiment and of "the reasons of the heart"; more and more they found themselves sensitive to Shakespeare unimproved. For choice they set him up as their true "natural genius," partaking of something divine. Poetic vision—so, in his *Conjectures on Original Composition*, dying Edward Young urged in 1769—when true, is a spontaneous growth of the soul, a living insight, not a contrived show; an original creation of the natural genius who alone can create originally; alone can "call forth shadowy beings, and unknown worlds as numerous, as bright and perhaps as lasting as the stars." Immanuel Kant defined genius as *Originalgeist*. Its powers are inborn; study and practice might refine and discipline them but cannot produce them. Genius is a gift, not an achievement, not a capacity for infinite pains, nor a practice that makes perfect. No law binds genius. Like God, it is a law unto itself, and its action creates, with the act of creation, the laws of that creation. So the powers of the possessing spirit are translated and revalued into the powers of the spirit possessed. Now, inspiration no longer descends from above but wells up from within, and like the Biblical wind, it bloweth where it listeth. It is creativity, at once the newsmaker and newsbringer, and both ineffably. Study cannot learn it, teaching cannot impart it. Neither the sciences of man nor the sciences of nature can attain to reliable knowledge of its causes, however efficaciously they may account for its consequences. Ideas of cause and effect are derived from experience of creativity, not the experience from the ideas. Causation, effectuation, are only modifications of creativity remembered; repetitions, imitations, not the original.

Yet, if we trust the record, the mind's endeavor to transpose creativity and origination into necessary causation and repetition is coeval with reason itself and intrinsic to mankind's humanity. The urge to account for the spontaneous, the new, the unexpected, in terms of the recurrent, the old, the forseen and foreseeable, seems as inveterate as the hunger for them. The urge to render the new, in one way or another, an event pre-determined by the laws of nature and/or nature's God—laws always and everywhere the same—may be as innate as the urges to feed or fight, or hate or love. It may entail a like survival-value in a world which was not made for man and in which no man was made for any other. In this world of ours to learn and know the causes of things and to attribute things to causes and thus be able to foretell future consequences of current events, is to make survival surer. It is to attain possession of power and knowledge, knowledge which our "instinct of workmanship" spontane-ously employs to steer and shape events into means toward achieving or maintaining ends of which the sum is survival. For the most part, the sciences are taken to be such knowledge. But the perception that the sciences stay such only so long as they do the same job better than their rivals, is not yet a part of the commonsense of mankind. The record tells that *genus humanum* has at different times, in different places, endowed all sorts of images and ideas with survival-functions. The record tells that the believers become convinced that certain ideas and images, in im-patterning activity or prescribing actions, enable the actors to direct, hold and manage the persons, the places and the things which they, the actors, know. Their knowledge is the power whereon, in this ambience, they bet their survival.

Since Francis Bacon, that knowledge is power has ceased to be news; nor is it any longer news that this power has a paramount role in human survival. To command and use it continues to be both the end and the means of the most blissfully ignorant. Command and use are the *terminus ad quem* of every culture. In each they model into its human form the animal forces which are man's plan. Each individual shapes up into a singularity of its own his personal role, a process in an ambience of processes, ever redetermining the laws of nature—and of nature's God if he believes in one. To learn God's *what* and *how* and *why* is to take possession of all power and to harness it to the service of man, alive or dead. For God's knowledge and power are one, not two. He is defined as at once the all-knower and all-doer. And this is what man would emulate, as he struggles to live on and not die. Our sciences, like our religions, function as bets that presumed causes can be made into workable means to these ever hoped-for effects; the presumptions figure as inventions

c*

wherewith to harness creativity, whether natural or divine, to the service and survival of man. Whatever be said about God, what else does any believing sayer expect from his saying?

And does not the same question arise respecting the creativity of the man of genius? Unlike the traditional answers, the "scientific" or "naturalistic" ones postulate causes of another kind than "possession" or "inspiration." Genius must be, it is assumed, a natural effect of natural causes. To know those causes should be to command the power which can shape the singularity of creative genius into a means for collective ends. Even if the "unconscious" is assigned the place traditionally held by the heavenly Muse, it is still a better means of fitting the social misfit into society, without castrating his creativity. Or, if he cannot be fitted, his unfitness can be accounted for as the social price as well as the personal fine paid for his creative urge. The literature gathers arguments and proofs that genius is an effect of schizophrenia, of glandular imbalance and other organic deficiencies, of autogenous intoxications or of those due to infectious diseases like tuberculosis, like syphillis, or of others due to habit-forming drugs like alcohol, hashish, opium, marijuana, polycybin, peyote or lysergic acid. The genius's difference is acknowledged, his social deviations are justified if not forgiven, for the sake of his creative works. Long lists of artists and thinkers are produced to prove that a man's defects are the conditions, if not the cause, of his genius. William Sharp, who wrote as Fiona MacLeod, believed that he wasn't much as William Sharp. He wrote to a friend that his achievements depended on his "aloofness and spiritual isolation" when Fiona MacLeod. "I believe that a spirit has breathed into me, or entered me, or that my soul remembers or has awaked . . . and that being so, that my concern is not to think of myself, or my 'name', or reward but to do . . . my finest and best." He felt himself a "we" rather than an "I", "sometimes I'm tempted to believe I'm half woman."

An inference of psychopathology is here obvious. But the odds are even that it could be irrelevant. William's role as Fiona is not unconscious; it channels the exercise of a different function; it does not project a different character. Many artists and thinkers choose pseudonyms to signalize what they would shut out as well as take in, the better to practice their arts. They undertake a new birth; they would be, so to speak, twice born, in order more excellently to answer their vocation; and for not a few the pseudonym bespeaks the "real" man more truly than the name of his christening. Was not this the case with fourteen-year-old Thomas Chatterton? He was a poet who hid his everyday identity behind the features of a fictitious Thomas Rowley, whom he described as a fifteenth century monk and author of the teenager's own poems? Was Chatterton a sick soul, a healthy and purposeful cheat or a timid adolescent naturally afraid that critics would judge his writings by his youth and station rather than by their poetic quality? Only seven years after his suicide at the age of eighteen, was it discovered that Rowley was a figment of Chatterton's imagination, an invented Other, creating what opinion would have rejected as creations of Chatterton's. There was Chatterton's older contemporary, James McPherson, who died a natural death at the age of sixty. He passed off original poems of his own as translations he had made from the Gaelic of one Ossian. As works of Ossian, his *Fingal* and *Temara* won the enthusiastic appreciation of celebrities diverse as Wolfgang Goethe, Napoleon Bonaparte, Thomas Jefferson. The last wrote to McPherson for copies of the original, and the poet's fellow countrymen gave money that he might travel in Scotland to gather the still ungathered works of the imagined Ossian. Was McPherson a charlatan and a cheat or a pathological liar in projecting the Ossian of his imagination as the author of the poems of the man, McPherson, and the poems as translations from Ossian's Gaelic? Or is the image which masks the artist's or thinker's ordinary self and deceives the public an aspect of the duality which tradition signalizes by "inspiration" or "possession"?

True, not a few acknowledged geniuses have attributed their creative urge to some defect of their own they were aware of. There was Heinrich Heine, for example, a poet and a sage, yet a spirit disillusioned, who chose the simplest, the most obvious of defects. "Krankheit," he said,

> Krankheit ist wohl der tiefste grund
> Des ganzen Schöpfungsdrang gewesen
> Erschaffend könnte Ich genesen
> Erschaffend wurde Ich gesund

But there is no consensus among artists and thinkers that creation is health and healing, that creation is salvation. There is no consensus that genius is the Siamese twin of disaster, as effect might be the Siamese twin of cause. Not many accept the image of themselves as split personalities, as neurotics or near psychotics. Not many would account for themselves by an inward conflict of propulsions aware and unaware, in kind or degree unlike the conflict which is unalienable to all mankind, as they struggle to preserve themselves and build up thus the works and ways which compound into their personal histories, and which could well be described as episodes of the quest for peace of mind and strength of heart. The terms of the union of genius with disaster have been provided by interpreters like Lombroso, Max Nordau, Sigmund Freud and his epigons (be the latter dissidents or true believers). All translate such powers as the gods of the ancients or the daimons of Socrates into the blood and brain and psyche of the genius himself, justifying "abnormality" as the inner cause of the singular outer effect. They imply that the effect liberates the genius from his bondage to the cause. Creating, he is a social asset; uncreating, he is only a social problem.

This soi-disant "scientific" accounting for genius neither displaces nor abandons the sense of its subject's uniqueness, the practice of taking its singularity (however explained away) for a superiority somehow charismatic and alluring. The "scientific" knowledge about it does not seem to contaminate the scientists' acquaintance with it. When they confront it, their analysis of it as a character seems little to influence their experience of it as a force.

Jean Untermeter, in her autobiographical *Private Collection*, writes of her "impossible" endeavor to reveal to a college class her experience of "inspiration," as a turning of herself "inside out." But she did it: "I had gained for a time, at least, the power of concentration that is almost a friction of the mind: I had experienced the unbelievable moment when heat turns into light, and I wanted to share it. Later I learned it cannot be shared nor even won; it is a grace." Carl Sandburg, who heard her, commented: "Jean, you're like the old Negro preacher; you try to onscrew the onscrutable." On another occasion she told an inquirer: "Anonymous writes all the poetry. It is we who are usurpers when we sign our names to it." The throwback to "inspiration" or "possession" is implicit. Emerson's notion of the vital difference suggests how in actual encounter with genius scientific explanation gets displaced by experiental tradition with its connotations of possession and inspiration. In a man's own experience, Emerson says, his genius is that in his psyche which never toils, never calculates, never argues or reasons, it simply and freely utters what comes to utterance as it comes. "In writing my thought," the sage noted, "I seek no order of harmony or result. I would not degrade myself by casting about for a thought nor by waiting for one. If the thought comes, I would give it entertainment; but if one does not come spontaneously, it comes not rightly at all."

The essential, then, is the spontaneous coming. Creativity, originality, novelty, uniqueness, surprise, are spontaneities. Their *haecceitas* is, for personal experiences, unforeseen and unforeseeable. We so experience them on every occasion, under every condition. They do not fit in, as they come, with the recollection, the imitation, the plagiary which they attend and which are the dynamic of so much of our experience. They are that in our experience which cannot be plagiarized, and their ultimate singularities get attributed to recurrent deviations from the ordinary in the custom of a community or a culture, *post hoc, ergo propter hoc*. Creativity (so goes the inference) is regularly a manifestation of some personal or social pathology—this in the face of the fact that such pathology is not less regularly a component of health and normality than fog, storms and other meteorological stresses are regular components of weather. Indeed, persons whom their neighbors appreciate as very healthy and normal are impelled by an urge to create, in whatever field and whatever form— only they get known as amateurs.

These whose public roles identify them as artists and thinkers, as prophets, inventors or discoverers, are known to be spurred by the same needs, urged by the same passions, the same wishes and desires, the same rivalries and emulations as people everywhere. They also want "success." They also measure it by the Joneses they have chosen for their pacemakers. They crave not only to keep up with their Joneses but to excel them, and the measure of their success—William Sharp's protestation notwithstanding—is as much the money, the recognition and the rank which opinion rewards their creations with, as the satisfactions in the originality and excellence of the creations themselves. "Fame," John Milton declares, "is the spur that the clear spirit doth raise, to scorn delights and live laborious days."[1] Many among the cognoscenti appraise Shakespeare as a man of genius impelled by some such aspiration, nor has it been established that artists and thinkers by vocation who lived with "disaster" were not in equal measure impelled by the motives of healthy mankind.

Healthy or unhealthy, "normal" or not "normal," originality, genius, whatever its field, is signalized by the novelty it introduces in the field, the unprecedented turn it gives to vision and action; the breaks that it now and again makes in the chains of habit and custom which their linkage can neither foretell before they happen nor account for after they happen. On the record, the healthy, the normal are no less penetrable by innovation than their opposites. No matter what the context of the variant, the context fails to serve as a sufficient cause of its novelty. Thus, for example, fails Livingston Lowes' *Road to Xanadu*. This is the critical expert's lucid and sedulous topography of a poem of Coleridge's. Lowes seeks, and, so far as I know finds, every experience, especially every literary experience of the poet's that he consciously and unconsciously remembered and repeated in the poem. The detecting is detailed, precise and persuasive, with an originality of its own—a notable academic *zerelgung*. But the anatomical chart no more discloses that by virtue of which the poem it charts is an original with an ineffable singularity of its own than an

anatomist's *zerlegung* of a corpse could disclose the personality of the
living man. Originality is a surd. We ever keep striving to render it rational
with every instrument of analysis and reconstruction we can devise: but
on the record, these bring to light only the opportunities and occasions
of the creative act, but not the event of creation—this keeps occurring but
eludes as it occurs.

Some, perhaps many, may see in this relationship of originality to
causality a confirmation of one or another Existentialist philosophy. But
if the human condition were what Existentialism says it is, its true believers
could not say it. Their dialectic comes as a tangent from it, not a demonstration of it. The sciences of man and nature are consequential as that
dialectic is not. They more reliably bespeak the human enterprise from its
development as a hairy ape struggling for its own survival and thus making
itself over in the course of aeons into the *homo sapiens* who, struggling
even as all his ancestors, remembers, imagines and records his own
enterprise with its ever-varying visions, works and ways, and its never-
abandoned strivings to catch the variations in the act and to fit them to
its passing inborn purposes.

The tradition of genius is one such endeavor to catch, tame, and
harness up creativity.

The word "genius" is traced back to *gignere* which is the Latin word
for *beget*. It is cousin to *genus* and *gens* and perhaps shared its paternity
with *gene* until the disclosure of the double helix, our modern sign for
those complex, self-repeating, originative chemical chains to which we
attribute the diversities of living forms. Another relative of *genius* is *genie*,
also written *jinn*, an Arab word for that protean daimon whom heroes of
the Arabian Nights call up and command to work the miracles their good
requires. Usage begets meanings on *genius* which assign it sometimes to
personal destiny, sometimes to fortune's magic, sometimes to the *Kismet*
that Allah wills, sometimes to the postulated fatality of nature's laws. We
imagine these imputed causes of genius as separate but equal forces which
compel our lives, shaping our ends and imposing our means. We imagine
that they work on us by prescription in the stars or as a daimon possessing
us or as an angel of good or evil persuading our wills. A man may live
in a state of war with this genius of his; he may without resistance submit
and obey it; he may welcome it and willingly cooperate with it; but as
ever his *Other*, never himself. When usage changed the meaning of genius
from *Other* into *Same*, a man's genius came to be regarded as his vital
center, his nuclear disposition and power, even his skill, so far as skill
could be taken to be spontaneous, instinctual (as Thorstein Veblen did in
his *Instinct of Workmanship*), unlearned, thus also an endowment by

Nature or by Nature's God and not the man's achievement through study and practice. Genius was another word for the man's True Self.

Philosophers, with Plato their pioneer, work out one or another of these alternative meanings of genius, endeavouring to establish that one and only one is the true one. But the alternatives perdure, and philosophic disputation only refines them. Is a poet or a thinker a born genius or one possessed or inspired by an *Other?* Is genius intrinsically a human trait or is it an outer power, a power of man other than human? The *periti* still keep laboring the alternatives. So far as I can judge, the creative act still puzzles the most learned of minds. Striving to establish it as the sure effect of a definite configuration of causes, striving to contain and graph its ever-eluding role, students simply uncover one more of its occasions or map one more of its milieus, while the act comes into experience and passes undefined, at once perceived and ineffable. When usage displaced the meaning of genius as outer power taking charge of a man, by the man's own drive and disposition welling up creatively within him, this but changed the locus of the philosophic issue, not the issue. To believe that genius is as human a trait as man's other traits renders accounting for it an exploration of human nature and its causes instead of an argument about a transcendent power mastering and suppressing the human.

To believe that genius is an attribute of human nature was to turn inquiry in a new direction. It changed the inquirer from a metaphysician or theologian into a psychologist; it replaced dialectic by description; it confronted appeals to reason by apostrophes to passion, eliminating the former and diversifying the latter. But continually now, creativity was said to start in feeling, and the discipline of reason was demoted, as by Joseph Addison, to a place beneath the spontaneities of feeling. The man of genius was taken for another sort of man than tradition's artist or thinker. He was an original who creates unchecked by any discipline and according to no rule, whereas artists and thinkers work by rules that they have learned, according to a discipline which has become a habit which they cannot free themselves from. True, geniuses may, often do, accept a like discipline and learn rules; nevertheless, the rules can only refine, they cannot heighten the geniuses' creativity, and might diminish it. The sure *haecceitas* of genius is spontaneity, wildness, extravagance, which rule and discipline serve only to drill and contain, thereby to cut down, even to cut off, the innovation and strangeness which genius brings into the most familiar of repetitions.

Just look at Shakespeare "warbling his native wood-note wild." His plays repeat old familiar tales which his genius transfigures, like his Ariel's sea-change, into something new and strange. His creations are thus imitations yet non-imitations and inimitable. He differs from men of reason and art, Edward Young remarks, as a magician differs from a good architect; he raises his structure by means invisible, while the architect raises his by his skilful use of common tools. Of course, there are, there always will be, true believers that genius is sheerly a human trait, who also insist that the trait requires discipline and rules if it is not to produce, like an earthly wilderness, weeds and brambles only. Their authoritative spokesman was Voltaire who found Shakespeare a savage. He advanced a view common among the Enlightenment's representative men: that originality draws upon models; that the creative act does not perform from nothing at all; that it must cultivate its material, that it grows from seeds in prepared soil, not *ex nihilo*.

But, that originality is originality only insofar as it grows otherness, uniqueness; only as it is not a replica of a same but a different from this same, is merely recognized, not accounted for: *how* the same and the different, the old and the new, are linked, the *why* and the *wherefore* of their linkage, elude discovery and definition. Some, following Plato unaware, see a disclosure of the relationship in the details of the conception and birth of *genus humanum*. They interpret man's creativity after birth as but one more actualization of a specific potential of his genes, a potential which his transactions with the world around keep actualizing from conception to death. They call attention to scientific disclosure concerning the form and functions of genetic forces that Voltaire or Diderot or Edward Young or Immanuel Kant could not even imagine. These disclosures are still news—news about all life's processes, from conception to death. But what they reveal, or only hint at, regarding the *haecceitas* of creativity in a personal history from its pre-uterine beginning to its coffined end is still closer to reasoned faith recalling Plato and Philo than to reliable knowledge.

Nevertheless, the news which the geneticists have brought stirs and challenges the intelligence and spurs the imagination. Take the tale of "vegetative reproduction": it is a tale of genes. A person's genes are decalred to be, each, an identical replica of every other, and to hold a place in the nucleus of each cell of his body, as of the body of every living animal. Lungs, liver, intestines, muscles, glands as well as eggs and sperm contain identical genes in each of their cells. But they exist in the cells like The Sleeping Beauty, inert. They have no discernible share in the organic functions of the cells: they contribute neither to breathing nor digestion, nor to other exertions. For instance, biologists experimented with cells lining the stomach of one species of frog. They extracted the genes from the nucleus and replaced them with genes from a different species. On several occasions the transplantation was followed by the formation of a complete individual of the second species; "vegetative reproduction" signifies this event. It is asexual, a sort of parthenogenesis or virgin birth. The alien generator, when intruded into the unsexed egg-plasm, begins to make itself, not only into the mature form of its own kind, but with its genes replicating the generative originals, repeated in every adult cell. The originals have generated by dividing, not uniting as in sexual conception. How indeed could they unite with an *Other* which is not there and whose place they have taken? Things being otherwise equal, each developed, we are told, by itself alone into a complete individual, an identical repetition of the original whole. Barring accident, it could keep on forever—a sequence which has a beginning but no end. There need be no death in its cosmos.

Death as humans experience it is an innovation. It figures in life's struggle to preserve itself long, long after life itself happened, and itself began by sheerly happening. Reproduction as fission of the same[2] somehow got supplemented by reproduction as union of the different—a transaction between those late-come variations of vital forms—the multitudinous, mobile sperms and the solitary ovum moving slowly on its autonomous way. Compared with the sperms, the ovum might be Aristotle's unmoved mover drawing all those wiggling particles toward itself. The race of the sperms towards the ovum is the initial *Liebestodt* since, after forty-eight hours all but the winner perish of the flight, and the winner's survival is only vicarious, while an ovum which no sperm has penetrated goes to pieces after twenty-four hours. Sex and death are, it might be said, Siamese twins, so bound together that neither exists without the other nor can endure to exist with the other. Sex is a happening which modified a repetition of identicals into differentiation within identity. Death is the *terminus ad quem* of organic differentiation; death is entropy consummated.

The individuals that the congress of male and female genes engenders do not share the immortality of their self-replicating genes. The individuals are each unique, each singular, each an identity that makes a beginning and comes to an end. Other things being equal, an animal's genes might reproduce themselves without the animal individual whose genes they are, and who figures for the long run as a simply accidental instrument of their preservation and self-reproduction. The genes, not the persons who grow from them are the genus, the race. If man, as Tennyson tells us, goes on forever, it is as genes: as human persons, men but come to birth and go to death. A person cannot be reduced to his genes. Nor can an individual life of any other kind, whatever be its genetic code—insect, reptilian, fish, mammalian or human. They are born, they grow up, they grow old, they die, while new generations of strugglers to go on struggling first displace and then replace them. This is the improvident providence that shapes their ends.

Somehow, somewhere, men learned to combat their providence by inverting this relationship to their genes. They took themselves for ends and their genes for means. This cost them their animal innocence. And there are those who, with Sigmund Freud, hold the cost too high. The person, man, they protest suffers unnaturally because he struggles not to serve as a mere agent of the survival by reproduction of *genus humanum* but labors to employ the genes to further his personal happiness as a freely growing individual. His strivings have, in idea at least, transvalued his sexuality from a means of producing posterity into an ongoing means of forming personality; from a blind urge to satisfy animal lust into the imaginative ardors and tendernesses of human love and human friendship in which the Word plays so pervasively powerful a part. Sexuality as a vehicle of storing and transmitting the genes which are the primal material of *genus humanum* is by this very humanity transvalued into a mode of so using up the material that the spendthrift shall keep making himself more variously and abundantly human to the day he dies. Thereby man's *Liebestodt* becomes a kind of death which animals, including the human one, can neither experience nor imagine.

It is no news that the innovation which reshapes an animal—a naked ape, if you prefer—into a human being is the latest, the most precarious, turn of an immeasurable flux of ages—a flux which our words can intend, our numerals purport but which not even God can perceive or imagine or conceive,save as words and numbers. We but postulate an initiation, a beginning of the sequence of alterations which we call evolution; we postulate new turns at moments of the perduring trajectory until this day, and our Utopians extrapolate newer ones for days to come. We perceive the evolution of *genus humanum* in the nine-month sequence of mutations which began after a fertilized egg has taken a place in a female's womb and which came to their term when the human somewhat hairy apish creature thrusts its pain-enfolded way out, having been in succession a form fishlike, reptilian, mammalian. We are told that the succession telescopes some 2,000,000,000 years of this evolution. Life in the womb shapes up as a sort of recapitulation of an original creative process, itself creative to those who believe that the recapitulation is also a scrambling of an original order of succession.

Nor does the new-born come quite into its human difference with birth. It takes some years to turn from crawling on all-fours to standing up and walking erect, from merely making noises to speaking words. Its life as human—whatever the story, however long or brief—is somehow compenetrated with its life as fish, as reptile, as primitive mammal, as ape. The later new formations add themselves to the earlier; thence older ones alter their roles and meanings and reshape their forms. Some, as we have seen, believe the process of innovation to consist of an explication of structures implicitly already present; they speak of "emergent evolution"; others take innovation for creation *ex nihilo*, adding itself to what already exists as the sperm adds itself to the ovum: they are the Darwinians, speaking of "spontaneous variations," "struggle for survival," "natural selection," "survival of the fittest." But whatever the image of evolution, its vital center is creativity. Persons who are persuaded by Carl Jung or Teilhardt de Chardin would be emergent evolutionists; they would talk of archetypes; those who acknowledge geneticists' findings would seek causes in the past for present and future forms. Both would endeavor to reduce innovation to repetition of identicals, spontaneous variation to necessary connection of cause and effect.

Nevertheless, the authentic process of evolution does not permit foregone conclusions. For example, it is not a foregone conclusion that the *terminus ad quem* of life in the womb is birth into the world. That presumably favorable environment of an embryo, the womb, need not be so, or may become unfavorable. It may fail as a whole or in some part to perform its function: a placenta may be unable to make estrogen or, being able, cease to make it, so that the womb's muscles become too weak to hold a developing foetus with the suitable flexible firmness; or a placenta's transactions with a foetus may fail to enable the foetal parts to keep in that configuration with one another which assures that the organism grows up as a *whole* of harmonious parts. More often than not, new births are normal—that is, they repeat the ways of earlier ones, but the possibility of untoward contingencies being what it is, this normality is much more remarkable than, logically, its absence would be.

Anyhow, we confront our diversity of births and hold them all, with or without reservations, for true potentials of human persons. As actual, these potentials are the battery of psychosomatic propensities already formed in the womb which with birth they bring from the womb to the world. Already in the womb the unborn is alert to heat and cold, to pain, to hunger; it is able to move all its movable organs in order to escape or avoid their impact. Its sleeping and waking are pervaded by a restlessness which its movements relieve.

In due course, the restlessness of the newborn would be the end of it were its ongoing presence not the concern of parents, nurses, doctors, siblings, police—adults who strive, by helping it escape what hurts and possess what helps, to replace restlessness with the felt calm and contentment which "homeostasis" presumably signifies. Of course, in the experience of infant and child elders may also figure as forces which hurt and only hurt. Figure as they may, their images get added to the unconscious past which lives on as the child's body and to the once-conscious one which extends and suffuses the unconscious one as the child's memory. The images compound into "the Joneses"—loving, hating, helpful or harmful but always powerful—that the child as it grows would emulate, would endeavor to keep up with or surpass. Its conscious career becomes a shaping of its futureward thrust with images from its perceived present which has become its remembered past, patterned into a flexibly stable configuration which new events penetrate as sperm penetrates ovum and (perhaps) similarly reorders. Its "nature" is continually reformed by the transactions which constitute its "nurture."

These transactions are an unceasing conversion of experiences—of perceptions external and internal—into memories, into the present assimilation of the coming future by the perduring past. The stuff of the future will be sights, sounds, touches, presences, movements, heat, cold, smells, tastes, feelings, attitudes, images, intentions, impulses, actions—any and every event we experience. It is responded to in the brain by some unpredictable new configuration among its ten billion neurons, with their axons and dendrites, its hundred million glial cells, its neuronic fluid which laves them all. Between the dendrites are gaps; none touches any. But electrochemical changes set up by activity in neurons send a flow of electricity down the dendrites, and wherever the flow is strong enough to leap gaps, consciousness is said to ensue. It is believed that the flow brings on chemical changes in the form of ribonucleic acid (RNA) and perhaps also of peptides and of whole protein molecules. The electric current traces a path which frequent recurrences fix as the single helix of RNA that holds and lasts, and might well be a "memory trace." It adds itself to the deoxyribonucleic acid of the double helix (DNA), with its paired forty-six chromosomes, whose sequential patterns are held to figure as the blueprint of the inborn configuration which directs the production of the body's thousand different proteins. The reordering goes from ribonucleic acids to the glial cells. The newly formed proteins receive the imprints of perceptions as they come. Some investigators identify memory as these imprints. They believe that a variety of experiments disclose that it can be transferred as such by injection or ingestion, from individual to individual from generation to generation. They believe that the rung-like portions of it can be damaged, even deleted, by intruders (such as X-rays or certain drugs or chemicals) and that it defends itself against such killing by processes analogous to the splicing of a film. The repetition of series of diverse identicals which encode our heredity comes as a succession of constituent units, like tapes in a computer, and when a break in the succession alters the repetition beyond repair, mutations occur.

Whether or not this be a true image of psychomatic man, living and growing, there are biologists who doubt that it is, who postulate that the gene is not an independent variable; they guess that it is one of a team constituting the cell and that the heredity of a living being is a consequence of the teamwork, of the transactions, within the cell. As human persons and not merely electro-chemical, cerebroneural mechanisms, we recall and we forget, aware of ourselves as whole individuals whose successive memories are so compenetrated that they suffuse one another into a single ongoing futureward propensity of pastness, into a deviation wherein the distinctions we make between *then* and *soon*, between *now* and *after* must needs be recovered or created as the exigencies of our struggle to live on impel us to choose.

Recalling the "time-relations" of an experience, setting it in a chronological order, become more dubious as the experience becomes remoter. Since we live duration and create time, since we live extension and create "space" by moving in extension and making geometric figures by our trajectories, time and space, space-time or better, time-space, are products of our transactions with the conditions of our struggle and function among our survival-values. By rendering duration and extension into patterns definite and precise, we make of them weapons to overcome with. Some say that in regard to time, definition and precision vary inversely with the intervals between an experience happening and its recollection. They point up a distinction—Bergson is conspicuous for it with his postulate of "pure memory," and James is remembered for it with his hypothesis of a "reservoir" of memories—between the reciprocal suffusion by one another of all our remembrances and their reciprocal exclusion. The first envisions memory as an ongoing act in which the latest happening of a succession compenetrates with all that preceded it, earliest to latest. The second so shuts each away from all that the order of memory is ineluctably the order of chronological succession. To date any item in the order requires, to "time" it, a field of reference, an assemblage of documents and other present residues (their own dates are also decisions on faith), and an arsenal of time-determining and time-measuring tools. It postulates that the date and field are functionally relevant to each other. Datings are open to doubt always, while the durational stretch hardly ever is. For that is the substance of our individual selves, as a personal history might present it in totality. It is each one's *haecceitas* of his struggle to live on, body and brain together. It is what we become aware of in reverie, during those rare moments when relevance becomes irrelevant, when the circummabience we are ever facing up to in fear and hope relaxes its aggression, and we live on for the nonce, freely.

By and large, our ways with it are mobilizations from our past of memories which our hopes and fears deploy, to make as safe and certain the intrinsically unsafe and uncertain future coming to enter the past; we strive to absorb and assimilate it; the striving is lifelong and is the all of our survival. Whatever we do and feel and say, all our faiths and works and values are, taken separately, our working hypotheses, our designs so presently to shape the shapelessness which is still future that the new shapes will compose with the old in reciprocal orchestration. How many and how diverse the remembrances we can so employ, what the range of recollection may be—its breadth and depth—seem to vary with the scope of our intellectual functions.

And more than any other, the measure of these functions seems to be the Word. Intelligence as well as intellect is preponderantly a faculty of the apt use of words; homo sapiens is homo loquens. And as with the other survival-functions of the race, it lives and grows with constant exercise, with the discriminating practice that makes perfect. Our survival as men seems so very much to turn on how well we employ images and symbols in order to direct, shape and orchestrate the physico-chemical and physiological processes which are our bodies as memories-in-action.

However the experiences we know and call memories arise, we recall them as images. Be they likenesses or unlike, we attribute them to originals. If our concern is the original, we endeavor to envision the whole, its parts and their relations as in such wise interdependent that none, whether constant or variable, is seen without the rest. The whole image has a style and order which constitute its singularity. If we are indifferent to the original, if any, our concern is not resemblance but the qualities of the image as such, the *haecceitas* of the transactions between the parts which make and sustain their togetherness as a whole. Or perhaps we vary the relations or the parts, or both jointly, and a new configuration appears which challenges yet satisfies, and is recognized in its turn an original, a first, to be imaged and recalled.

How far these, among our activities as persons, do or do not replicate the behaviors imputed to our genes is a speculation for the creative reverie of a bold imagination.

NOTES

1. That he does call it at the same time "the last infirmity of noble minds" comes as concession to utopian prejudice as to what strengths noble minds should have.

2. "Amoebas at the start
   were not complex.
   They tore themselves apart
   and started sex."

Imagination and Image-Making

IN ANY personal history the distinction between image and original is an event of experience. As they come, the happenings which compose into the flow of consciousness are all originals. They impinge on eye or ear or nose or tongue or palate or hand or foot or on trunk or on all together, as successive presences. Each arouses one or another of the movements which make up our struggle to keep on struggling. It is as, by the feel of them, we take these presences for friends or foes, helps or hindrances, goods or evils, truths, falsehoods, beauties, uglinesses, that we segregate them into originals and images and finally qualify them as formations of reason or creations of imagination.

This qualification has on occasion been interpreted as "polarization" of reason and imagination. More or less, it pervades the philosophic enterprise; it is, indeed, a convention of the philosophic tradition, whose preponderant logic works from a belief that universals are prior to particulars, that wholes are prior to parts and that the relations between them are internal, world without end. In this logic, connexion is necessary, literally unyielding; it is ongoing activity which repeats identicals according to a law and in an order which are always and everywhere the same. Difference, in this logic, violates the law and breaks up the order; it renders connexion contingent and repetition incidental; it displaces necessity by chance and law by anarchy. In our experience it is Imagination which signalizes differences, which perceives the new as though they are authentic realities, and not merely one or another shadows or reflections of the one original, but following from it, and ever dependent on it. Whatever the presence be that Imagination affirms, it is only a seeming, only a distorted reflection of the original which reason envisions or reveals. The reflection comes as news, but neither good news nor true news; it can come only as falsification of the good and true by a change that we identify as one happening in a confusion of them which challenges the rule of law and dispels order in chaos. There is a hazard from Imagination against which Reason insures us. Reason provides safety and certainty. The God who is the guarantor of both in our struggles not to die is lastingly the providence of Reason, only occasionally the grace of Imagination. His creations, including our uniquely sapient selves, are, in truth, but reflections which inspirit the lawlessness of Imagination with the law and order of Reason.

Reason must needs tame Imagination and harness it up in Reason's service. Countless as may be the worlds which the divine Word might transform from a future possibility into a present reality, the one we do now from moment to moment experience is the very best of them, the *ne plus ultra* of goodness—the forever unique manifestation of God's providential Reason, lovingly forever repeating itself in those moments, its creations, its images. God-Creator may be as protean as omnipotent, but his omnipotence is Eternal-Reason-in-Action, alike the sustaining cause and the sustained effects which repeat and represent it—the cause which ineluctably must underlie the changes and chances of the infinitude of images, of shadows, illusions, hallucinations and self-deceptions that make up our experience.

So, for our salvation from ourselves and our world, the *periti* of religion and philosophy, each in his own manner, have assured us, denying with their gospels any saving power to Imagination. However, in recent years their comforting has been receiving a new configuration and its workings a new intent which restore to the visage of their God the Imagination so long purged from it. The potency is no longer Reason's alone. It has been again realized that authentic creativity cannot be separated from Imagination even though it require that creature necessarily *follows from* Creator. Must not every babe have, at least, a mother? And can there occur, in reason, a new beginning without an old but unaging original to begin from, an original which it implicates, and from which it gets explicated? For logic, creativity must be one *totum simul*, ultimately one sole cause of all effects, which our own reason then links up into "chains" of unyielding connexion, so that a chosen *terminus a quo* may be always and everywhere united to a preferred *terminus ad quem*.

We name what we conceive to be the ultimate binding power by many names, usually unaware that our namings signify valuations of the events of our experience, each an item we strive to possess and cling to, or to avert from, reject, render null. "Matter," "mind," "spirit," "reason," "love," "nature," "law," "order," "God," and their alternatives and opposites intend existence and value so compenetrated that neither can be realized without the other. Each intends a metaphysical substance not only, with its singular ways and works; it intends also the dialectics of approval and disapproval which establish, nourish or alter the arts and sciences of it aficionados. What happens with those discloses their role in the struggles of the true believers to keep on struggling; struggles for which, as we need to continue reminding ourselves, "existence," "self-preservation," "survival" are synonyms. The values we set on any which we decide is ultimate give it primacy, ordain it as a temporal, not a logical, *first*. This, religionists and philosophers—Kant is here modernity's classical representative—transvalue into eternal instancy, rendering the temporal *first* cause or *final* cause the one abiding timeless cause *semper ubique idem*, somehow the master, the ruler, the savior, the imperishable scapegoat that enables congenitally immoral man to give himself moral holidays for which he is sure to be forgiven. And not only this. The ever self-identical instancy guarantees to the struggler's ever-changing struggle the peace, safety and certainty which he believes unalienable from his survival. It transvalues the continuing experience of their alienation into mere appearance.

The creeds and codes wherewith this act of faith keeps working itself out get grounded on Reason by one kind of intellectual violence, one form of the absurdity of Reason. On the record, their genesis is in Imagination. Any ground once it has been imaged, can be taken for a first cause repeating itself endlessly in a self-representative system. But an authentic first comes attributable to no prior happening nor to any unchanging activity. It joins an aggregation of *eaches* already there; and after it, or concurrently, come others either not yet there or not yet anywhere. Thomas Mann, discussing his own imagery in *Joseph and his Brethren*, indicated a vivid awareness of the already there. He conceived, back of any beginning, an indeterminate depth of spacetime, without an authentic *first* or *last* anywhere. He argued that origins can be only "provisional"; that "practically and in fact" they figure as images of the initiations starting some community's singular tradition; as the start of its folkways or its religion. Even though persons and peoples have become aware that the depths which their memories reach do remain in fact unplumbed, they may and do take their stand, for all that, "at some prehistoric period of time"; assessing it as their authentic beginning, they "perennially and historically speaking, come to rest there." Yet such stands are fixations, pauses which in and by themselves are temporal happenings, images used to found personal or communal histories. On the record, they are items in an indeterminate sequential aggregate which the image-making struggler chooses shall serve as points of departure toward forming the symbols he keeps compounding and the myths he keeps shaping. Both the formations chosen and the acts of choosing are, we feel, happenings, free partners in a transaction which produces the symbols and the myths that pervade man's cultures.

If, as some have felt and said, Imagination is "the faculty," which creates these events, then its creativity must itself work in quanta, come in drops or bursts, each a unique happening, or come not at all. The comings are not identicals repeating one another; each is different in some respect from all the rest. Nor is the difference of any attributable to a ground or cause. Each is a *first*, coming like Fred Hoyle's particles (perhaps like them also contributors to the his "steady state") *ex nihilo*. In the tradition, nevertheless, they rank as images, and our traditionalists imagine the originals they prefer them to be the images of. On these imagined originals they confer the ultimate values; beside them, the designated images are indeed defective likenesses—defective in that they are formations of time passing and by nature incapable of assuring the safety and certainty which Reason proves are, and must be, *semper ubique idem*. For alone the postulated originals guarantee to man the struggler these conditions of the future unchanging peace and safety and certainty he is struggling for. William Blake called these originals the real and eternal world of which this vegetable world (of our experience) is but a faint shadow. In the imagery of Thomas Traherne, if not in his meaning;

> The thoughts of men appear
> Freely to move within the sphere
> Of endless reach; and run
> Though in the soul, beyond the sun.
> The ground on which they acted be
> Is unobserved infinity
>
> Abiding in the mind
> An endless liberty they find.

It is unhampered immortality both poets imagine.

Imagination, *Mimesis,* in the
Struggle for Survival

IMAGINATION IS a word for an activity of ours. To the grammarian it is a noun; to the man imagining it is a verb. It signifies a doing of ours which finishes in images—not only the images which the eye sees, the ear hears, the hands touch and feel, the muscles and joints design, separately or together: but it stands also, and perhaps especially for formations which the tongue articulates and its wordings intend, be they spoken or written. In brief, Imagination is the power of the Word producing forms and figures of persons, places and principles which either represent originals or are originals. If an individual's productions are reproductions, his imagination is occasionally qualified as "empathic"; his imagery is attributed to an identification of himself, in feeling, with the originals, an identification which works out in a likeness made with materials other than the original. The likeness is the repetition of a role on a different field in a different form. Enacting the role is sometimes identified as sympathy—literally, feeling *with* the original rather than feeling it fully, becoming it. In either case, the quality of feeling, its *haecceitas,* is called intuition, and the awareness of its inward configuration, insight. What the original may here be does not matter; it may be anything—an ineffable presence in a mystic experience or the most effable construction which a mathematician or an analytical philosopher is capable of. Soon or late, the act of identification, perceived as insight or intuition gets to be identified, Bergson-wise, with sheer creativity. However achieved, its non-rational spontaneities of variation, its contingent divergences and convergences, all bringing news into the world, get attributed to Imagination, and Imagination is taken for more or less of a synonym with creativity. It is believed that the surd of the flow of the transactions which constitute our experience is the un-patterned energy which patterns into the experiential sequences we call reason, law and order. Traditionally, philosophy records a war absurdly waged by aficionados of reason, law and order against Imagination.

Nevertheless, often enough reason or intelligence is taken to be truly creative, to make news rather than newly disclose forgotten or hitherto unperceived events, and intelligence is thus endowed with the powers of imagination. But the wars of the rationalists continue to be waged. The philosophic subordination of imagination perdures. Plato set the style of it with his translation of experienced oneness into metaphysical unity, experienced mobility into instant eternity, experienced singularity into undifferentiated universality, limited reasonableness into universal Reason or Logos. Without these absolutes always and everywhere the same, mankind could never be saved from the fragmented images, the hazardous opinions and the fictions and practical illusions of fantasy (imagination) that at best can only arouse blind and self-destructive feelings. The absolutes are our salvation. Perhaps it is not an irony worthy of Socrates in his matter-of-fact moods that, when it came to such ultimate values as Plato concerned himself with in the Timaeus, he could not help invoking Imagination (fantasia) to account for creation. To do so, Socrates had, however, to hypostatize "fantasia" in its turn. He exalted it into a power transcending reason, an intuition of a super-rational psychic energy which reveals its demiurgic self by means of myths.

Aristotle somewhat collapsed his teacher's fantasy into something closer to commonsense—tempered, however, by the academic privilege of his time. As he expounded Imagination in the *de Anima*, he kept it ancillary to reason (for him that hierarchy of forms or principles which he believed give the cosmos its structure). But the ranks of the hierarchy do not exercise their functions by themselves alone; each is companioned by a power of fantasy peculiar to itself, which works along with it, yet is a lower kind. Faculty psychology, at best but a standardized distortion of Aristotle's *de Anima* and for a thousand years regarded by Academia the one correct understanding of the human psyche, kept the psyche's behaviors of wanting, remembering, reasoning and imagining segregated as indemiscible activities of hierarchial powers, and described imagining as an action on our intake through the senses which patterns their stuffs for reason to conceptualize.

During more than a millennium, alternatives were either disregarded or condemned as heresies. But in due course their proponents had to be listened to, disputation conducted, refutation heeded. The traditional notions of the *what* and *how* of imagination became recessive. Although they no longer dominated, they were by no means abandoned. They never quite displaced the Platonic conception of fantasy's nature and role. For the school of the Stoics, for great rhetoricians such as Quintillian or Longinus, for more than one neo-Platonist, imagery could be vivid and lifelike only with the teamwork of imagination and passion. Many others— for example, Plotinus, Iamblichus, Synesius, St Augustine—drew upon the transcendentalism of the Timaeus for their restatement of the nature and workings of "fantasia." In time this identification got challenged and imagination was demoted, as by Albertus Magnus, to an activity of *re-production*, and "fantasia" restored to its postulated transcendental creativity. This is what Dryden's vindication of poetic imagery in fact involves: *ut pictura poesis* does not direct the poet's makings. Fancy, which alone gives life, is the creative power, not reason.

By and large, the belief that in the nature of things, imagination should be the handmaiden of reason, as once philosophy had to be the hand-maiden of theology, prevailed during most of the Renaissance. I have read of only one writer—the 16th century Fracastoro—who challenged the unique creativity of the Word, and left to the poet's imagination only the power of *mimesis*, while he assigned to the mathematician, the musical composer and the architect the power to make original combinations, to create unprecedented unities. It was this power which, as the liberating age of Enlightenment dissipated centrifugally into the liberated life of romanticism, was restored to the Wordmen. Samuel Coleridge, translating the German philosophers' *Einbildungskraft* into *esemplastic power*, rein-stated in man's original nature the creativity of imagination whereby *Homo sapiens* is indeed the image of God, unless it be that God is indeed an image of sapient man. Was it not the first Bonaparte who declared: Imagination rules the world? The overall trend, from the Democratic Revolution on through modernity into our post-modern times, has been toward exalting the creative imagination above the creative intelligence and interpreting both as items of an ongoing creative evolution. The pregnant word is "creative."

That creative imagination and creative intelligence are traditionally segregated, even opposed, is due rather to philosophic prejudice than to insight of how they work. Their isolation from each other is an outcome of dialectic, not of observation. In our struggles to live on each is a function of the other, and the creative act starts as imagination and finishes as intelligence. The creations of the imagination come first; their reshaping and fitting by the intelligence follow. The novelties of the first come *ex nihilo*; their adjustments and refinements are works of the second, and are intrinsic to the quasi-terminal "wholeness" of the creation. The creative intelligence reshapes the new image by workings which are themselves innovative but harmonizing. It might be said to steer and refine the ongoing suffusion of the past by the future, altering the blind determinations of change and chance into designed determinations, or better, perhaps, *re-determinations* performing a survival-function. The procedures of the creative intelligence are not repetition, whether habitual or customary. They are originative. But not as the imagination is originative *ex nihilo*.

These innovations of intelligence do not come as invaders rupturing an established order; they come as harmonizations of the old with new, as a fitting them together in such wise that they make a newer and more reliable safeguard, if not enhancement, of survival. Experience goes on; but, through the survival-function of the creative intelligence goes on as an altered orchestration of the passing future with the past whose growth the future feeds. While the intellect works toward closure, the intelligence works toward growth; it seeks the diversification, not the repetition of identicals. The diversification is what *mimesis* achieves.

Intelligence without imagination is intellect or "pure reason". Imagination without intelligence is but as the primal flux of experience; it is the present inward passing of sensations, percepts, concepts, feelings, doings, wantings, takings, havings, and refusings, as they come any which way—without selections, without direction, without goal. It is the becoming of the past and the aggregation of its happenings into the unique person, whom the happenings shape up. They are his substance, he is their configuration.

From birth to death a human's character and career keep forming and reforming as such orchestrations of images. We note again that the traditional name for this process is Memory. We conceive it to be composed of present residues of past experiences which we refer to also as genes and brain-traces of the body and images of the psyche. We take brain-traces for effects that we attribute to causes in the circumambience outside or in the formations within. We take the images for imitations or reflections or reproductions of the originals that came to be used for models in image-making.

One ultimate concern of every system of philosophy is to establish forever the difference between original and image, to resolve the persistent doubt which is which, by disclosing the original as beyond question that for which the image is a representation, a symbol, a sign, a token. In relation to its image, the original is past; it has come before, the image has come after. Even if the original perdure, and the two became contemporaneous like parents and children, it belongs to the past of the image, and the image belongs to the future of the original in the order of their time together. Philosophy's quest for the original is perhaps its paramount survival-function in the human career. To disclose what the original is, how it works, varying old images and eliciting new ones is the game of that name, the Word of the beginning. Since the philosopher can hunt only among images, they are all he has available to signify, express or "mean" the undisclosed originals he presumes they imitate, repeat or signify. But the originals are *meta*physical, "beyond" "*trans*cendent." They continue never present, ever absent; they are "things-in-themselves"; and either like the much-touted *Deus Absconditus*, altogether out of reach of perception or to be reached by an intuition, an act of faith, commensurable in no way with the ways of knowing we call commonsense and science and perhaps even art. Those may hint at originals, but they know only images and images of images.

There are of course philosophies which teach that images are originals and originals are images; that the difference is one of role, not nature; that it signalizes a decision about its function in our struggle to keep on struggling for which our cliché is "self-preservation". In our daily lives, images repeat an identity. Which of a pair or a multitude is believed to be image and which original turns on which repeats which in time and on their roles in the fortunes of the believer. Is man or God the original or the image? What is he imitating who imitates Christ? The survival-value decides, it institutes the status of the form. Conventionally, an image is a likeness in another medium; it discloses dissimilarities as well as similarities, with now the first and again the second playing the more vital role. The role of the image is to serve as a surrogate for its original as our reflections in water, on glass, or on metal might serve us, or as our portraits in paint on canvas, or in stone or plaster or metal, or in configurations of words or music or pantomime; or in symbolic shapings of some other practicable material. Our concepts and abstractions, including such philosophically ultimate ones as Being, Becoming, Number, God, Devil, Nature, Law (whether of nature or of God), are also images. They are images which, over the milennia, the hairless ape compounded, homogenized, stream-lined into a shorthand of words and symbols from the multitudinous originals of his experience, and thus made himself without aiming to, body and mind, into *homo sapiens*—the image of God able to translate and transvalue the ever-diversifying flux of his experience into the single, real, eternal, universal function of some aspect of his struggles to live on and not die.

Moreover, the mutation includes an inversion; it renders the original, image; the image, original. The practice of this inversion may be said to have become the art of philosophy with Plato. But it has been throughout history the common practice of every sort and condition of philosophic thinker. There are exceptions such Protagoras or William of Occam or William James, not numerous and not frequent. Since the image is a residue of a present which is no more, the original is no longer available to check its reliability by. How be sure that it now truly discloses a formation now forever absent? That is prophesies certainly the unprecedented event which has still to come to be?

"Objective" or "subjective," conscious, unconscious or subconscious, the image is a remembrance which together with all other residues of passing experiences, Memory includes. A person's memory comprehends everything he has lived through, body and soul. It is the substance of his individuality, of his personal history as he alters his selfhood by his struggles to preserve himself between birth and death. Every remembrance is like a pseudopod of this selfhood, thrust forward in its struggle, to grapple with some felt challenge from the world around. It is a use of memory wherein imagination and intelligence function together as tools or weapons of the self's striving for survival—that it, to be not stopped from striving. It is a use of memory which has been recognized in all the cultures of mankind as becoming the art which generates and nourishes every other art, however we distinguish it—religious, economic, political, scientific, esthetic, philosophical. There is an insight in the Greek myth which presents Mnemosyne (memory) as the Titan mother of the Muses, and Zeus, the father of the gods, as their father. Historians may know this better than other artists.

However successful or unsuccessful, using memory in *ad hoc* acts of remembrance is the method of the self's struggle to live on and not die under the strains and stresses of its transactions with the circumambience. By means of the latter it strives to sustain at peak an ongoing personal history of growing up, growing older, growing stronger and wiser; strives to resist aging, to resist remembering less instead of more, remembering less quickly, less relevantly. Until, at last, remembrance ceases to function, the stream of consciousness quiets into non-selective reverie which death terminates by hardening self into a soma without a psyche. To resist aging is to resist entropy; it is the drive of our struggle to keep on struggling. Growing up and growing older and wiser is our victory in the struggle; and tradition holds aging and old age our defeat and the victory of entropy.

In terms of our fight against entropy, remembrance plays various roles. Sometimes its suffuses an original with an aura of "pastness" such as we experience naturally in images. The feeling, *dejà vu* which this communicates complicates the perplexity that genuine novelties occasion; the commingling seems groundless and absurd—sometimes we want to remember an original, but "memory" fails to bring on the one image which will fit the space our want shapes. Or else images may come up whose originals we are endeavoring to forget. And of course, we forget as wilfully as we remember. Remembering and forgetting come like acts of decision in our transactions with the moving world around. They are present workings of a past in order to form a more satisfying future if we can, to face an unsatisfying one if we cannot. To *survive* is to keep living

D

beyond the present, and first and last our struggle for survival is the action of the past we keep becoming which assimilates into itself the future by which it grows. Some words for the dynamic of our part of this transaction are *will, hope, aspiration, anticipation, expectation.* They signify various ways in which memory-images embody this dynamic, all shapes for the future which the images prophesy and intend, whether that be tomorrow's weather or the weather of the After-life we hope or fear to live when we are dead. But in whatever role, the survival-value of the image is its function in our escaping, delaying, entropy by diversifying our past, enriching and strengthening it through the future we join to it, by using our present past in relevant remembrances. In sum: by refining and perfecting the transactional role of the memory-image in the practice which makes perfect, and in distinguishing and improving the variations which come as the practice recurs.

This is what stops when death reduces the Self to a soma without a psyche. Of course, the soma in *rigor mortis* does not cease to change. But its changing is another phase of entropy. The body crumbles, dust unto dust; the brained soul has only an imagined maker to return to, unless the nothing it came from be the maker. It is put out of existence as the flame of a candle is put out; it ceases to be as the melody of a fiddle ceases to be when the bow no longer crosses the strings or the strings break. Candle and fiddle, surviving flame and melody, might be prized as monuments or symbols of the light and music which had been the life of them. Soon or late the configurations which constitute their identities will also dissipate in entropy, till the very dust to which they return shall be no more. Survival is a self-altering action going on, not a state always and everywhere the same; it is a past enlarged and diversified so long as a future keeps joining it, a living past so long as the future feeds it and it grows by what it feeds on. Our authentic sense of our selfhood is the immediate feel of this ongoing transaction. It is, in William James's simile, the direct awareness of this *stream* of our consciousness rather than of the multitudes of diverse images whose succession is the streaming. As in a subway rush-hour, we feel the strain and squeeze of passage rather than the forms of the passengers. Yet we feel the propulsion to be nevertheless the self-orchestration of the passengers, with the newcomers joining the earlier arrivals peacefully or aggressively and reshaping the movement as they come, making over yet sustaining the identity of the Self struggling to preserve itself by its unceasing give-and-take with every sort and condition of otherness, of not-self, that surrounds them.

This usually overlaid and unheeded immediacy—it may well be the ultimate original of our images of creativity—is certainly the original of

what we have come to call possibility and to distinguish from actuality—
the thrust of power spending itself, using itself up as patterned waves
wherein pause seems to come as a phase of process passing on. "Now"
signifies such stretches of pattern—the present phase of time passing.
Tradition calls these phases actuality, but determines arbitrarily which is
later, which earlier. Determination is a succession of patterns which transvalue "what might be" into "what is likely to be," possibility into probability. The transvaluation reduces and limits both the range and variety
of alternative patterning. When a sequence seems, and is believed, to
repeat itself in one and only one series of patterns, probability becomes
necessity and the order of succession gets ascribed to "law".

Experience has led us to invest every actuality with possibilities. As
William James remarked, a possible chicken is an actual egg. But the same
dynamic in the sequences: *actual, possible, probable, necessary,* is the
confluence of events we call time—each a particle, an atom, a molecule, a
drop, or a configuration of such, each with its own stretch of existence,
keeping itself going between nothing and nothing. Our images of a thing
intend not only whatever it *now* is: they intend as well all it *might* become;
they comprehend the present dimensions of its past and extrapolate some
variation toward its future. Our present perceptions of it are at once also
retrospective and prophetic, and are the latter in the light of the former.
To "know" anything is to be aware of it in terms of its past and to believe
one now anticipates its future coming. The thing is a history, a course of
happenings compenetrating, not a standstill identity.

Such is the import of the images which make up our knowledge of
things. Although evolutionary biology postulates this belief and tends to
take biological actualization for a synonym of evolutionary recapitulation,
although psychoanalytic theory similarly envisions present personal
character as past personal history, the disposition is inveterate to hold
that the image is a constant, always and everywhere the same. Especially
so among the scientists, whether of nature or of man. To them mathematical equations postulating the universal repetition of identicals are the
only reliable means of designing probabilities and implying necessities in
the happenings of nature and the thinkings and doing of man. It is
indifferent that, on inspection, metric configurations turn out no less
images than other figures of speech, and no less contingent actuals,
possibles and probables than are eggs and chickens. On the record, the
figures of the mathematician are man-designed images, eventuations of his
struggle to live on and not die, functions of the give-and-take between
himself and his circumambience. In view of their role in his career as man,
Homo sapiens reinterprets these temporal inventions of his into eternal

truths he found, not made. In view of their uses as instruments of survival, he crowns them with godhead, enshrines them in holiness, establishes them as unaltering and unalterable monadic principles, instant absolutes, with the stretch—beginning, to middle, to end—of the events of experience, out of time, anti-time, yet the source and ground of time, and therefore to be cherished, worshipped, obeyed and defended from outer challenge or inner change.

What else, according to the tradition, do challenge and change achieve, if not to confirm by their doubting, to repeat by their changing, the presence they purport to mistrust? Doubt and change contradict themselves. The mutations they would effect, the fluidity they would melt the ever-unmeltable permanence into, turn out to be at best only appearances of this permanence, its reflections from the nothing which, in imaging, can only distort and falsify the permanence. The images are many, the original is one. The images are shadow, the original is substance. The reflecting Nothing it is which morcellates the unmoving One into the mobile Many and darkens substance to shadow. The reflecting Nothing it is which segregates the truest of images from their original. It is the distortions and falsifications that are of its essence which figure in the image as an autogenous originality other than its Original.

Image and original, appearance and reality, individuality and universality, many and one, time and eternity, existence and value, can be taken as synonyms for a Siamese-twin-like twosome which, on the record, all schools of philosophy agree pervades experience, however aggressively they dispute over which is which, and how human reason and human imagination relate to the duality. Belief in the parity of the image's originality with that of its Original came late in the history of thought to rival and to overcome the entrenched faith in the higher status of the original. Disillusion with the latter seems to me to pervade all the disputations of the semanticist and analytical schools of the recent past. But the pragmatists began it, the logical positivists gave it a turn of their own. One thinks of the divergent pragmatisms of Charles Peirce and William James and John Dewey, of the logical positivism of Ernst Mach and Otto Neurath. One thinks of the diversification of "analysis" from the penitent Bertrand Russell through Ludwig Wittgenstein. As Russell wrote at eighty, reviewing the history of his opinions:

I set out with a more or less religious belief in a Platonic eternal world, in which mathematics shone with a beauty like that of the last *Canto* of the *Paradiso*. I came to the conclusion that the eternal world is trivial and that mathematics is only the art of saying the same thing in different words.

What difference, then, does the art of saying the same thing in different words make in mankind's struggle for survival? Does it help? Does it hinder? And how? Whichever it does, it so channels the energies of men in their transactions with the circumambience as not only to repeat the older originals but to remake them into new creations, and to create authentic novelties, originals in no wise images, such as man-made elements. But the difference of the image, too, the difference of that in the repetition which is novel, is as reliably original as the originality of the original "same" and may call for our entering into quite a different transaction. Persons make themselves, peoples make their cultures and civilizations by the acts of imagination which originate differentiations in the "sames" that they are repeating, and by their intelligent orchestration of those diversities. Perennially artists and thinkers, whatever their media and their skills, draw on personal memory and public records for images conserved either as repetitions of identicals or as variations upon them no less original than their originals, and no less excellent or less cherished. They orchestrate their selections to configurations of faith and works, beauty and use, impartially for war or for peace. Those orchestrations compose the cultures and give direction to the *human* behavior of mankind. They constitute the variations in whose originality *Homo sapiens* is a different species from his cousins, the hairy or the hairless ape. No "reductionism," be it the physiologist's, the psychologist's, the anthropologist's, the "social scientist's," or the philosopher's can denature that difference—to say nothing of abolishing it. What is human is not animal, however little it may be a variant upon animality; what is animal is not human, however much the human may resemble it.

Perhaps the ape is all the more other than human if, as varieties of existentialists mourn, it be not merely possible, not merely probable, but truly necessary that the "human" shall be a synonym for a life of dying, in freedom, anxiety and dread, into an all-prevading Nothingness. But as the struggle to keep on struggling (which existentialities carry on while deploring it), the human is all of the *haecceitas* which keeps affirming itself after it is born and before it dies, even by its own hand. The trials and tribulations which condition it are no part of this affirmation. They are what it repudiates and would annul. If, in George Santayana's words, there is no cure for birth or death save to enjoy the interval, *Humanitas* is the affirmation of enjoyment. Whatsoever other value priests, prophets, poets or philosophers may proclaim for mankind, it is *flatus vocis* if it be not knowingly or unknowingly postulated on mankind's existence here-and-now, between birth and death.

That is the alpha and omega of value. For the dead man, the moment of death turns to nothing all other values his existence cultivated and cherished, as it turns his existence to nothing. Only as he lived could any other value have had for him any ground or meaning. In and out, first and last, for *Homo sapiens* existence is value, value is existence, and his life is at once thus their seat and their content. All values, other than his life, all divergences into the abstractions of value "as such," are creations of this identity, are its images which vary from it while repeating it. Their vital function is to reaffirm it, each with its own diversifying identity. Protagoras recognized this long ago. "Man" he declared: "is the measure of all things; of those that are, that they are; of those that are not, that they are not." The key-word is "measure" which we may hold a synonym of "evaluation".

Existence as Value: Culture

IT IS when we take "measure" as independent of man, when we hypostasize and sanctify it, that it is rendered irrelevant to value. This seems to be so largely what many scientists think they are doing and must do. This is why the equations and other measurements of the natural and social sciences intended as a correct bookkeeping of values are irrelevant to values. The balance sheet is ever wrong. As William James wrote Henry Adams in comment on his *Letter to American Teachers*, "the *amount* of cosmic energy it costs to buy a certain distribution of fact which humanly we regard as precious, seems to me to be an altogether secondary matter as regards the question of history and progress. Certain arrangements of matter *on the same energy level* are from the point of view of man's appreciation, superior, while others are inferior. Physically a dinosaur's brain may show so much intensity of energy exchange as a man's but it can do infinitely fewer things, because as a force of detent it can only unlock the dinosaur's muscles, while the man's brain, by unlocking far feebler muscles, indirectly can by their means issue proclamations, write books, describe Chartres Cathedral, etc; and guide the energies of the shrinking sun into channels which never would have been entered otherwise—in short, *make* history. Therefore, the man's brains and muscles are, from the point of view of the historian, the more important place if energy exchange, small as this may be when measured in absolute physical units".

Existence as value is ineffable. Its criterion is itself, alike for those who are killed, who kill themselves, who are executed or who come to their deaths as they were born to die, in or out of bed. History is replete with instances of humans who scheme and labor to reduce the *haecceitas* of others to images of themselves because to them the want of such repetition endangers their own existence, because they believe that self-repetition is the guarantee of peace, is the necessary preventive of war and thus the *sine qua non* of survival: "Be not my equal, be my brother, be my image, be the shadow of my substance, or I'll kill you." The passion is the animus of all totalitarianisms, of their animosity toward the different-and-equal. But the totalitarian animus is only one variation of a yen which seems universal and pandemic. We all like other people to be like us in their beliefs and preferences, their thinking and doing, but no so like that *they* become our identical twins and rivaling equals. They must conform to us, believe us, obey us, and fight for us, not seek to share our powers and privileges. There is a menace in that kind of likeness we must insure ourselves against, as there is a menace in the ineluctable unlikeness of things to our personal identity, a pressure toward conforming it to their own. Yet, once others have been forced or persuaded into likeness, they bore us. First we avoid them, then we ignore them, then repel them, and would shut them up and cut them off forever. Our struggle for *survival* also craves the differences we think to destroy: at least for sparring partners, optimally for team-mates. As every totalitarian discovers, the game of life is voided if the players are all on one side, and they never can be. This is why such words as *imitation, reflection, echo, takeoff, effigy, shadow, parody* signify that repetitions can be only approximate, that diversification is intrinsic and that each image men perceive or create constitutes an identity with a touch of uniqueness all its own.

Perhaps this is what Ralph Emerson had in mind when he wrote that "quotation confesses inferiority" or that "genius borrows nobly"; that perhaps Cowper recognized when he originated the now commonplace sentiment that "variety is the very spice of life." Our metaphors, all our figures of speech, our myths and allegories, our fables, our proverbs, our histories, our sciences and our philosophies are images we keep diversely multiplying, of an original which isn't there: recall the image of metaphysics as the vocation of a blind man in a dark room hunting for a black cat which isn't there. This image is one valuation of the great tradition of philosophy which, the cultivators of this image believe, keeps taking for originals the *haecceitas* of images that *are* there because we have put them there. What Plato and Aristotle signalize by *mimesis* and we translate by *imitation* is the act of origination, the creative act suffusing all repetitions of old things with newness and of making news independently of any repetition.

Nevertheless, metaphysicians like Josiah Royce argued that the universe is a "self-representative system"; knowledgeable social philosophers like Gabriel Tarde argued that imitation is the dynamic of the entire human enterprise and follows certain invariant laws of variation. In his exposition, the main action would be that which our American cartoon series, *Keeping Up With the Joneses*, images. Persons are singles, by nature emulative of the feelings, thoughts, attitudes and actions of others whom they regard their betters: the poor want to become like the rich, and the rich like the richer, the weak like the strong, and the strong like the stronger, whether in body or mind. The ambition of some is to image saints like the imaged saints of their experience; the ambition of others to image sinners like the sinners they've read of or seen or seen portrayed. None is *born* a saint or sinner, or for any particular role at all; all choose, aware or unaware, out of their cultural circumambience characters, attitudes, beliefs, works and ways to imitate, yet not altogether to repeat. They want to better their betters. The repetitions orchestrate into customs, mores, styles, fashions which in their turn get taken for models to imitate, world without end. Tarde images for us an imaging of images which he believes is the dynamic of group behavior, the power in society and in history. It is a process which assimilates the different into a same and adjusts the new to the old. The American psychologist, James Mark Baldwin, held that imitation is the mechanism basic to learning and that personality forms itself from birth by taking on and assimilating roles which image others. In principle, this was also George Mead's brilliantly verified working hypothesis. But no more than Tarde could Mead or Baldwin explain the "mechanism." They could only observe, generalize and postulate their generalizations as working hypotheses or as "laws." Walter Pitkin was struck how a certain species of flatfish he observed—at Woods Hole, if I remember correctly—changed color and spots to repeat on their skins the patterns of light and shade of the waters where they lay and swam and had their ichthyous being. He speculated that the repetition his eye observed consummates a sequence from fisheye through fish nervous system to fish skin and that the entire process was a protective coloration in the interest of survival. Charles Peirce's notion, that our images of the circumambience as conceptions, principles, "laws," are reflections in "man's glassy essence" might be regarded an earlier and more metaphysical image on like lines of *mimesis*.

Original and Image: Truth

AMONG OUR *now* artists and thinkers, *mimesis* no longer holds the place it used to from Plato's times to our parents' and teachers'. Variation and originality have been gaining precedence from the days of Romanticism on. But *mimesis* is still the event of experience it always was, is still among our activities as autonomous and unconscious as breathing—as vital and as commonplace. Obstruction renders it, as it renders breathing, conscious and purposeful; it changes a reflex action into a conscious goal. Overcoming obstruction requires the increase of effort that lifts action above the threshold of instinct or habit to the level of conscious drive or "will." So with *mimesis*.

"Compassion," "sympathy," "empathy"—all three could be synonyms for *mimesis*. "Compassion" and "sympathy" both intend "feeling-together-with," which is to say, imaging the feelings of living things as their forms express them, be they humans, animals, insects, even plants, that are hurt and suffer. Usage excludes feeling-images of the happy, the healthy, the gay, the mighty, the triumphant. Although images of such feelings arise, although we do impart and receive feelings of joy and delight, strength, skill and triumph, they go by other names, perhaps such as "Keeping up with the Joneses."

"Empathy," by contrast, would denote not only all that "sympathy" and "compassion" intend, but moods drawn from non-living forms as well. All three signify a contagion of feeling we become aware of when its source so takes our attention as to divert the flow of our own feeling toward itself and channel it there. The experts tell us that we then "live in" or "live with" the object; it becomes, so to speak, both our identical and Siamese twin—"two minds with but a single thought," "two hearts that beat as one." The object, whatever it be, has become our Other. Person or no, it may be anything that comes to pass in the course of human events, subjective or objective. Simply, it is an encounter of the Self with an image—whether a creation of its own imagination, a product of nature, a work of God, as you prefer—and the consequent transaction between Self and the other force and form in the encounter. Those of us who value the act of empathy or sympathy above the object which evokes it, tend to regard the object an imitation of the act, and the actor a Narcissus imaging

96

himself in the object. Those who cherish the object more highly than the act tend to regard the action a reflection of the object; the Self is then the mirror, the object the Narcissus, and the Self may speak with Charles Peirce of "man's glassy essence"—if it also includes in man's essence his senses, his perceptions, his feelings and his willings to commingle with his conception. Others, who portray truth as somehow a repetition or image of an Original which reproduces the Original by one-to-one correspondence with all its parts could perhaps speak of "man's glassy essence" without incurring reproach from the logicians. So could those to whom truth is not the trait of an image but the same as the original itself—the original's self-awareness.

But so, also, could those who do not intend by truth an image, but the original itself. Or those to whom truth is not an image which its original assimilates in such wise that the two become one, whatever the form of either may be. For the image is an event of experience with an identity of its own, a happening neither true nor false. What renders it the one or the other is its role in a person's configuration of values. This role is also a happening. It accrues when a person takes an image on trust for reliable prophecy of future consequences, for foresight of the shape of things to come. Its truth is his faith *now* that it now images what is not yet but is coming to be, or what has come and is no more. This image is true for him if and when he trusts it as a reliable present sign or symbol of an absent past, which was and is no more, or the filling and shaping of an empty future which is not yet, but will be. Neither original, past or future, exists *now*. *Now* is the time of the image pointing beyond itself toward a future in which the past somehow acquires presence, or a future which itself becomes present as events fill and shape its emptiness. The image is true if what follows confirms the believer's trust in it, whether it intends what was, or what will be. Truth is not a function of *mimesis*. A true image need have no likeness whatsoever to that which it is true about; however patterned, it is the believer's reliance on its guidance that endows it with truth, and in many cases the reliance survives the failure of the guidance. Most such cases involve religious images, such as the gods and the immortal dead. But science also has its instances, such as Lysenkoism in biology, and anti-relativity in Stalinism and Hitlerism, anti-catastrophism in Shapleyite astronomy.

Imagery of past events is also prophecy of future comings in quanta of duration. If there be any other way for this to come, it has not yet been either imagined or discovered. Since we live irresistibly forward, future-ward, from birth until death, since all our experience is an ongoing enhancement and diversification of our past, an enrichment of it by adding now what had not yet been to what had already been, the truth of its image which figures in this addition is the survival-value of its working futureward. Somewhere, if I remember correctly—si non e vero e ben trovato—Thomas Henry Huxley remarks that where religion says The just shall live by faith, science says the just shall live by verification. Literally, 'verification' means *making true*, and the *making* is the works that follow from the faith—that is, from the working hypothesis—of the maker, who postulates it *as if*. Its truth is his trust in it, his readiness to rely on it as he experiences it without evidence; his readiness to bet that it will bring the evidence needed to confirm it. His act of faith is an act of trust that the image will lead to the original or to other evidence which confirms his trust. He trusts the leadings, the procedures, the process before, and the product after. He accepts the product in virtue of the process, and takes that in its turn for a working hypothesis on which he bets for successful future consequences.

No such bet, indeed no bet whatever, can ever be a bet on a sure thing— not even a bet on the "laws of thought" or the mathematical repetition of identicals where they are believed to work infallibly. Belief is a choosing between alternatives none of which can ever be necessities always and everywhere the same. Some may be probables. All can be possibles. Which shall eventuate, work out, get trusted and verified is no foregone conclusion. It is a wager on the future that may be won or lost. The one sure event is the act of faith which bets.

This act is another way of denoting the force and form of our human struggle to live on and not die. To our last breath it keeps verifying itself via every formation of the struggle to keep on struggling which is our existence. Religion with its rites and rotes, housekeeping (the academic word is "economics") with its arts and crafts and bookkeeping, the sciences with their rites and rotes so divergent from the religious, all with their different images in words, signs and symbols, folkways and mores, are diverse and diversifying patterns of this ongoing self-verification in and by which we live and move and hold our being.

In the most elementary sense, this self-verification is our ultimate concern as human. It discloses itself in the bet which some of us—say certain Buddhists of South Vietnam—believe they win when they set fire to themselves to burn alive to death, or that soldiers make in combat on the battlefield, or that martyrs make anywhere who die in their faith for their cause, whatever it be, rather than surrender it. It is the bet all humans bet—the bet of life on life against extinction, but more visibly the bet of those who bet their lives and know that they are betting their lives. It is the experience Josiah Royce had in mind when he consecrated "loyalty" to be the supreme value and "loyalty to loyalty" to be the topmost peak of supremacy. For in the transaction by which we suffuse another existence—whether image or original—with value, that value is an accrual from the sympathy, the compassion, the empathy of the valuer; it obtains only so long as he exists. His singularity is, that for him only his existence can be his value, his value ineffably his existence; that the value of the objects of his loyalties, of his loves, his hates and his "causes" are functions of this singularity, and become null when it perishes. Those who die thus believing and loyal have been killed for their faith only in the judgment of the compassionate who survive. In their believers' own judgment, in their "conscience," it is not their faith which killed them. It is the infidel, the misbeliever, the heretic who is the killer, even of the suicide by fire. With his faith, by his faith, far rather than for it, the true believer went to his death living, unafraid, even rejoicing. Its survival-value was the essence of his existence, and thus the truth on which he bet his life.

The truth-value of images varies with the stake that the bettor puts on them. When a person bets his life, the image he bets on is his truest, his most reliable anticipation of future consequences; its survival-value is ultimate. If he dies believing in the consequences—optimistic, pessimistic, or melioristic—the leadings of the image have been its truth for him.

But, successful or not, the image is therein the determination of the original, not the original of the image. For, let me say again, the image is used to shape the unshaped future, and if successfully, belief in it has created its own object; if unsuccessfully, belief in it has sustained its truth. "Error," "mistake," may signify deviations of the original or of the product from the image. It happens sometimes that the deviations turn out more satisfying than any production or original could be. The luck of Columbus is an oft-repeated instance. History reports many others in which faith creates the facts which embody, but instead of verifying, falsify the faith. One such predicament under perennial discussion is the arms race, consequent on the faith that *force majeure*—in the idiom of a Confederate cavalry general "gittin there fustest with the mostest,"—is the assurance of security if not of peace. However, the consequent invention, production, and purpose of weapons impels rivals to adopt and work from a like belief, so that the consequence of an increase in weaponry is a decrease of security, a growing danger of war and an increase of anxiety. Also a nation's life is a bet on the future, a collective bet, but the enfleshment it bets on is by no means a sure thing. What else then can the truth of the image be, if not the trust of the true believer. It is such a trust, I believe, that led early translators of the Book of Job to the gargantuan mis-translation of Job's refusal to trust omnipotence: to write "though He slay me will I trust in him" instead of "I have no hope. I know that he will slay me."

The images on which individuals or groups, whatever their configuration, bet their lives are, ultimately, creeds and codes composing systems of philosophies, supernaturalist or naturalist. Each is an individual orchestration of images of the artist's human and non-human circumambience, his selfhood, and his warlike and peaceable transactions with that world around. Completed, it is a design of compenetrations and compositions which present, as a unified single whole, an image of man, his world, his way with it and its way with him to an end either immortally self-fulfilling or utter extinction, sheer nothingness. In one style or another, the least aware, the most unlearned and most unknowing of humans holds to some such world-image and steers his life by it as well as he can. Somewhere Bernard Shaw remarked that "reasonable people adapt themselves to the world; unreasonable people adapt the world to themselves. All progress is made by unreasonable people. To err is divine."

Are then not all mankind divine? And are their dominant faiths not divine?—the Taoisms, the Confucianisms, the Brahmanisms, the Buddhisms, the Judaisms, the Christianisms, the Islamisms, the Comunazisms, the Naturalisms, the Humanisms—in all their likenesses and differences, unreasonable, reasonable, or both, as they send missionaries to adapt the rest of the world to themselves? Perhaps all are irreparably both. The true believers of each judge all the others as heretics committed to devilish errors leading, not to salvation, not to angelic consummation of selfhood, but to damnation or extinction. To true believers, if error be divine, then Satan, that spirit of dissent, that Goetheian *Geist der stets verneint*, that rebel in Heaven who became the autocrat of the Hell he provoked the King of Heaven to create—Satan, not Jehovah, is the true, the trustworthy God, and the spirit of progress. To be sure, Bernard Shaw would rage and repudiate this. But, on the record, dissent, although ineluctable and indispensable, is not enough. By itself alone, the imagination, which intrudes the Other, intrudes the Stranger that ruptures and confuses the routines of sames repeating themselves, must be surely the anarchist emissary of chaos. To adapt the old to the new and to orchestrate them into a new yet freer and safer pattern of togetherness such as "progress" purports, requires the planning and the orchestrating skills of creative intelligence.

Figures and Configurations
in Philosophic Images

WHATEVER BE the phase or region of his circumambience where *homo sapiens* struggles to keep on struggling, he there shapes his transactions into an image with at least five features. The tradition repeats and accounts for the five over and over again, each time differently. They function, singly and together, like amoebic pseudopods in an amoeba's struggle for survival. Most pervasive and perduring are the tradition's abstracted and imaged configurations of extension and duration, which it geometrizes and counts as space and time and which it has come to rejoin as space-time. Immediate experience is seamlessly spatio-temporal and time-space rather than space-time, for it is the pulse and rhythm of feeling which structures the formlessness of space. The boundaries we intend by the *present, future* and *past* that we draw within the stretch of any pulse of feeling, are positional allocations. Without space, *now*, *soon* and *then* could not be distinguished, to say nothing of separated. Their center of reference is our own perduring *now*; "present" signifies some otherness alongside its "future," an other otherness ahead of it; and "past," still another otherness behind it. In our selves all three are permeating one another. Without the room for the allocating action, present, future and past fuse yet continue diverse. Our *now* is activity in itself, by itself and for itself, change without change of place, differentiation without translocation, flow without direction and without goal, save as it is itself both direction and goal. As such, its successive phases suffuse one another and its differentiations come as seamless present pulsings of future into past, pulsings without measures or shapes such as mathematicians and geometers create.

Now might be compared to the beating of a monadic clock with no hands to move, no time to tell. Telling time requires space for moving hands—or moving shadows—to pass over and for the passing to trace a pattern in. Time patterns are creations *ex nihilo*, which the divisions on the face of a clock or a sundial embody. No space, then no tracks, no times. Without space, whether because we do not heed it or it otherwise falls out of our awareness, we "lose count of time." We revert into the immediacies of reverie, aware of images passing but not of time. We forget, in our struggle to keep on struggling, that its immediate space is indeterminate—not chaos, for chaos is the orderless actions upon each other of becomings, of processes of eventuation within the formless void of space and thus informing it, creating geometry and arithmetic (has not Plato advised us, God geometrizes?). The two are forms and images of tracks in the void deposited by events. They are trajectories of things which geometrizing man perceives being made by their motion or which he makes himself by repeating selected images in sequences he chooses. Common words for his choices are *tempo, rhythm, balance, harmony*. Arrangements of them or their likes are pure designs.

The sciences project such designs in the form of mathematical equations. Since designs in no way pure pervade the circumambience, the arts select, purify and repeat the purified selections; the sciences study their own selections in order to achieve purifications of their own; as is sometimes said, "to distil their essence," and with the resulting abstractions to inpattern chaotic nature's ongoing diversifications, macrocosm to microcosm and back. The patterns are of the rhythm, balance and harmony postulated for pure design. Theologians prize the patterns as implying if not revealing a designer whom they call God. Together with the scientists they cherish the patternings as "laws" which the scientists argue are "laws of nature," the theologians, "laws of God." Sometimes they celebrate the designs together as "laws of Nature and of Nature's God."

"Laws," to both callings, signify in practice rules of repetition which are eternally and universally the causes of the courses of nature and the ways of men. "Cause" is a somewhat ambiguous word. But by and large it signifies powers and forces which events not merely follow, but *follow from*. Causes are coercions. The events which follow *from* them must follow as they do and not otherwise. They may not follow either contingently or by habit, next to next. The philosophic tradition carries on a continuing debate over habit, contingency, necessity and over the direction and mode of causation: Does "law" produce its effects deterministically by pushing from behind or teleslogically, by pulling from in front? And what have push and pull to do with change and chance?

Although the courses of experience disclose transactions in which all three of these modes of effectuation could be said to be in play, each alternative has its true believers to whom the others are heresies. During recent years chance and freedom have received more attention, not unironically in a climate of opinion expressive of the behaviors currently named the scientific-military-industrial complex. Not unironically, because this complex postulates a deterministic naturalism with an aura of teleological supernaturalism. The knowing and skilfull persons who

profess the naturalism employ it, however, in order to free human enterprise from nature's determinations, in order to achieve human purposes
by harnessing the purposeless forces of nature into means for human ends.
Often they reinforce and prolong man's struggles to keep on struggling.
Some frame this determinism of theirs in an even more explicit teleology,
a super-naturalist one; but by and large, the Providence which shapes
their ends shapes them as they prefer. A few others resort to a *tertium quid*,
neither natural nor supernatural, yet providential. Bergson's *élan vital* or
Creative Evolution is such a quiddity; transcending entropy, it provides
somehow an assurance of deathlessness.

But whatever the philosophic image, it presents the fourth of the five
features. The third, causality, is linear; the fourth images the original in
depth. The image is of a whole with parts in such relationship that none
can exist without the others and all *follow from* the wholeness of the whole.
But the whole's efficacy is not causal, and the parts which are its consequences are not effects; nor is the whole an agent nor are the parts
products. The parts are constitutive. Their relations to one another and
to their whole are "internal" and each involves all, all involves each. The
relations are logical; the whole is premise, the parts are conclusions on
the model of the syllogism; *All men are mortal, Socrates is a man, Socrates
is mortal*. The usual word for this relationship of whole and part is
"implication". The whole is an identity, *totum simul*; the parts, however
diverse they seem, are repetitions of this identity—the infinitely many
images of a Unity which is, in Josiah Royce's words, a "self-representative
system" that logic and mathematics are believed most reliably to portray.
This solution of traditional philosophy's perennial "problem" of the One
and the Many is somehow an ineffable mystery which the mystic's intuition realizes as self-evident, real like Plato's idea of the Good, truest of
the true, best of the best; or like Spinoza's substance, *causa sui*, the self-
grounded ground of all other grounds—thus without a ground and in
need of none. *It is*; that is all we know or need to know.

True believers hold that in our transactions with this *totum simul*, our
attention takes hold of a part without in reality separating it from the
infinite multiplicity it figures in, but that, being *homo sapiens*, we treat it
as if its relations to its circumambience were external, as if it were a unit
in an organization instead of a cell in an organ of an organism. We
endeavor to realize the whole by way of some of its parts, to understand
its wholeness as the consequence of placing simple next to simple, next
to simple, next to simple, in a progression of complications until the
patterns reconstitute and repeat the wholeness of the original whole. The
tradition's "laws of thought" are basic rules for such image-making. They

direct our affirming and preserving identities and explicating "implications". Focal is not the most widely invoked "law of contradiction"; this only would shut conflict out of identity and pursues "consistency". The "law of excluded middle", however, is directed not at conflict but at compenetration. "Contradiction" concerns Being; "Excluded middle" concerns Becoming, concerns the indeterminacies of present, future and past that are the stuff of our immediate experience. Alfred Tennyson symbolizes the "excluded middle" with his *Flower in the Crannied Wall*:

> Flower in the crannied wall:
> "I pluck you out of your crannies,
> I hold you here, root and all, in my hand
> Little flower—but *if* I could understand
> What you are, root and all, and all in all,
> I should know what God and man is"

Francis Thompson, a generation later, bespoke it thus:

> All things by immortal power
> 　Near and far
> 　Hiddenly
> To each other linked are,
> Thou canst not stir a flower
> Without troubling a star

We may, I think, distinguish in the tradition two images of the "excluded middle." One is the eternal and universal Identity which commingles and homogenizes all diversities of Existence and Value in a single system of absolute and necessary Being, the changeless dialectic of all change, its ground at once, and its consummation. The other is the indeterminate confluence of diversities spontaneously diversifying, the process of Becoming, with its contingencies and innovations as experience learns it. Becoming is the middle which the "laws of thought" ever seek and ever fail to exclude, regardless of the devices logicians keep inventing and employing to exclude the middle and to render the discourse of reason consistent and infallible, thus the sure thing we would love to bet our lives on.

In the struggle against the middle we may recognize the survival value of reason, and the import of logic as a differentia of *homo sapiens*. Like the teeth, claws and tails of other mammals, reason with its logic denotes instruments for taking hold and holding onto something "good" or "true" or "right" or "beautiful" that would otherwise pass on out of our experience. Reason and logic also serve to cut off and shut out whatever might alter the object of our choice, or otherwise speed its passing, whether by a spontaneous variation or heightened momentum from within or a push or pull from without. In reason and logic a valuation is at work, at work so long as a life strives to preserve itself, strives even without hope, to proportion the force and scope of its actions to the immediate impact of its circumambience and its imaged consequences in its survival. Its survival is a process of rationing, rationalizing, fitting together, orchestrating, taking in and pushing out. It is a transaction seeking to confirm and advance itself. When it is such an action by means of words and symbols being fitted to those of other persons, we call it "intellectual." When the circumambience we act toward is not alone others' words and symbols, but persons, institutions, events and things, we call the transaction "intelligent". As noted, intelligence is creative as intellect is not, for intellect is postulated on implications, intelligence on efficacy. Intellect seeks to repeat identicals, intelligence to discover or devise differences. Both are differentiae of *homo sapiens* which render him another kind than the rest of the mammalian world; they are tools of survival so serviceable that they get transvalued into idols.

Valuation is the fifth feature of the five that compose our images of the changing world around. Whether we image it piecemeal, like the arts and sciences, or *in toto*, like religion and philosophy. I list it fifth because I find it to pervade the first four features of the image, to give them their singularity and role in the portrait of the original, be that visible or invisible reality or fiction. From one's perduring awareness that one's existence is one's value, one's value one's existence, branch out the processes of valuation whose divergences are directed to transvaluing both the forms and the forces with whose upsurge and subsidence this identity passes to the nothingness of death. Survival is the actuality of value. That which it values is the content. Humanly, to keep on existing, to survive, is to feel, to remember, to hope and expect, to reason, to imagine as certain, a future of well-being among happy companions; and by dint of facing and fighting down the images which arouse them, to allay and overcome all feelings of anxiety, fear, weakness, apathy, failure or despair. Survival is living on even as dying, and to die living on.

Certain valuations, which are consequent upon awareness that Value is is the ongoing struggle for survival, keep recurring in the history of philosophy. The tradition singles them out as *the* values: *Goodness, Beauty, Truth and Right* are perhaps more familiarly such than *Immortality* and *Freedom* for ourselves, and *Spirituality, Unity, Eternity* and *Universality* for the circumambience. These are less familiar perhaps, although no less recurrent. None images existence as we experience it, with its multitudinous changes and chances, ever in passage. All image existence as we want it to be, therefore as it "ought" to be. All develop as imaginative reshapings of remembrances, of images from our past, so as to envision and prophesy the future as we want it to be. All are ideas which our hungers bring up and render ideals; that is, shapes of satisfactions which should satiate. Sometimes, the satisfaction sought is to keep what we have as we already have it, to prevent its changing. At such times, image and original are confluent; each reinforces the other. Sometimes the ideal is a design for altering what we are and have into a more satisfying future form, and a program to reshape the existent into an incarnation of the design. Sometimes, image and original are so incommensurable that the first is in no way a rendering of the second or a design to alter it, but is a contradiction, a total rejection, of its very being. Then the present actuality of the original is transvalued into a shadow or reflection of the image, and the image is endowed with the actuality of the original. Its role in the struggle to keep on struggling is to compensate in image for the nullifications and failures due to the original in fact.

Each such image is an ideal. All can excerise the four functions, but it is as compensatory that most figure in the philosophic art. For *genus humanum* they are *Immortality*, or that we continue alive when we are dead; *Freedom*, or that we may be and do and have what we want, when we want it, as we want it, wherever we want it—by definition God has such freedom, no one else—no angel, no devil, not even rebellious Lucifer. For the circumambience, the ideal compensations are *Spirituality*, or that the universal Being is the original of which the Immortal Substance, our Humanity, is the image; *Unity*, or that Being is ineffably One and not Many; *Eternity* and *Universality*, or that Being is always and everywhere One and the Same. Thus Being is transvalued from Martin Buber's *It* into his *Thou* by an act of humanization which long ago John Ruskin had named "the pathetic fallacy." Henri Bergson and Teilhardt de Chardin have been among the late comers so to transvalue Becoming, save that they give Evolution a modern turn in imaging it as an everlasting propulsion onward and upward, whose proper name is God. Whether as Being or Becoming, we reluctantly make God in the image of man and account for man as an image of God. "That God," Alfred Tennyson consoles himself against death in *In Memoriam*,

> That God which ever-lives and loves,
> One God, one law, one element
> And one far-off divine event
> To which the whole Creation moves:

Our humanizations appear to be pandemic, and locally concrete. Images of Gods and Devils symbolic of natural processes are individuals repeating some male or female local individuality who, having become outstanding, has been taken for a Jones to keep up with as well as to worship. *Imitatio* goes on of all gods and devils, not alone *imitatio Christi*: the supernaturals seem ever to be made in the image of some natural human chosen by the other humans who make it. And not of a human alone—of an animal, a fish, a bird, an insect on which the choosers depend for food or clothing, safety or other satisfactions. We call such humanizations totems, and images on coats-of-arms are often residues of such totems; so are names of men and women. As symbols of collectivities and aggregations of all levels of purpose and complexity, they recur with new meanings (like the Elks or Moose of fraternal orders by those names), and serve to communicate in brief the faith, works and life-styles of the groups who have taken them for their symbols. Just as crosses portend the Christian drama of salvation, flags the forms and functions, the life and laws of nations, so do male personifications like "Uncle Sam" or female ones like Bartholdi's "Liberty Enlightening the World"; so do images of a group's dead leaders, heroes, or heriones, all present the compenetration of the group's remembered past with forecasts of its feared or hoped-for future. As well as a church or a state, the group thus communicating its communality and aspirations in a symbolic image may be a financial or business trust, a school, a trades-union, any configuration of individuals who give their group a proper name, share in making its life-story and thus in generating a collective identity which the laws recognize and sanction with the legal fiction, *the corporate person*. Over the years, also the Roman Catholic establishment made use of this fiction to assure its own prosperous survival and growth.

Such images, each with a certain uniqueness of its own, communicate to the initiates patterns of faith, of works and of destiny by which they hope to live until they die, and in which to live on forever when they die. As schools of philosophy present them, the traditional role of these world-pictures is compensatory. Philosophers keep reshaping them and hypo-statising their renewals, so that much of the history of their art is a rehearsal of argumentation after argumentation, to *prove* that the images are not consequences of our experience but its ground; that they are the originals which we distort by our endeavors to reproduce them, and that our destiny is truly the immortal safety and freedom of living forever in the pure presence of the originals. Somewhat recently, the programmatic has begun to challenge the precedence we so easily give to the compensatory function of the image as ideal in the hierarchial configuration of values whose stressful compenetrations constitute human existence.

Aristotle, that mostly straightforward and matter-of-fact observer of the human comedy, remarks in his *Nichomachean Ethics* (VI-1140-1726)

All art is concerned with coming into being—contriving and considering how a something may come into being which is capable of either being or not-being, and whose origin is in the maker and not in the thing made . . . Making and acting being different: art is of making, not of acting. And in a sense, chance and art are concerned with the same object; as Agathon says, art loves chance, and chance loves art.

Aristotle did not, of course interpret philosophy as an art, and would no doubt have denied that it was intimate with chance. And in the *Eudemean Ethics* (VII 14) he draws the line.

As in the Universe, he writes, so in the soul, God moves everything. The starting-point for reasoning is not reasoning, but something greater. . . . For this succeeds without reasoning.

Deliberation is no advantage—"they have inspiration but cannot deliberate." The inspiration comes as the *nous poetikos*, the intuitive reason which is the rational principle aware of itself, God the Being and God the Image one and the same. Aristotle could, one might guess, generalize experience until it came to generalizing the generalizations. In our experience, things begin, things end; we make things, we destroy things. Why then, should the universe of all things together not also be a making and an ending? How can we argue from happenings and disappearances that these depend on something which neither happens nor disappears but stays on self-identical, world without end?

The Image as Dream

How CAN we without self-deception contend that the real world, the true world, is eternal and universal, uncreated, always and everywhere one and the same? We cannot come to this realization as a conclusion from a premise; deliberation cannot lead it to it. If we do not arbitrarily assume it, we must receive it as its self-revelation, without motive, without cause. It discovers itself to us humans in virtue of our being what we are—figures of earth, like all our earthly kin: able to see, hear, touch, taste, smell, feel, break things up, put things together, remember, imagine and deliberate, hence able to learn, to anticipate, to fear and to face what we fear, to love and hate, to work and fight. But more, we are able, as our earthly kin are not, to talk about the transactions in which these functions figure. For each, our bodies have an organ, and we use each and every organ in order to conserve the experiences we cherish and to eliminate those we do not want repeated—that is, we deliberate, we reason. And still more, Aristotle tells us we have a faculty our earthly kin have not, a faculty not linked to the body or any organ of it. This it is that grasps and participates directly—not by imaging—in the *Nous Poetikos*, is that Unmoved Mover who like Faust's "Eternal Feminine," draws us on unto itself. It also draws the rest of existence, but only *homo sapiens* arrives, and stays until he dies. It is his immortal part, but not his personal self; that is his mortal part. Spinoza's definition of immortality, one might argue, is a sort of personalization of Aristotle's without the personal survival which the religious establishments base their economies on. Insofar as the latter purported to derive from Aristotle their certainties that we live on when we are dead, they only quoted Scripture for their purpose. Personal survival is what scientific students of body-soul relationships tell us depends on an ongoing give-and-take between parts of the mechanism of our brains. By that, mobility becomes orchestrated into behavior, reaction into transaction, and whatever we appreciate as "meaning" is ongoingly created. Personal immortality would consist of the future's entering the past and reshaping it without the action of the brain mechanism, doing this although the brain has gone dead, and the individual as body-in-action has become extinct.

Extinction, death, when transvalued into a "beyond" between life and

109

after-life, is often imaged as sleep—"not dead but sleeping" is a metaphor intended to console, although it at once concedes and denies the extinction which death signifies. The sleeper who does wake from his sleep wakes to the continuing world he had gone to sleep in, not to an Otherworld, and while asleep he has lived on, his organs had kept functioning, his flow of experience had continued unaware more than aware, his emotions re-patterning the configurations of its images, making different forms, giving these different directions from his waking life. We call the succession Dreaming, and the images, Dreams.

Dreams come as successions of images which somehow do and do not fit together. However they come, they evince a singularity so diverse from the events of the waking life that we feel them unreal and absurd, yet ominous. The waking life is a shared life; it is public, commonsense, and divergently rational. The dream life is private and by comparison, irrational. It makes no waking sense, yet is ominous with "meaning." Where the events of the waking life are normally not difficult to recall, those of the dream-life are largely forgotten; those we recall come with stronger feelings than are common in the rememberings of the waking life.

It is this otherness, not its imputed unreality, which separates dream life from waking life. It is this singularity which renders the image of the dream after waking a challenge unlike the challenges of the waking life. Those, the dreamer once awake has ready ways of facing and overcoming. Their rationality consists in the personal habits acquired, aware or unaware, from the folkways and mores of his community (we often call them commonsense or custom) and it is contingent on a repetition of identicals that his transactions with the day's challenges may be made up from. But he also encounters challenges strange, new and upsetting.

To meet those he has available the human rules of logic and scientific inquiry. Through the latter, he may channel the propulsion occasioned by the encounters into searching and seeking, with its risky trial and error, and thus perhaps assuage the uneasy curiosity aroused by the new, the unprecedented, the unique. He spontaneously attributes the challenges to causes of which he presumes them to be effects. He would like, by reason of scientific inquiry to discover those causes, to harness them up and work them toward making himself master of their effects.

But, not yet quite, with the causes of dreams, monitory and challenging as he may find his dreams to be. The scientific conquest and taming of dream life is still more endeavor than achievement. By comparison, its history is brief. It may be said, not unironically, to have taken a positive naturalistic direction with Sigmund Freud's researches into his waking recollections of his own dreams. Its present place is spanned by the current studies of the behavior of sleepers, dreaming. These studies take dreams as psychosomatic events following from impersonal (physiological) causes. They take the causal relation to be measurable and reducible to general laws which may be directing a survival function. They seek to work up a sort of Darwinian biology of dreaming. Men and women, whose dreams have been experimentally interrupted, are reported to come awake irritable, tense, anxious, bad-tempered, inattentive, and forgetful. And hungry. Completion of dreams might, hence, be an insurance of ongoing mental health in the waking life, since in the latter the alternative to the imagery of dream life would be hallucinations, delusions and illusions.

Psychoanalytic studies, on the other hand, take dreams and the dream-images as events in specific personal histories. Psychoanalytical inquiry is empiric inquiry into living biography. Its "model" of the structural dynamic of dreams, its discussions of their meaning, aim to disclose the role of his past experiences in the dreamer's memories as his personal history, and in his present anxieties and hopes and fears for his future. Already in 1922 Freud had noted (*Traum und die Telepathie*) that dreams serve as a safety-vale and protect sleep. By relieving the overburdened brain they are able also to heal and calm the psyche. As "behavioral scientists" might say it, the mechanism of dreaming is the physiological homeostat that keeps sleep unbroken. But however bespoken, the psycho-analytic interpretation of dreams confirms and nourishes mankind's perduring faith that the otherness of the dream life and its events warns *homo sapiens* about his waking present and forewarns him about his waking future.

These alerts have been said to compose the dream's survival value in all cultures. The tradition of the mystery of dream-interpretation may have started with articulate speech. Certainly philosophers from the pre-Socratics and Plato to Philo and the post-Philonics, certainly poets from Hesiod and Homer to Virgil and after, concerned themselves, no less than prophets, priests and politicians, to find reliable knowledge regarding the nature, the source and the meaning of dreams. Dream books with recipes for their interpretation may perhaps be counted as authentic antiquities of great age. The tradition attributes dreams, with no exception, to super-natural inspiration: Gods, daimons, demons send them. They are messages of the spirits of the earth, the air, the water and the fire, and of the human dead. To attribute them to the impersonal forces of nature is heresy. Advocates of these forces, however disillusioned—psychoanalysts not a few among them—hold the dream-image as no less imaginary and unreal than illusions, hallucinations and delusions. To hold it thus is to place its cause in the person and plight of the dreamer himself. It is to keep on challenging the prevailing belief that our dreams are caused by powers in the circumambience without, the peers of the astrologer's Zodiac, the Pythogorean's numbers, the fortune-teller's cards, tea-leaves, crystals and palm charts, the priest's entrails of beasts, flights of birds, pecking of fowls. What dreams mean calls for similar discernment—and only specialists are prepared to practice such discernment. Cause and meaning often coincide or overlap. Traditionally, their import transcends every normal value of the waking life. Self-repeating as this life we live may be, it still spans, perhaps corrals, a sequence of change and chance, of an uncertain future through an insecure present into an eluding past; it is still a flux of challenges against which dreams are harbingers of relief, be what they foretell good or bad. To such as can read them, dreams, allaying anxiety about the future, impart certainty for the uncertain, assurance for the insecure; while such as cannot, seek out the professional interpreters— the priests, the prophets, the psychologists, the mystics, the fortune-tellers, all learned in the skills of translating the images of dreams into the words and symbols of the waking life. So, forewarned of the future, the seekers can the more confidently meet it as it comes. For indeed a truly imaged evil assures greater determination than a dubious good. It calls out a firmer and freer will to overcome and live on. In our struggles to keep on struggling, the vital force is not the actual course which events take but the very often ineffable feeling of its fore-ordination. Such a feeling is religious. Similarly ineffable is the scientific belief that the course is pre-determined. Dreams are taken for secret ciphers of fate and fortune, for a supernatural or natural cryptography, which once deciphered, serves our survival.

Ciphers are images each of which has an identity of its own, regardless of the secrets it hides from the unknowing and reveals to the knowing. Functionally ciphers are symbols created and shared by certain groups of cryptographers to serve as helps in their struggles with other groups. Athletic teams, such as baseball and football, have their ciphers; businesses, arts and sciences, religions, all have their ciphers. In effect, symbols are ciphers, ciphers are symbols, some as public as a flag or crown or other emblem shared by multitudes or intended, like the emblems of the United Nations, by the ostensible cryptographers of all mankind, to be deciphered and shared by all mankind. Of such the key, whether or not used, is provided with the cipher; the symbol is a function of the meaning, not the meaning of the symbol.[1] Of others, the key is a private possession like the key to a safe or a crossword puzzle and the symbol, like a safe or the spoken and written words of a language one does not know, may be public for any one to see or hear. It is natural that the cipher should be, and often is, first taken for what it seems—a mental image that enters a person's experience to be suffused with meanings which the person, not the image provides. His perception of it is a transaction whereby the image gets its value and meaning from his feelings of its role in his struggle to live on. These may or may not repeat the secret transactions of the key-holder; they may confirm or displace the latter's meaning or values. How a dreamer interprets his dream and how any other interpreter—professional or amateur—does, discloses the divergence and the changing of the image.

NOTE

1. This is notably the case with such value-words as *Liberty, Equality, Fraternity, Justice, Law and Order, The Beyond, Power*. They signify transactions between the user and the situations which occasion them; as general terms or concepts they are empty of content other than the feelings which prompt their use.

Image, Learning, Myth
as Survival Values

READING A sign, opening a safe, learning a language deneutralizes the image. They suffuse it with values. Transvaluations keep changefully recurring, at a pitch and in a rhythm by which we identify the image, despite deviations, as this-and-no-other. The image, initially private, becomes public as more and more individuals take for granted its repetitions and both pool and share their differences. Taking-for-granted, pooling and sharing are processes of identification. They do not abolish the differences; they submerge them in a created sameness. By and large, they are critical steps in the transaction we call learning, which we take to be completed when others are satisfied with our own repetitions. It need only be mentioned that learning is a particular pattern of our struggle to keep on struggling, that it varies from person to person, that it varies within the sequence of transactions which suffuse as they succeed one another on their way from the simple or complex challenge by the circum-ambience. The challenge may come as one image alone, or as a configuration of image with teacher, or image with any other person. Its impact is, to evoke the attraction we call curiosity or the aversions we call disinterest or boredom or apathy or resistance. The consequences are the "learning process"—intensification of curiosity, dissipation of aversion, satisfaction of curiosity as acts of exploration and appraisal, each repetition reinforcing its predecessors; for the learner, the consummation of all is the satisfaction expressed by the "teaching" others. Of course, the propulsion to learn need not be exhausted by this completion. As often as not such completion becomes a barrier to curiosity that would push beyond the public boundary, beyond the prescriptions and taboos against discovering or creating new images stirring up new curiosities.

It may be that the world's cultures, its folklores, its myths, its arts and sciences, are learnings consummated in some such sequences of re-valuation moving from originals to images of images of images, world without end. Maybe their substance is the residue which outlasts the imaginations and intelligences that, generation by generation, transform and transvalue the inherited images without eliminating them, as

114

"evolution" is believed to have transformed and transvalued some hairy ape into *homo sapiens*, altering but not eliminating the apetitudes.

The yen to strip from the original the overlay of images which mask it, the curiosity about *first* causes, and the play of imagination and intelligence in the will to search and seek or to create satisfactions to both, are differentiae of *homo sapiens*, intrinsic to his *haecceitas*. So also are the anxieties intrinsic to his *haecceitas* lest satisfactions, once attained, should be lost, the chances of survival thus diminished. So are the passions for the repetition of identicals that should compensate for their diversification —for diversifications darkly felt perhaps more than the openly observed. With these passions come also the xenophobia, the fear and enmity toward the different, the new, the strange, that are evident in all human establishments, the most sophisticated as well as the simplest.

The notion that the sciences might be—uniquely—free of these emotions is itself a compensatory idealization of the actualities of behavior in the sciences. I think of two instances which seem to me representative. One is a remembrance Darwin tells about in his Autobiography. It concerns a notable geologist, a contemporary of his, who warned him that the finding of a "tropical volute near Shrewsbury would be a great misfortune to geology, as it would overthrow all we had known about the superficial deposits for the Midland counties."

Another is an American astronomer's denunciation of the research and hypotheses of Immanuel Velikovsky and the defamation of his character because he proposed alternatives to "the laws of mechanics" which "have been tested competently and thoroughly . . . if Dr. Velikovsky is right, the rest of us are crazy." This, without having read Dr. Velikovsky's evidence or tested the adequacy of his inferences. The American astronomer was Harlow Shapley, then a professor of astronomy at Harvard. He initiated a lifelong vendetta in defense of a public image—"the laws of mechanics", which had already been challenged by proponents of other alternatives, such as Max Born: in play was an urge to defend the astronomer's *status quo*, its insurance by the repetition of its identicals and the fear and hatred of whatever might break into the succession of repetitions: ". . . if Dr. Velikovsky is right, the rest of us are crazy" projects the survival-value of the image "laws of mechanics", for Shapleyan astronomy.

Velikovsky, for whatever reason, seems to have been a learner whose curiosity propelled him across the barriers set up by the satisfactions of the establishment. He assumed that mankind's myths, symbols and other purported forms of *mimesis* of an original might not be sheer creations of man's imagination reworked and finally recorded by the generations, but experiences overlaid first by authentic images of their originals, then by images of images. He assumed that by strpping away the ovrelay, the primary image could be brought to light, and a strong curiosity led him to do this regarding the Hebrew scriptural image of the sun and moon standing still. For Shapley this was no astronomical original, but utter human fantasy, and any one who took it for such an original must be either a fool or a knave. Velikovsky, no fool, no knave, but a man of notable scholarly parts, felt he had reliable reasons for so taking it. He inferred that an Old Testament miracle could have been an actual historic event which Adam's posterity remembered, suppressed, yet diversely recorded, and he set out to dig up the records. The image shaped of his findings, as he drew it and argued it in three books—*Worlds in Collision, Ages in Chaos, Earth in Upheaval*—is a reasoned picture of events in the solar system recent enough for men to have observed and recorded in historic times. His imaging is an orchestration from all the available records: it composes them into an evolution compounding itself of catastrophes. The resulting portrayal is a signal achievement of imagination and intelligence working in close harmony to restore authenticity to an early image of an actual happening. A physician skilled in the theory and practice of psycho-analysis, Velikovsky postulated that the actual happening must have been too disastrous for *homo sapiens* to remember as such. The memory image gets remodelled; it is given human features and the remembered event gets converted from a bringer of defeat and destruction to a bringer of victory and survival. By imaging happenings as acts of the tribal god, the Bible story infuses them with human meanings and values. The imaging is a transaction which remolds a cataclysmal experience into a satisfying human myth.

By and large, all myths might be regarded as humanizations of the non-human or deifications of the human. Certainly the philosophy, like the scientific study of them, involves searching and seeking after the non-human originals which they are believed to image. But the image as myth is repeatedly an epic or a drama or a collection of them accounting for the course of human events—its *wheres* and *whens*, its *terminus a quo* and its *terminus ad quem*—and prescribing what humans must do and refrain from doing in order to keep on living also when they are dead. The religions of mankind ever repeat the story and imitate the drama with their rites and rotes. To the true believer they continue to be ineffable incarnations of meanings which establish and sustain the values of the common-places of the daily life, with its lusts and labors, its friendships and enmities, its wisdoms and follies. The myths wherewith they are measured and policed are taken by the true believers for revelations to shape their own conduct by. They are "gospel truth". Their dramatis personae are images of gods and of men like gods—whose ways are ways to salvation disclosed to the true believer alone, and rendering him holy as the holy ones are holy. *Imitatio dei* is the incarnation of a myth in a personal history.

But the questions Which God? Which myth? have their infallible answers in the wars of religion. The wars of religion are wars over myths. There is a widespread belief that modernity has dispensed with myth-making, that the mankind which has bet its life on science and its methods for reliable knowledge bets on a more trustworthy agent than the mystique of "the Beyond" with its chronicles and rites and rotes of salvation. Instead it stakes its prosperously postponing death on the knowledge and knowhow of the farmer, the healer, the engineer, the industrialist, the banker and the soldier who have been indoctrinated in the teachings and disciplined in the skills of the new culture built upon science and machinery. This "now" generation of mankind purport to have no use for the old myths and their old images. In today's usage, "myth" is a term of scorn or derision. It is taken to signify an involuntary deception or a wilful falsehood. However, that some discard certain myths of their cultural heritage is as nothing beside the multitudes who do not, who cherish them as reliable value-systems which suffuse de-humanized images of nature and man with the features of humanity and the human warmth. For these multitudes, the *It* of the seesaw between *Thou* and *It*—which William James first called attention to and Martin Buber transvalued into an unambiguous exaltation of *Thou*—*It* is not denatured but is rendered precious by *Thou*.

Nor do those who presently discard the myths of the past refrain from myth-making and ordaining their creations as religions for the future. Myth-making is as inveterate as breathing and the displacement of myth by myth as the displacement of breath by breath. Myth may follow myth as unaware as healthy breath follows healthy breath. Or they may intrude on each other with the characteristic violence of religious wars. Leaders may be imaged, after they have died, with god-like features and traits, as were Moses and Lycurgus, George Washington and Abraham Lincoln, Winston Churchill and Martin Luther King and other spokesmen for Democracy. Such imaging transvalues their actual *haecceitas* into symbols implying the values for which they worked and died. Or leaders may choose an image with which to mask their actual identity, order it designed and imposed as a true portrait, symbolizing the value-system by which, godlike, they take and hold power, and have themselves revered and worshipped as gods, descendants of gods, or men like gods. So the sanctified value-system we call Communism has its symbolic, concretion in the images of Marx, Lenin, Stalin, and Lenin's corpse; of Mao, Che Gueverra, Castro and the rest. Fascism has its symbolic concretion in the images of Mussolini and Franco, Nazism in those of Hitler, Goering and Goebbels. The ancestors of all are the live Roman Emperors, worshipped like the gods; a survival is the divinely descended decent man, the Mikado of Japan.

On occasion, again, a pantheon of images may be designed, as by August Comte. This extraordinary genius—Bertrand Russell, very strangely has not a word about the beliefs of this philosopher of science and society in his "History of Philosophy"—projected a "religion of humanity" and designed a temple where the symbol of the race, *homo sapiens*, should be a living woman and the lesser gods images of men and women who had benefited the race. He ordained feast days for them on the model of the Saint's Days of the Roman Catholic religion into which he had been born. The Comteist myth won believers. But possessing only its intrinsic merits and neither money nor arms to impose itself, it had a brief vogue among a few intellectuals and faded out. Perhaps it came nearer than the faiths which preceded and those which followed it to "telling it like it is". With respect to its whole image of man, his world, and his struggle to live on and never die in it, Comte's "religion of humanity" also challenges the appraisal: symbolic truth or wilful deception? Only the act of faith affirming or denying provides an answer.

True, "history", once it purports to be "scientific," searches and seeks after the authentic original of the image. Its announced goal is to disclose whether the image is "only a myth" or a "true" likeness of the original. But of course, history cannot bring the original to light. It can only compound a new image from the fragments and residues of older images of the original. Should a historian's new image diverge from the established one, and he be approved as a truth-seeker exposing a deception, a debunker refuting by his feat Henry Ford's revelation that "history is bunk", he will figure as an authority until his truth, in its turn, is debunked. Like the images of men, movements and events devised on behalf of their clients by the image-makers we call public relations specialists or advertising agencies, the images composed by historians do but serve present purposes for future realization in purporting to reveal past events. Their truth is the trust in them of the believer, not their likeness to any original.

Myths multiply and their rivalries multiply with them. What concerns true believers most is not the goodness, the beauty or the rightness of their myth, but its truth, however much the former might shape the latter. How far may they trust their myth to steer them over the stormy seas of Thisworldly existence into the snug harbor of salvation? For

generations the specialists in salvation of our part of the world simply
denounced or scorned or deplored the deliverances of the sciences as
blasphemies against "the Word of God". Then as the consequences of
those deliverances in bettering the works and ways of men's daily lives,
became too evident to ignore, the specialists began to construct myths
imaging "the harmony of science and religion". Philosophical systems
intending these myths became units in academic curricula. Nevertheless,
the sciences, theoretical and practical, increased and multiplied. They came
to pervade an ever larger portion of *homo sapiens*' daily life. Like the
astronomer-mathematician Pierre Simon Laplace, who replied to the first
Bonaparte's question, *Where was God in his system of celestial mechanics?*
that he had no need for that hypothesis, so the later generations of
scientists. They not only could "do their thing" without God, they could
do it better without him.

This deeply disturbed theologians to whom the myth was the ultimate
concern. Their appreciation of the myth as truth changed. Many ceased to
believe that the myth, in whatever mode, was a reliable image of the
universe, *terminus a quo* to *terminus ad quem* no longer then successful rival
of the scientific image. But they continued sure that in the realm of values
the scientific image could not successfully rival their myth. Science can
treat only of existence, not of value, but myth homogenizes value and
existence. It is truer to the *haeccitas* of our struggle as *homo sapiens* to live
on and not die. The myth expresses, as science cannot, the meaning of life
to itself. Not theologians alone are apt to call this meaning "transcendent".
The adjective is philosophical, and the first transcendentalists were
philosophers with subtle affiliations to religion. On the record, nevertheless, the meaning is immanent and cannot be otherwise, since we experience
and know it as the very push and pull of our self-altering self-preservation
—at once our existence and its value. Moreover, we know it immediately
as an event in "nature", not as an intrusion of a supernatural grace. To
experience grace is a natural happening or an act of the imagination of the
natural man. Its orchestration with the order it breaks into is the work of
this man's creative intelligence.

More than one true believer in scientific naturalism has taught that
science is tangent, if not inimical, to values. I mention only Bertrand
Russell, Max Born and Julian Huxley. Russell and Born each had a
creative role in giving the sciences of nature new patterns and turning them
in new directions—Russell in logic, Born in mathematical physics, Huxley
in biology. Their rhetoric initiated mutations in the bodies of knowledge
which were their primary concerns. Russell and Born can be said to have
been to mathematics, physics and mathematical physics what, broadly,

E

Darwin had been to biology: they created new images which first challenged, then displaced, the idols of the scientific establishment. Russell, nevertheless, condemned the successes of the sciences as the self-defeat of humanity. Born's powers as a mathematician and physicist were no less singular than those of Laplace. He played a leading role in rivalling, if not displacing, the Newtonian celestial mechanism which Laplace had in his turn proved beyond all reasonable doubt, by the quantum mechanics whence come the working hypotheses of our *now* physics. Born believed that the this-and-no-other determinism of the Newtonian tradition was deception or self-deception; that neither its successes nor the successes of quantum mechanics gave evidence that they could contribute to any bettering of human relations. That, on the record, these successes had worsened them.

Julian Huxley, grandson of the apostle of Darwinism, Thomas Henry Huxley, brother of the Bloomsbury novelist and later spokesman for "the perennial philosophy", Aldous Huxley, has been a Darwinian in the great tradition. He had come first to believe that the progressive compoundings of the discoveries and creations of science and of the machinery they led to, wherewith we subdue the forces of nature to the wants and will of man, would bring a new religion, a post-Comteist religion of humanity by which each individual human would be so linked with the individualities of all other humans as to compose a single organic spirit, the spirit of humanity. But over the years, Huxley found his not implausible Utopianism obstructed by the ever-expanding configuration of science, industry and invention. He noted that with this expansion came a regression and destruction as actual as the progress which first had stirred his imagination. For the scientists, the inventors, the industrialists and tradesmen are anticipating only the immediate satisfactions which their enterprises might bring them, and elaborate those in gargantuan measures. They give no thought to, or if they do, neglect to heed, the other consequences of their works and ways. It seems not to have occurred to the captains of science and industry that the difference in scale between man and his machines alters their relations: it puts man at the mercy of his machines. It imperils the welfare of the earth and man's tenure of it. His survival as *homo sapiens*, always precarious, becomes a losing bet.

So Russell, Born and Huxley. They charge in principle that by concentrating on existence to the exclusion of values the scientists and technologists of the age have put existence in double jeopardy. It seems not to have occurred to them that the concentration on existence we call science is a specific valuation of existence no less struggled for than the concentration on what we call profit; that science and profits are both humanizations of non-human existence, diversifying formations of man's struggle to keep on struggling. At any phase in the history of these struggles the charges against the exclusion of value from existence could be restated as charges against isolating value from value. Long ago, Harald Höffding argued that religion is "the conservation of values." Once we recognize that the conservation of values is the self-preservation of a life, every single human activity may be defined in this way, not only religion. On the record, religion is constituted by the self-conservation of each by force of its war upon all, by force of its always denying that others, however wrong it may believe them to be, have alike the same right to be wrong as it has to be right. The inhumanity of man to man does not follow from the differences of man from man. The difference is his value as himself to himself, is what makes him this-man-and-no-other. It is at the same time what makes his value to others, since if he and they were only identicals repeating each other, none could be or have any other want. The humanity of mankind is the consequence of the free orchestration of their diversities, on equal terms. Its inhumanity is to penalize the different for their difference, to deny them the equal right to live and grow. It is, to nullify their existence by annulling its value.

Back to the Word and the Name

SO DEEP, so perduring has been the influence on philosophy of Plato's image of the real as a hierarchy of eternal and universal ideas, that his role of pioneer in the investigation of language and the making and use or words has fallen into the background, and is discussed incidentally. But he was the first to declare the spoken word an image and to argue its nature and function as knowledge. This is the theme of the earliest of the dialogues in which Plato is no longer remembering Socrates but is using him as the voice of his own attitudes and insights. It is the dialogue *Cratylus*. Significantly, Cratylus had been the first of Plato's teachers, and a disciple of Heracleitus. In the dialogue Plato confronts this first teacher with his preferred master Socrates, but makes the opposition between them less than might be assumed. As was his wont, he had Socrates' opponent concede many of the former's points, but as was not his wont, nothing essential, nothing that need be contrary to the teachings of Heracleitus. As the latter saw the world, it was a flood of transformations in cycle. None of the formations which the Milesians identified as its ground and substance but is seen transformed into some other—water, vapor, air, ether, fire and back again all self-modifications of a stuff which is none of those modifications, but is the process of modification itself. The stuff is the flow of all things—*panta rei*—and the flow is an ineffable push or thrust (Aristotle's word for it was *hulé*, Bergson's word for it was *élan vital*) which ever liquifies solids, vaporizes liquids, turn vapor to gases, gases to the incandescence of fire whose burning is never at rest, whose heat is the animation of life. This thrust and flow, from fire to fire, "is the same in all." It is not the creation of any God or any man; "it was ever, is now, and ever shall be an ever-living fire with measures of it kindling and measures going out." We observe the process as a sequence of opposites. Day and night, summer and winter, hunger and satiety, war and peace, living and dying, pass each over into the other. They are becomings. A later generation would accuse Heracleitus of self-contradiction. Aristotle did. But he might better have accused him of identifying the reality with logic's Excluded Middle, declaring "mortals are immortals, and immortals mortals, one living the other's death and dying the other's life" as the flux, which forms itself into all things and cannot be found the same as any, flows its concurrent up and down ways in fixed measures of stress tending to balance each other. The flux is a war of the ways. This "war is the father of all and the king of all". It is the universal and ever-lasting struggle within which particular victories and defeats come. Yet the ways somehow transcend the events they produce and destroy. They provide the law and order of the flux they impattern. They are its truth, its *Logos*; our reason is our faculty which images this *logos*, shaping the flux into its sequent formations, keeping them in measure and bringing retribution or compensation for overflowing measure.

Presumably, it is with some such philosophy that Cratylus confronted Socrates. How otherwise could he imagine the *logos* of Heracleitus than in terms of the spoken word of man written to outlast both speech and speaker, and somehow to signify, if not to contain and impattern, the power of the speaker whose speaking is the act creating the creative, the commanding, Word? In the Hebrew Scriptures, this seems to have been the sole concern: Egyptians seem to have signified it in their hieroglyphs, Sumerians in their cuneiform ideograms. It is what could plausibly have been intended by the devices created by other cultures so as to have sight stand for sound. In Sumerian, we are told, the equivalent for *logos* as the name of the felt power of speech to rule, to create in the uncreated deeps, was *mummum*, sometimes the "word of wisdom," sometimes the "word of wrath" as we experience both in the courses of nature and in relations of man to man. The Hebrews used *davar* (word) for many meanings, of which *davar Elohim* is among the most telling; with the word *ruah* (wind, spirit), it signifies like, if not interchangeable, powers, as the Psalm tells us:

> By the word of Yahweh were the heavens created
> And by the breath of his mouth, their host.

And the Deuteronomist warns regarding the commandments at Sinai . . . "the Word is very nigh unto thee, in thy mouth and in they heart, that thou mayest do it. It was not with our fathers that the Lord made this covenant but with us, the living, every one of us who is here today."

Not surprisingly, the relation of the Word to the World became itself an occasion of the wonder which, it is said, philosophy was created to assuage. It is the now somewhat banal issue that Plato debated in Cratylus. *What, if anything, can we know if we have no name for it? Is it possible to know an anonymity?* There works underneath the question the assumption that what is not infallible cannot be truly knowledge, that true knowledge must be absolute certainty, and always and everywhere the same. In *Cratylus* Socrates seems not yet so committed as he was in the later dialogues. But he does argue that naming implies authentic knowledge, sure as the conventions of word-use cannot be sure because names, rightly given, are the likenesses and images of the things they name. In the nature of things the responsibility for rightness must be his who gives the names—ultimately the lawgiver's who first gave names, and who might have been a god rather than a man. The names we presently call things by may well be deformations or falsifications of the first names. If any is to be taken for authentic knowledge, knowledge as certain as Cratylus agrees it should be, we must needs discover how the first spoken word relates to the object it bespeaks. If, however, that object be but the heracleitan flux, no word can present it. For authentic knowledge is infallible. It is of that which is always and everywhere the same. It is one of the object's unchanging essence and what can better disclose such an essence than an image of it? Every first name must be such an image, portraying the object's nature, and the purpose of the name-giver as he shapes sounds and syllables into the "absolute or ideal" name befitting the object's true nature. Only that phonation can be right which by a sort of sympathy echoes the function of the object it names. For evidence Plato draws first upon poets—Homer, Hesiod, and others. He has them show that sound must make sense of sight, sight of sound—*ut pictura poesis*—if a name is to be a true image of whatever it names. This, regardless of whether we analyze the phonations shaped into the names of the gods, of heroes or ordinary humans, of men's bodies or souls, or of the heavenly bodies, or of the elements of Terra—earth, water, air, ether, fire—or of the four seasons, or of the faculties, the virtues and vices of men, or of maleness and femaleness.

But how can there be a true image of anything in flux? Such a thing both is and is not, and never the same.[1] Cratylus agrees. That is, he agrees that the flux is an identity which does not stop to be known; but he believes, nevertheless, that the name (or word) also in itself a passage, can be and often is a reliable image of its original. He agrees—did not Wittgenstein join him in thus confirming Socrates?—that a sensible man should never submit to the control of names or trust either them or their makers. But he prefers to trust Heraclitus rather than the Socratic suggestion of the alternative of eternal and universal ideas as the objects of true knowledge. "I believe," Socrates had said, "that name-givers believed that all things are in motion and flux. Still, in reality that is not the case, and the name-givers, themselves having fallen into a kind of vortex, are whirled about, dragging us along with them. Consider, my worthy Cratylus, a question about which I often dream. Shall we assent that there is any absolute beauty, or good, or any other absolute, or not?" Can this be the truth, on which true knowledge depends, or are only the untruths of the flux accessible to us, the flux itself being beyond knowledge? He urges Cratylus to inquire and tell him; and Cratylus replies that he had already inquired, that he thinks "the doctrine of Heracleitus" is much more likely to be true, and hopes—perhaps ironically—that Socrates will continue to keep on reflecting on the same questions.

The *Cratylus* reads like a moment of the process which advanced the hypostasis of *logos*, the word as we speak it and experience it, into *the Logos*, the word transcending all experience, yet creating, ruling, sustaining, destroying it as the words of men do in the business of living. Perhaps because of this role of words and their ways in the daily life, Plato's hints, in the *Cratylus*, of the resonance of things and events in our vocalization —his hints of the origin of language, shall we say, as onomatopoiea— stimulated such diverse artists or thinkers as Emanual Swedenborg or Robert Burns, or perhaps Edgar Allan Poe, or Benjamin Pearl Andrews or Benjamin Paul Blood, to speculate on what Blood named "the poetical alphabet." Each, and no doubt many others unknown to me, sought what Blood called "a natural alphabet" in the experience of talking, and Blood became aware long before the swarming of the analytic schools how "logical truth is held to the arbitrament of language." Each imager gave his own version of how letters and syllables correctly image things and relations and events. It may be that the renewals of Plato's perceptions are indications of intellectual turning points analogous to puberty of the body, and the feelings of wonder, anxiety, and delight that often come together go with puberty. There is a hint, perhaps, in the pleasure with which small children keep repeating their own first articulations after hearing them. And of course it is no news that the experience of speaking does, on occasion, fill the speaker, if not the listener, with wonder and delight. The sense of the word, the marvel at its role and power, the concern over its matter and manner, seem to have come to early expression in the recorded history of our culture. Perhaps, in man's beginning as man, the word was the all of philosophy: Aristotle, as everybody knows, charged philosophy to wonder, and his teacher Plato provides us with an early philosophic wondering about the wonder of the Word, that Snark of survival which ever turns out as the Boojum of extinction.

Every so often survival is accounted for by "homeostasis". In such accounts growth can figure as solely addition of the same to the same. That is, growth can figure as increase, not alteration, of an organism and its organs during the struggle to keep on struggling which is its survival. The roles of the whole, its relationship to the parts, and the relations of the parts to one another are believed to perdure unchanged. Thus homeostasis is another synonym for a self-preservation which signifies the teamwork of the organism's organs as they take in and render flesh of the organism's flesh and bone of its bone anything in its environment which it feels may nourish its identity, while it keeps out and thrusts out whatever it feels may hurt or starve it. The energies are "physiological". For the most part, eyes see, ears hear, noses smell, tongues taste, hands and skin feel and touch, when hunger prompts; blood flows, heart, lungs and glands meet each other's pushes and pulls and those of the world around in such wise as to bring the organism back into 'balance'. Balance is satiation; it is a temporary *terminus ad quem* of an action, of an action which has itself for its lasting terminus; by comparison, balance is rest; it is inertial; the satisfied animal falls asleep, it stays in repose until a hunger impels it again to fill the void and restore the balance. All its existence is a flow back and forth, from want to want-not, have-not to having, hunger to satiety, imbalance to balance to imbalance. Homeostasis is now one name for this imaged self-repeating cycle; another is cybernetics. Soon or late, however, the patterns of intake and output fall apart; balance becomes less and less recoverable. Entropy takes over and death follows, perhaps with infinite slowness. Existence may become an immortality of dying, like the immortality of Jonathan Swift's Struldbrugs. Survival fossilizes. The brain has ceased to function, thought and feeling happen: they happen without purpose. Living is experienced as the deathlessness of dying.

While the brain functions, the intake from the senses compenetrates into commonsense, without the senses ceasing each to do its "own thing". Subtly, eyes see sounds, ears hear sights, noses smell both and tongues taste both; hands and skin feel, touch and take in what eyes see, ears hear and tongues taste. Commonsense is the survival-function of an ongoing reciprocal permeation of the intake of the different senses into patterns of action, each a field with a fringe. Images keep resulting. They are formations consequent to our transactions with the diversifying ambience that our senses reach or that reaches our senses. In them our living past is joined by our changing present; perception and remembrance unite and form a new configuration of behaviors. Hallucinogenic chemicals—the current preferences are said to be lysergic acid, heroin, marijuanna, peyote, as against the more traditional drugs: hashish, opium, cocaine, alcohol and tobacco—can help disfigure the vision and action of commonsense into unprecedented diffluent shapes far more original than the unorganized immediate compoundings revealed—we have Mr. Marshall McLuhan's word for it—as the creations with which "the media" are destined to abolish the Word.

But to abolish the Word is to abolish the Human in human kind; let the images which the generations live by be as protean as Proteus, they are

Man's singularity as man. From the caves of Altamira to the houses of Congress, names, drawings, pictures, hieroglyphs, symbols, statements, tables of numbers, acronyms, ciphers, handworked or machine-produced, preserve the image which perishes as we create it by speaking, miming, gesturing. It survives only if we repeat it by a different means in a different material which can and does outlast us. Images so repeated come to be as creations which survive their creator, survive him at least as Lenin's corpse survives the once-living person whose corpse it is believed to be. It survives as the person's fossil residue, kept from extinction by the embalmer's art—an art of which the old Egyptians are believed to have been masters. And whatever the image images, Homo sapiens finds ways of preserving and multiplying it as he cannot the once-living original. Let the original be words thought—i.e. subvocalized and then written or printed on parchment or paper; let it be a shape or meaning worked into clay or wax or stone or metal. So materialized, it outlasts the original original, and hopefully, its creator. So materialized, he takes it for his immortal residue, for his ongoing presence that his children and children's children can not ever be. In and by itself, however, the image is nothing of the sort; it represents nothing, it means nothing, not even itself. It simply *is*, like all things, a becoming, neither true nor false nor good nor bad nor beautiful nor ugly. One or the other value accrues to it only when some living person encountering it brings it to life, to vicarious and passing life, as his awareness of it develops in empathy and is voiced in words, heard or unheard. If he takes it as well for the image-maker's residue stating a meaning of the latter's, he endeavors to fit the two images and present them as one. Much of the world's literature—whatever it projects, portrays, reasons about—comes to birth as the *re*imaging of the images produced and left behind by the dead, incarnating in the recreations other lives than their makers'. Of all, the first, all-powerful, all-pervading image is the Word: "in the beginning was the Word."

NOTE

1. Change changes. The phrase "change does not change" intends a process always and everywhere the same. But this is exactly what change is not; it is not eternally a this-and-no-other. It is ongoing diversifications, a flow of beginnings into endings, a sequence of differentiations, none of which becomes a same with any other. Whether the new comes as a drop or a wave, it is a passing break from its predecessor and a barrier to its successor. Neither the logic of illation nor the dialectic of polarization can qualify it as, say, an absolute—Hegelian-style or any other—bounded in self-polarization. The Other of change is not change itself becomes its own opposite. The Other of change is sheer nothingness. Should change not change, there would be

E*

left the vast inane. The Parmenidean aphorism "Being is, non-being is not and cannot be thought" signifies neither the state of the universe nor the human condition. It signifies the human struggle to achieve an identity which survives change, to hold fast to what humanly is prized. It does not image either the *what* or the act of prizing. Changes come out of nothing as somethings which soon or late disappear, maybe into nothing. Maybe because existence seems to be happenings succeeding each other and suffusing what they succeed. Even as the plasma of the new physics it is change arising and going on *in vacuo*. What, as such, does it "mean"? All that it can mean: itself going on as we learn to know it in our struggles to preserve ourselves by striving to arrest and harness it to our uses.

The Logos of Language

THE BEGINNING! As we of the West have been taught and most of us continue to believe—the beginning of the world of our struggles to preserve ourselves, of the world wherein we come to experience ourselves, where we come to "self-consciousness!" But, in the context of our manifold, diverse and diversifying perceptions of this world as somehow a likeness of ourselves, it could well be that our image of the World beginning as the Word is but an imaging of the beginning of the World from the beginning of Man. Man began when to the powers and arts of the hairy ape was added the power of articulating noises into words. For what more distinguishes man from his cousin the ape, even as from other things alive, than the power of the word, of logos in the course of time hypostatized into *the Logos*. By his uses of the Logos, the hairy ape became the hairless one, *Homo sapiens*, and was no longer an ape. Exercise of the power of speech, experience of the roles of its divergent voicings— *Homo sapiens* identifies them by such sounds as *telling, reasoning, reckoning, counting, arguing, commanding, creating*—built the power of the Word into the power of powers: Jehovah God's unique instrument of creation and control (God *said* "let there be", and there was); the Demiurge's *Logos*, creating a cosmos of law and order in chaos, and both Jehovah and Demiurge making man, solely man, in their own image as masters of the Word!

So *Homo sapiens* is Homo loquens. He began with the Word. This became the commonest medium of man's image of himself, and of the ambience of war and work and play wherewith he shaped his image by means of his religions, his philosophies, his arts and sciences as his wars and works produced them and they then produced his arts and sciences. The Word became the creator and sustainer of this self-image, the ultimate inwardness of the Humanity of man. One might take this as the secular sense of the words of John: "In the beginning was the Word, and the Word was with God, and the Word was God. He was in the beginning with God: all things were made through him, and without him was not anything made that was made. In him was life and the life was the light of men. The light shines in the darkness and the darkness has not overcome".

Cavil the Word as some philosophers do (there's Wittgenstein for example). I submit that these verses can be accepted with little scruple as a reliable image of the role of language in the life of man from naming day in Eden to the latest namings in the sciences, the arts, and all the other goings-on of *homo sapiens*. Names produce boundaries, they enclose and preserve identities. They are each person's *Kaa*, his soul, his ghost, his double, his Other; they are his immortality that he can be remembered by when he is dead. They are believed to crystallize the diversifications of his struggles to live on in an unchanging formation that compenetrates the events of his personal history in a single symbol—a concept, a One comprehending all the Many which his life has compounded and will compound until he dies. The survival-function of the name is to serve as one means of handling together a diversity of things and thoughts, from a single pair to an infinite multitude. Naming may be compared to shorthand, an economy, a device for getting the largest, the most satisfying results for the least effort.

Naming is capitalism's original. The "master of the name" is the master of that which is named. "Give a dog a bad name" and you transvalue him into a bad dog, however unbad he may continue to be. The power to give names is the power to value and transvalue, to create and recreate. Remember the wonder-rabbi of Prague? His legend tells he modelled a man in clay and endowed it with life by fixing in its mouth a parchment inscribed with the never-to-be-spoken name of God whom true-believing Jews refer to only as *ha-Shem*, the Name. Our own time's rabbis of Prague would be the public-relations counsels, the commercial artists and copy-writers, the journalists, the critics and speech-writers who work at creating for their employers the image each seeks to have of himself and of the goods and services he wants the public to be persuaded or scared into buying. The words and figures of these "masters of the name" are expected to transvalue the questionable clay of their originals— the clay of the corporations which produce, first of all only to sell, actual foods, cosmetics, drugs, vehicles and other machines; the clay of the agencies of government which purport to serve the general welfare, to protect it from the harm with which the market ever threatens it. The images which package these clays endow them with the saving power of beauty, goodness and truth: Give a dog a good name. . . . Of the magical power, the capacity for miracle in naming, as the creation of a new image of a familiar original we may read in Joseph McGinnis' account of the re-formation of a politician into a president. He called it "The Selling of the President." The name is the power. He who demands "in God's name," "in the name of the law," or of "justice," or of "love," or of "reason," demands by right and the power credited to right. "Blessed be the Name."

"Where two or three are gathered together in my name" the New Testament has Jesus say, "there I am, in the midst of them." Language increases and multiplies with namings. It may begin as the simple lallation of infants but it diversifies into complex systems of articulation, each a sound-pattern altering by usage in its own way in order to signify at once both its own singularity and the multitudes of divergent likenesses it is used to mean. As the former, as one formation orchestrating a multitude of boundlessly diverse forms, it embodies "the universal and eternal," the always and everywhere same. As the latter, its oneness figures for but a convenient fact in our struggle for survival amid the Many which it signifies. *Man*, in its singularity, is but a word, *flatus vocis;* in our use of it, it exercises a different function with each use; its singularity alters with the situation we apply it to, its universality becomes indeterminate and dissipates into an interminable sequence of particulars which we record and explain in dictionaries.

This process, although more readily noticeable in language, seems to be the career of all manner and condition of symbols and signs. But language bespeaks the human difference more than any other kinds. Some four thousand tongues are believed to be in use, and each of a man's interests, each passion, each vocation, each sport, each amusement, gives rise to a new mode of speech relevant to its own configuration of transactions. It is not unlikely that the birth, rivalry, and death of languages is an ongoing process in *Homo sap's* struggle for existence, and that it turns on our success or failure by means of the Word to conform the chances and changes of the world around to our strivings to live on and grow. Reasoning, when we examine what actually we do as "rational" existences, is seen as the labor of this conformation, the impatterning of events in the grammar and logic of the Word. On whatever level, in whatever phase, this is believed to be more reliable, more "scientific", than imaging or imagining. Yet William James, talking to teachers generations ago about the use of logic warned them: "The science of logic never made a man reason rightly, and the science of ethics (if there be such a thing) never made a man behave rightly. The most such sciences can do is to help us catch ourselves up and check ourselves, if we start to reason or behave wrongly, and to criticize ourselves more articulately after we have made mistakes. A science only lays down lines within which the rules of art must fall, laws which the followers of the art must not transgress, but what particular thing he shall do within those lines is left exclusively to his own genius." Left exclusively, I would add, to his creativity which alters the rules in following them. The science of logic and the logic of science serve alike for alterations, not reproductions, of the order of nature, if any. So, likewise, is what is now being called "the philosophy of logic" with its import for the divergence of logic from philosophy. On the record, language has never been off on what Wittgenstein suggested as a holiday, nor are the language "sciences" likely to harness it up to services they would have it perform. "Our grammar and logic," William James wrote in another connection "violate the order of nature as on reflection we believe it to exist."

And why should they not, if we take the "order of nature" to be the ways in which our grammar and logic had come? Had not Carnap suggested in *Philosophy and Logical Syntax*, from quite another outlook than the pragmatist, that we are the prisoners of our languages; that our questions can have only such answers that language can convey, and experiment verify; that what cannot be verified by experiment and refuted by dialectic has to be meaningless; that since no symbol can signify such a *what*, the *what* is unthinkable? Thus, so much of philosophic language is at best only the utterance, not of reason, but of hopes, fears, and desires. It is like laughter and tears. Carnap, like other "logical positivists", like many philosophers of science, was interpreting the scientific enterprise as Max Weber interpreted modern business enterprise, in terms of what might be called the Protestant ethic in the philosophy of science. As if, first of all language had not set us free, and continues a tool of liberation, also from its own unanticipated effects! As if desires and feelings were not as actual as sensations and perceptions, nor their objects and images as memorable and as available for hope and fear and for other moods or forms of anticipation! As if desires and feelings could not, as they were, be reasonably imaged with the languages of mankind! On the record, this imaging is what our cultures prevailingly achieve. It is the humanization of the environment which we ever practice as we live and move and struggle to preserve our being as in it, yet not of it. The practice produces the familiar reasons of the heart which Pascal tells us "the reason" cannot know, and which Kant with a not unlike insight segregated into "pure" and "practical" reason.

First and last, we find, wherever we turn, that language consists of images created by tonguing and giving voice in countless ways; that each way gets imaged in formations of materials designed for eyes to see and hands to feel and grasp. For, let me repeat yet again, what the tongue speaks perishes as it is spoken. By comparison, what the eye sees and the hand takes hold of, perdures. Its stuff is the configurations of signs and symbols whereof language (literally tonguings) consists. They are the presences with grammarians anatomize, logicians analyze, poets orchestrate and philosophers transvalue into their "objects of ultimate concern" of which one ineffable is the sensory flux (that certain denominations take for *terminus ad quem*, as well as *terminus a quo* of their vocation) of whose waves or drops the images are spontaneous variations, no less substantial than they.

Homo sapiens the knowing man, the wise man, is I must repeat *Homo loquens*, the Wordman—the expressions are synonyms. Of course, like other animals we could survive without talking or fingering words like deaf mutes even though some psychologists train chimpanzees to produce phonations and give meanings to visual forms which resemble human speech as heard and seen. For a life and a living as men, we do a great many other things besides, needful and unneedful. Some of our pundits have assigned to one or another of them an equal, if not a greater, role than the Word as the difference which renders man the unique Other among animals. They have added to the traditional classifications which distinguish him others such as *Homo Faber*, *Homo Ludens*, *Homo Ridens*, *Marxian man*, *Freudian man*, even Human man, and have composed verbal images of him for which these expressions are acronyms. Their verbal configurations fit together old words and new, words remembered and words invented, thus to shape up images of men, together and apart, their life-styles and cultures, with their survival-functions. In this, the fitters have not accounted for the Word but taken it for granted, whether as a memory-image of events outlived, whether as recollection and design that an unborn future will or should incarnate, whether as an invention wherewith to identify a surprising present or to distinguish an expected one. Our wordings, persisting and altering as memories, function and alter as anticipations. Often they get taken for the shadows which coming events cast before. Our experience of the future is not of a coming-out from behind the present, but of a coming-in from in front. Before it happens, the future simply *is not*; when and as it happens, it enters the present as from the void which is the present's front and boundary. So the *sapiens* of *Homo sapiens* signifies the difference which the Word has been making and will keep making in the human struggle to continue struggling, with its consummations in ecstasy or despair. The ever-recurrent divergence of intellect from intelligence, "pure" from "practical" reason, comes whenever men segregate the power and skills of the Word from their other powers and skills which the Word orchestrates and channels. Segregated, the Word becomes pure Reason; a systematic repetition of identicals each representing all, all, each; orchestrated, the Word works as creative intelligence, the ongoing diversification of consequences, altering the past, keeping it alive, and enriching it; the Word works as the struggle against, and lifelong conquest of, entropy. And let it be remembered that *the Word* is an abbreviation for all mankind's dictionaries—past, present and to come—and that we must needs join to them all the residues of man making himself from his beginning, which the Word transvalues from the left-overs, the garbage, of his dead into meanings of the living.

Seeing that the original comes into existence perishing, seeing that its more lasting images themselves change and finally perish, we imagine for all an imperishable original immune to entropy, staying always and everywhere the same—hence an original of a substance other than its images. Thereby we produce and elaborate the problems whose solution is by choice the philosopher's sisyphean vocation. Imaging this substance requires new words which the generations of philosophers keep creating. Ever and anon the innovations are assembled and ordered in dictionaries as the language of philosophy. Again and again a new word is offered as a new, a final, solution of a new-returning problem. In our lives, words figure as independent variables, each an identity with a history and configuration of relationships to other words and to not-words which our use of them suffuses with life and meaning. A dead language is an aggregation of once-used signs and symbols that no one uses and are slowly crumbling to the unmeaning presences they were made from. Any dead language can be brought to life whenever a human takes its words for signs and its symbols for expressions not only to mean again what they meant when the language was alive, as humans still take biblical Hebrew, classical Greek and classical Latin. For the language is brought to a new and different life when its words are used purposefully in new ways to mean new and different things, as modern Greek and modern Hebrew are used. Such use is not resurrection, but new birth; not ongoing usage, which is intrinsic to all living tongues, but alteration and redirection. However, the perennial concern of the philosophers has been a meaning which survives (isn't the professional word "transcends") all meanings; has been the *eternal* Logos as if it were not also a human one—maybe ultimately the dead end which the signs and symbols of logistics and mathematics intend for the infallible or almost infallible measures of all things.

That the Word figures in our culture as an independent variable from which the rest of culture somehow depends has been a spring of both philosophic ecstasy and philosophic despair from Plato to the Preacher, from Heracleitus to Ludwig Wittgenstein. Here is the Preacher, in the Hebrew Bible, again and again avowing that the Word is *flatus vocis*, concluding "the more words, the more vanity, and what is man better?" As if, without words, the Word could be condemned. As if Plato's image of the happiness of the immortals among the eternal ideas (what other than words might they by us be known as?) could be drawn in any other medium than words! As if a wordless culture of eating, drinking and whatever else that animals do or that poets might picture (*ut pictura poesis*) of a heavenly original, could be human! If "progress" means bettering the human conditions and not merely altering it, more words and more have been tools of progress; have been and continue to be with all their imperfections on their heads, anything but vanity, save only as "all" might be vanity.

Is there not something quite other than vanity in the platonic ecstasy before the Eternal Logos, in the Spinozist blessedness, in the Royceian loyalty to his self-representing Absolute? To the Biblical Preacher's disillusion and "vanity" we might join Ludwig Wittgenstein's agony in discovering that by itself alone the Word is not measure enough: if the living man measuring is ignored, he needs identities to measure the Word by—and maybe the measures are forever incommensurable. The vital problem of philosophy is the Word and its ways. Thus Wittgenstein argued that we should be silent about whatever we cannot discuss precisely. In his later mood (Investigations) he described philosophya as a battle against the bewitchment of our intelligence by means of language." As if intelligence were a power apart from language that can use language in order to cripple its parts and pervert its functions! But all such actual bewitchment is a self-bewitchment: It is the narcissism of the logic of illation, with its design for so repeating identicals that nothing other may intrude to alter any whole or any part, thereby making sure that all stands together forever the self-repeating same. Om! Om! Om!

It is this narcissism which translates the survival-value of the changing word into the bewitching power of the so precise unchanging Word that our philosophic systems strive to depict. Rationalist or empiricist, scientific or mystical, mathematical or allegorical, they signalize a quest for a One that shall bind the Many in law. Law must needs so unify and order the Many as to enable Wittgenstein's "intelligence" to image the real un-bewitched by the deceiving imagery of words, yet not the Many like the invisible chaos of chance and fortune they are, nor like the visible orders they happen to make up. This, even though no philosophy has yet been created to bespeak the real as at least like a song without words. What compositions of words have philosophers not put together to signify their One as the Yogic void, or the Heracleitan flux without its sequential patternings, or as the sensory comminglings-minus-commonsense now being glorified by the McLuhans of the age! Even if the *terminus ad quem* of all philosophy were those silencings, what other ways to them are there than the ways of the Word? Without language, the authentic philosophers are the animals; and is not this, indeed, the import of Kohelet's deprecation of language and evaluation of the word. His "real" world is one where memory is not and neither past nor future signify in self-repeating cycles of Heracleitan sequences. There is no news in his flux. Existence is a vanity we are born into where we receive a name which perishes in the darker vanity we die into. Is it not then better to die than to live, and best never to have been born only to be sharers of the impenetrable ignorance, futility and worthlessness which is the destiny alike of the wise and the foolish, the righteous and the wicked, yet the events of whose course none can foresee or prepare for? Since time and change happen to us all, talk about what happens is vanity. It can disclose neither past nor future, nor is God and his ways more knowable by the wise than by the foolish; the future is a blank to both alike. But the fool keeps pouring out new words, as if whatever has come to exist had not already been named. The more words, then, the more vanity "and what is man better?" Our good is but to labor, eat, drink and be merry, therein to find surcease from the toil, the strain, the pain and vexation we humans are born to endure until we die. Best for man is to enjoy living his life and never mind scrutinizing the inscrutable, never mind trying to cultivate wisdom by words and writing books: "of making many books there is no end, and much study is a weariness of the flesh . . . Vanity of vanities (says the Preacher) all is vanity."

Here was a counsel that of course called for contradiction and denial, and how else could this be had, if not by referring the human condition to God and subordinating the courses of nature and the ways of man to the *Word* of God, commanding both. Because of this Word, wisdom and righteousness cease to be vanities, toil and sorrow cease to be meaningless futilities, life stays significant also after "the silver cord is snapped, or the golden bowl is broken, or the pitcher is broken at the fountain or the wheel broken at the cistern, and the dust returns to the earth as it was, and the spirit returns to the God who gave it." Of this Word "the Preacher also taught the people knowledge, weighing and studying and arranging proverbs with great care; he sought to find pleasing words, and uprightly he write words of truth."

Obviously, he cannot be the same Preacher who taught that "he who increaseth knowledge increaseth sorrow" and that "all is vanity". It would be another, who to make an "end of the matter," wrote in summary "these pleasing words of truth: 'Fear God, and keep his commandments, for this is the whole duty of man. God will bring every deed into judgment, with every secret thing, whether good or evil'." With these words the other Preacher transvalued the vanity of all existence into values ordained by the Word of Words and with words vindicated the Word and its transcendent creativity. Alas, poor Ludwig Wittgenstein!

As obviously, the confusions which make up *Ecclesiastes* indicate that there were among the Judaist formers of the Scriptural canon authorities whose hearts acknowledged the rightness of the original Preacher's sentiment, as of Job's, and who could not not-want to include them in their ingathering of sanctified books. Include them they did, but in such wise that the inclusion subdued them to the Word of God and to that human wisdom which is obedience to God's Word. Except for his counsel that life is to be enjoyed, there is a likeness between the original Preacher's *Vanity of Vanities, All is Vanity* harnessed to the second one's Word of God which nullifies vanity, and the anguish which our age's Existentialists harness to the Transcendence that quiets and comforts their anguish. In God's name, in the ineffable incandescence of Transcendence, books get purged from libraries, libraries get burned to ashes. What other rationalization did Theophilus have for destroying the great library at Alexandria, Gregory the Great, the Library at Rome? Why else the Roman hierarchy's Index Expurgatorius? Why the Inquisitions in defense of the tonguing, which was *the* Word to the Inquisitors, from the menace they feared in the flux of other men's words? Why else the Stalinisms, the Hitlerisms, the McCarthyisms? For what reasons are all free societies no more immune than servile ones from the war against the word by the devotees of *the* Word, be it that revealed by a Socrates or a Marx, a Zoroaster, a Mohammed, a Paul, a Hitler, a Gautama, a Gandhi, a Lenin or a Mao? For devotees, the truth of their Word is the silencing of disagreeing wordmen, the imposition of a grammar of assent, and thereby a liberation of life from its bonds of verbiage and its return to the unverbalized security of self-confirming animal sensibilities and spontaneities guaranteed by *the* Word.

If now we imagine Ecclesiastes to have been a living man whose heart and mind were given to teaching his philosophy as a logical system of existence and value to young pupils, we may recall again Cratylus, that open-minded pupil of Heracleitus who, we have read in the Platonic dialogue named for him, could both concede the possibility of Socrates' suggested eternalism and hold fast to his belief that Heracleitus's image of the real as Becoming was the truer, the more reliable, image. We may even be reminded of Bertrand Russell's Ludwig Wittgenstein, and, for the matter, of Preacher Russell himself.

But on the record, doubt of the Word seems neither to have restricted its use nor arrested its geometric multiplication. The voice of no philosopher of silence wins converts as do the voicings of those whose revelation consists of phonations compounded into *the* Word, a patterned Whole or logical system which its revealer discloses as either *the* sole true image of "the real" or as the absolutely real in, by and for itself. That 17th Century's innovator among philosophical entreprenneurs, Francis Bacon, undertook perhaps quite unaware, to emulate the Plato of the Cratylus by looking behind the philosophers to the poets for the truth the philosophers never knew, since hitherto philosophers had not taken their principles from observing nature, but from the "laws" of disputation, from dialectic and mathematics. This truth of the poets Bacon called "the wisdom of the ancients." It was, he urged, except for what we have of it in Scripture, "enveloped in oblivion and silence" save as the poets' "fables" preserve it. In *de Sapientia Veterum* Bacon undertook to restore this pre-Hellenic wisdom to remembrance and to break the silence—but in Latin. He seems to have equated each of the thirty-one divinities and heroes he named with such non-Aristotelian conceptions and opinions as he himself favored, incarnating his anonymous ancients with the newer images of his own age. For example, he interprets Proteus as a symbolization of *matter*, inasmuch as matter as such consists of the totality of all that *is*, *was*, and *will be*. After Bacon, explorations of the word and its ways have increased and multiplied. To speculations whether nature be original or image, to appraisals of the structure of language as the grammar of reality, of the logic of words as the logic of events, have been added inquiries into the history of the diverse formations of human speech and their roles in men's dealings with one another.

Pursuit of Precision,
Hunger for Certainty

BY AND LARGE, apart from a curiosity whose searchings and seekings are means which are their own ends, the goal of these explorations has been a precision and certainty regarding our ways with our words, which would render communication maximal and its meanings permanent. The arts of the grammarian, the logician, the philologist, no less than those of the mathematician, seem to me to pursue this aim. Their practitioners are never intentionally soliloquists. They want also their subvocal phonations, together with the letters, words, phrases, sentences and paragraphs to be communications.

We see those as made to remain, each, a this-and-no-other, always and everywhere infallibly repeating itself. Their creators or discoverers crave an everlasting fixation of forms wherewith the multitudes of *Homo sapiens* might express themselves to one another, infallibly yet freely, sure of being always understood and never misunderstood. To many, it is only the mathematical disciplines which promote such fixations. Whether as "pure" or "applied," mathematics and only mathematics possesses the inalterable precision and unshakeable certainty which identify authentic knowledge of reality and sure our unsure selves against the doubt, the insecurity, and the anxiety which beset all other experience. Some hopefuls, however, invent new languages, such as Volapük, Ido, and Esperanto, to do the job which they feel the actual tongues of the peoples fail at. And do not sports, arts, crafts, sciences, all sorts of human interests and activities keep producing preciser languages of their own? Do not practicing scientists and mathematicians crave to have the vernacular of their disciplines attain global functions like those intended for Volapük, Ido, and Esperanto?

As universal languages serving all mankind, Volapük, Ido, and Esperanto and their likes fail. Much nearer success is the late Otto Neurath's invention of the Isotype. Neurath was a notable disciple of Ernest Mach, a leader in the Vienna Circle, and a creative intelligence of compassion and courage.

Logical positivism did not suffice him as a creed merely; its import for him was also a code of social action which he believed the program of

"democratic socialism" could fulfil. The breakup of the Austrian Empire
with the First World War, the overthrow of the Hapsburg power-structure,
brought on both the occasion and condition enabling Neurath and his
associates during a few years to implement their code. For the first time
in the history of the still feudal Austrian society, workers and peasants
would have a chance to participate in deciding on the *how* and *what for* of
their lives and occupations. Essential to this was a kind of education
formerly out of their reach. Neurath's especial concern was good housing;
and that the people should share in providing it for themselves. To this
end they needed to learn the entire economy, its *what* and its *how*. To
provide the information and to stimulate a desire to gain it, a Museum of
Housing and City Planning was set up; and because all such enterprises
willy nilly postulate a network of interpersonal and intergroup relationships which plans can block as well as facilitate, several sections of the
Museum were set aside for the social sciences. Soon, however, it was
discovered that these had best be shown separately, in a building of their
own which became the Museum of Social Science. Then it was noticed
that the materials on show failed to catch and hold interest; that documents, diagrams, statistical tables were bad rhetoric. They failed to
communicate. What was needed, Neurath decided, was a single "visual
language" whose clear and simple formations would move the onlooker
to take in a diversity of subjects in "one visual style".[1]

This "visual language in one visual style" is Neurath's *Isotype*. It does
not dispense with words and figures but gives them a focus of reference in
standardized images analogous, says Neurath, to old Egypt's hieroglyphs.
The images present the object of discourse. They come closer to the
formations of heraldry than to those of hierography. They present more
of a likeness than words now do and they present it in its relations to
others of the kind clearly, distinctly, all at once, and "neutrally" as words
cannot. Whether or not it occurred to Neurath that the logical conclusion
of this worldless image is the object-language of the words-rejecting sages
of Dean Swift's Laputa, he stopped short of this absurdity, claiming only
that the Isotype "humanizes" any careful argument by saving it from the
obscuration and prejudice which words often effect. Be this claim valid
or not, it is of record that the Isotype has come into global use as a device
helping communication and guidance of all sorts and conditions of *Homo
sapiens* from the illiterate Sudras of India or Vietnam to the scientific and
literary pundits of Europe and America. The press, the "media," the
schools and colleges, even the churches, keep words to their representative
functions by joining them to Isotypes. There are now Isotype Dictionaries
with more than 2,000 symbols. There is an Isotype grammar. There is a

set of rules for Isotyping scientific findings which Neurath called "scientific transformation." There are schools of Isotyping for all ages and Isotype Institutes in England and other European countries, all concerned to render communication clearly and distinctly intelligible by means of this *I*nternational *S*ystem of *T*ypographic *P*icture *E*ducation, whose name, ISOTYPE is the acronym constructed by joining together the initial letters of the title.

The Plato of the *Cratylus* might find in ISOTYPE another confirmation of his opinion that names are first visual images of sounds which themselves image originals. But George Magnan, in his Preface to *Using Technical Art as an Industry Guide*, indicates a like judgment implicit in his quite unlike context. "It is," he writes, "almost worth doing this book on graphics just to see one in print which does not begin with an essay on Chinese proverbs and a picture being better than a thousand words. One might think that if a single picture is all that good, a few hundred pictures could substitute for acres of text. But it does not seem to work that way, as I discovered, because it can take a lot of words to explain a picture. The function of the picture or 'visual tool' (as if the word were not a visual tool) is to present a clear and distinct image of the articulation of the original. It is a well-accepted fact that a presentation which combines words and pictures is much more effective than one which uses words alone. One reason is very basic—the nerves connecting the human eye and brain are known to possess twenty times the capacity of the nerves between ear and the brain". It seems not to have occurred to this lucid artist-engineer that words are also visual as well as auditory events, and that the word is a creation of at least the two senses acting together, and if words illumine pictures, pictures transvalue words. As Mr. Magnan observes, the news which scientific discovery and technological invention produce calls for new and unprecedented names to identify it by, and the picture crystalizes an initially indefinite into a definite meaning; it hones the name toward the ever-besought precision and reliability. As Emerson, discussing *The Poet* had observed more than six score years ago: "Words and deeds are quite different modes of divine (omit "divine" if you prefer) energy. Words are also actions, and actions are a kind of words". The picture saves time, improves performance, reduces costs; it helps to desegregate information which specialism segregates; the electronic economy distinguishing our age renders such segregation a wasteful anachronism for—this is one of McLuhan's few relevant points—our electronic-powered machines, our so speedy computers, our automations and the rest contract space and bring time nearer to never attainable instancy; wherever a person may live he may see the "same" sights and hear the "same" sounds at the "same" time as any other person anywhere. That this rarely happens now does not diminish the likelihood that it will happen *en masse* later.

Whether or not Wittgenstein was aware of his logical positivist and democratic socialist fellow-Viennese, Neurath, whose brave loving-kindness devised and put to use the Isotype, it could well have been a like craving, balked in Wittgenstein, which impelled that Utopian to rule: "what we cannot talk about precisely we must consign to silence." Utopian, because the *élan* of human speech consigns nothing to silence, yet keeps liquidating all would-be infallibilist fixations, keeps rendering their precisions imprecise, keeps suffusing anticipated meanings with unanticipated ones. Grammar and logic, rules of usage and laws of thought work at best like our traffic laws, effective when and as followed but with no power of their own over words and their ways in the flux of language. Postulating problems of repetition and tangent to innovation, they serve to correct and prevent rather than to create, to shut out the new expression, not to welcome it. Words like *symbol, metaphor, fable, allegory* and the like purport to signify sequences and compenetrations of meanings to which the precedents of usage and the laws of logic are either tangent, incidental, or irrelevant. Meanings just do not reveal themselves as the eternal and universal identities which our anxious quest for precision and certainty postulates: the infinitesimal monad turns out as changeful of meanings as the infinite one. Whatever the words wherewith we identify them, the meanings come as drops or waves of the flux, and the words for them signalize processes of commingling which are logically absurd. Yet we welcome them from poets and find their meanings hardly less clear, distinct and lucid than the most appreciated logical prose, and vivid as the latter fails to be. Their images come as self-orchestrated wholes from which meanings flow to some as clear, vivid, even self-evident revelations; to others, as configurative incitements for them to break up, to anatomize and define, to interpret and appraise the commingled whole, each reader determining for himself a *terminus ad quem* of meaning. However, on the record, also revelations get experienced as incitements which lead to still other meanings that the actions they evoke create or disclose. We call such actions criticism, and persons who choose them for their vocation, critics —in the literal sense of the Greek root for the actions, the word *krinein*— separators, analyzers, breakers-up who disrupt wholes into parts, and therewith also judges and interpreters against whom the artists and thinkers whose orchestrations are anatomized wage a cold war. Functionally this signalizes the divergence of logic from imagination, repetition from creativity. It may have been some aspect of this divergence that

Disraeli had in mind when, in *Lothar*, he wrote that critics are men who failed in literature and art. It seems not to have occurred to him that in the nature of things criticism might also be an imaginative art.

As we experience them, new formations are happenings, chance fore-gatherings of diversities teaming up into configurations more or less lasting. Take, for example, such an epigon of the monsters of the mythologies as this actual or fancied commingling of images which generations of professors of rhetoric have exposed and dissected for their pupils as a peak of absurdity, a peak far above the absurdity of "angel", "centaur", "minotaur", "mermaid" or "dryad". Its creator has been said to be an Irish member, admonishing his fellows of the British House of Commons: "I smell a rat," he warns them, "I see it floating in the air; I will nip it in the bud."

Comic? Foolish? But can this mixed metaphor not have been to its creator and to such of his hearers who felt as he did, a kind of poem as Robert Frost, introducing the 1949 collection of his poems, writes of "the figure a poem makes"? A poem, Frost says, "begins in delight, it inclines to the impulse, it assumes direction with the first line laid down, it runs a course of lucky events, and ends in a clarification of life—not necessarily a great clarification, such as sects and cults are founded on, but in a momentary stay against confusion. . . . It is but a trick poem and no poem at all if the best of it was thought of first. . . . The logic . . . must be a revelation, or a series of revelations, as much for the poet as for the reader. . . . A poem . . . may not be worried into being. Its most precious quality will remain its having run itself and carried away the poet with it." Do not the metaphors of the parliamentarian compenetrate into a *now* poem, with a single meaning?

In fact, no metaphor however communicative, can fail to be "mixed" and to clarify life at least for its creator. Even the most likely identification of differents comes about as a formation of irrelevancies commingling and thereby becoming relevant to one another and conveying the speaker's meaning with a lucidity and force perhaps beyond any utterance in which the later sentences figure as logical explications of the implications of the earlier, figure as unfoldings of an infolded identity. However laughable be any commingling of images in a metaphor, its consequence is a meaning which perhaps the speaker himself perceives that he intends only as he hears or reads the metaphor. Maybe poets are more aware of this than storytellers, storytellers than painters and sculptors. It is more intrinsic in religion than in philosophy and in the dialectics of philosophy than in the logic of the sciences; but the practice of all these arts consists of procedures that transform the immediate altogetherness of the mixed metaphor into a sequential design which transvalues a happening into a formation that images its original as a sheer experience which at once seems and seems not a structured presence of fitted parts. The drawings, paintings, sculptures of our Cubist, Futurist and post-Impressionist schools are such mixed metaphors. The creations of their "now" epigons are even more such. All solicit either an uncovering of covert meanings or a creation by the beholder of different meanings uniquely his own. Avant garde poetry and fiction, drama and music, are in like case. Men of art, whatever their media and instruments, strive to image Becoming as non-Being, movement as if also at rest. What they present is at best like a still in a motion picture somehow in motion, at worst a deformation of a form of commonsense. Those who welcome these turnings off the usual tracks of cultural communion appreciate them as new turns in new directions generating new meanings. Those whom the divergences disturb denounce them as another Babel, with a like God-created confusion of tongues. In their disturbance, they forget, if they ever knew, that in the flux of history the confusion of Babel became the good order of the after-years. The revaluation was an irrelevancy.

Yet it does appear that what begins as a mixed metaphor changes into a lasting symbol in the languages of commonsense, each with a meaning singular to itself, rendered visible and lastingly repeatable by means of an alphabet. Repetitions tend to repattern confusion into order, to transvalue the mixed metaphor into an orchestrated image with survival functions or meanings that the older generations pass on to their successors, until the successors in their turn find the figures of speech functionless, pass them by instead of on, and create other symbols to embody images. Religions produce a diversity of such symbolic concretions of mixed metaphors. Their rites and rotes are overloaded with them.

I offer only one as a representative sample—call it the Godhead as Fishhead. The belief is firm and widespread among knowledgeable people that the populations of the Near East from the Persian Gulf to the Mediterranean took a fishform for divinity incarnate. The overall name of this god was Dagan or Dagon. He had a peer, perhaps sister, wife or both, with the name of Atargatis or Ashtaroth. The Babylonians, the Assyrians, the Canaanites, the Philistines, perhaps the Phoenicians, built temples for their diverse mixed-metaphor ikons, half fish, half man, half woman, with powers of life and death and good and evil which alone the gods possess. Even the Sumerians worshipped such a fishform divinity although under a different name than Dagan; and the Babylonians used Dagan as alternate to Bel, En-lil, the earthgoddess. Among the other titles of the celebrated Hammurabi of the admired Code was Warrior of Dagan, that god-as-fish who, a myth tells, came ashore out of the Persian Gulf to teach the land-men of Asia Minor the arts of civilization. In the Old Testament narrative Dagon figures as the fearful idol of the Philistines, who are said to have joined him to their Ashtaroth-Atagarsis and to have erected temples to him in Gaza and in Ashdod.

Whether it was Ashtaroth-Astarte who was the mermaid-like Goddess that Lucian tells of in his *de dea Syria*, or an ikon in a different fish-story, belongs to another kettle of fish than this. For this, it is of particular interest that worship of Dagon was fairly common into the Maccabean Era and after. The mixed-metaphor image of the fishform God perdured, while its devotees came and went, people after people, generation after generation, giving it new meanings without much changing its looks. What linkage might there not have been between pagan Dagon and Christian Jesus, whose secret symbol during many generations was an image of a fish, *Icthys*. With his birth as the savior of mankind began the age—doesn't St. Matthew tell it?—of the Zodiacal *Pisces*, and those who accepted his salvation were to live and labor as fishers of men unto salvation. A sort of rationalization of the ichthy-form imaging of the savior of humankind is provided by putting together the initial letters of the Greek words which thus identify the second person of the Christian trinity —*J*ESUS *CH*RISTOS *TH*EOS *Y*IOS *S*OTER. These letters form the word ICHTHYS, fish. Perhaps a descendant of the line of Dagon is Herman Melville's White Whale, the allegorical evil Moby Dick. Perhaps, also, Dagon's perduring role is evidenced in the ongoing English usage which scorns unfortunate humans as poor fish. Wittgenstein, it would seem has appraised the plight of man in a far more poignant metaphor: "What," he asked in *Philosophical Investigations*, "is your aim in phil-osophy?" and answers "To show the fly the way out of the fly bottle." That his fly was imprisoned in a bottle and not entangled on fly paper gives one to think again about the Excluded Middle and the meanings of meaning.

And are not the distinguishing postulates of latter-day physics also instances of the logician's Excluded Middle? Of the comminglings of the rhetorician's Mixed Metaphor? For this, physics presents a congeries of communications about both microscopically and macroscopically remote events, about existences infinitesimal and transfinite. Physicists assume that by means of their new, immensely complicated and expensive instruments they have translated those events into the visible and audible symbols, signs and mathematical equations which serve them like an experimenter's pointers on a scale. He can see those with his naked eye; he can read and refer them back to an invisible original; he can arrange them in whatever formation he feels shall disclose to others, his peers not only perhaps, both the original of his image, and what he has done to create the image and how and why his creation reliably represents and points to its inferred original—that is, to the *whats* which his creation "means." In this wise is it that physicists have disclosed the complexity of their traditionally indivisible crumb of matter—of the hitherto unatomizable atom, now atomized into electrons moving around a nucleus of aggregated particles in orbits which some of them arbitrarily jump. Endeavoring to magnify, trace and map the movements, our physicists have found themselves balked: although they could fix the position or measure the momentum of an electron, they could not do both in the same experiment or in the same system. Their image of the balking? A "principle of indeterminancy" within and beneath the overt and operationally valid determinism of Newton's celestial mechanics.

But more: is not science at heart a diversified art of measurement, be that which it measures a thing, a man, or a god? Determination is measuring and indeterminancy sets measuring at naught. Still, the "principle of indeterminancy" is reluctantly admitted into, if not yet quite naturalized among, the articles of the scientific credo. It can be said to extend to the very substance of the original as event. For the measurer images its happening now like a drop and again like a wave. His logic forbids that it should happen as both, this topic requires him to choose: *either-or*. His commonsense, his intelligence, prompts him to take the two together, to decide that the original which he intends his representation shall mean is more reliably signified by both-and. So he invents a "principle of complementarity." This enables him, logic not withstanding, to disregard the law of Excluded Middle and to advance his inquiry by postulating the excluded, by taking its field—is not the stuff newly named by the new word *plasma* such a field?—to be a compenetrated and compenetrating variety of changes any one of which may serve him as a runway for rolling up a logical repetition of identicals that would either shut out or ignore the differentiations or translate them into sames. (This was long the case with the First and Second Laws of Thermodynamics). But for the experimenter's experience, as against his experiment, it is the commingled togetherness with its indeterminables and instabilities that is the subject—to the logician, the "mess"—of which the mutually excluding systems of images are alike predicates. Their survival function is to serve the learning and teaching of the original mess, by either their supplementing or displacing one another or by both supplementing and displacing, as may happen or be intended. The mathematics of them is named "probabilities." The waves are then not independent events. They are "probability waves."

According to Albert Einstein who also held that each such major concepts of physics as *mass, force, inertial systems* "are free inventions"—the "probability wave" is only a means of answering "sensible statistical questions." To Max Born, the waves were genuine "facts," but he recognized that the alternative was by no means excluded, and that the choice between the two depended on the taste—or prejudice—of the reporting observer, whose role in the definition cannot be excluded.

Heisenberg and Schrödinger preferred to imagine the waves as "realities": the latter because of their role in experimentation. So, for imaging any one original, the role of waves and particle is like Dagon's—to compose into a mixed metaphor which portrays the original more reliably and vividly than either by itself alone.

In sum, the Excluded Middle, the metaphor both mixed and unmixed, conceptually comic and logically senseless as analysis repeatedly shows it to be, is a mark of creative intelligence which involves not one sense alone, but the many of commonsense. It more tellingly bespeaks the actualities of our immediate experience. Not by a fallacy of sense did the doubting Thomas of the Fourth Gospel become convinced of Jesus and a believer in his salvation. All of the doubter was focused in his touching and it took the Christian Savior as somehow present. The touch was his mixed metaphor. Nevertheless, the Savior, in this Gospel also a mixed metaphor, at once the God and the Word, *the Logos*, is made to deny, as the Word requires, the prepotency of sense: "Is it because you have seen me that you believe? Blessed are those that believe without having seen me." Here the Word as original makes more sense than the image as sensory event. If this gets taken for a predicament as, it appears, Ludwig Wittgenstein did take it, the taker falls into that state of anxiety which made Wittgenstein's philosophical turnings so intriguing to other philosophers. His own metaphors seem not to have reconciled him. If Language, as he first argued, truly repeats the structure of reality, then what could, what would, be the logical form of, for example, a gesture which renders the truth of *ut pictura poesis* absurd? Was not logic, then, a game with the Word as football is a game with a ball?

Suppose this is the case, what then, so far as it affects our struggles to live on and not die? Does appraising, imaged as a game with words, deprive the word or the game of its survival function? Is not breathing by the same logic a game with air? The record seems to be that likenesses, word-images as homogenations of diversities—that is, as metaphors simple or mixed—become symbols, configurations of irrelevancies literally thrown into reciprocal relevancy by some person's act of imagination. All such symbols could be identified as "double speak", "double think", those epithets with which George Orwell in his 1984 pillories usage imposed by Big Brother on the Utopia where he deceives, overpowers, and enslaves his millions of little brothers. But *"speak"* and *"think"* are *doppelgängers* only in such Utopias. When honest and friendly, the two act as one; the one's intent: the better to liberate, to heal, to nourish and help. The double is not a repetition but a figure in a new configuration of relationships which diversify an identical experience by setting it in new perspectives and investing it with new meanings. Is not the history of human relations replete with such transvaluations by means of such identifications of the different? From, say, St. Ignatius Loyola's directive to his Jesuit subjects—he them called brethren—that they should see black as white should the hierarchial church declare them one and the same, to our no less wizardlike revolutionaries who would make synonyms of police and pigs? It is traditional knowledge how the word "adultery" changes the identity of the experience of "true love"; does not everybody who reads "love" as "luv" look for an altered presence? Honestly to call old men and old women "senior citizens" is to make them figures in a configuration which to some degree transvalues the natural and social handicaps of aging with political responsibility and social dignity for good or ill. And so on. Some say language is all metaphor. Very often, metaphors function as euphemisms for different strategies of attack and defense. Although they defy logic, which cannot fail to analyze them into nonsense, they carry the sense of their makers and users and carry it live to their auditors and readers.

NOTE

1. There is a certain resonance of Otto Neurath's ISOTYPE in the latest styles and techniques of the painter, the etcher and the sculptor. Their methods bring together selected identicals each repeating the others and their sameness measurable, so to speak, in millimicrons. On the record, the methods are diversifications of the methods which produce ideagrams, alphabets, denominations of coins, symbolic images employed in games with cards or tokens such as chessmen or checkers. The products' expression and communication serve like the "mass media". As such they look back to the printing-press which, from Gutenberg's day to this, has been an ever-altered tool whose construction and use engage a knowledge and skill that people must give years to learn. The Press may be imagined the institutional nerve-center of our culture and a *sine qua non* of our arts and sciences. The vital function of printing is to repeat identicals, thus to serve as a major means of social equalization. Hence freedom of the press is an imperative of modernity's free society. Before Gutenberg the precise and certain repetition of identicals was a rarity to be marvelled at. Even as images of the transcendent reality which is always and everywhere the same, all writings were originals because full of diversificatiins, not only from the reality they purported to copy but from one another. Each was thus unique but false, even when

carefully transcribed to be a true copy. Willy-nilly the act of copying made the copy different from its original. A true copy, indistinguishable from its original could be only a marvelous happening precious beyond measure.

Because of the printer's art it is now many generations that the true copy is a commonplace of modern man's experience and that, as already observed, the original, the first, the unique is held, like the rare human first-born, the rare and precious thing.

What has happened with the written word seems, these two or three generations past, to have been happening with the graphic and plastic arts. Its occasions could well have been: first, the ongoing invention, use and modification of the ever more costly machines which are more and more the indispensable tools of the "pure sciences"; and secondly, and configuratively, the invention, use and diversification of the engines of "the military-industrial complex" which put "pure science" to work as engineering. Stirred by these occasions, painters and sculptors were moved, each, from refracting nature and man in images shaped by his own singularity of vision and action, to constructing images of his subjects according to the determinist configuration of parts in a machine fitting together with geometric precision. For some, the skills of chisel, brush and pencil were supplemented, for others displaced by the skills of the assembly lines of "the military-industrial complex". From the nature made over by man into his "military-industrial culture" with its geometrizings so alien to Plato's God, men of art have come to draw and adapt tools wherewith to produce forms for them apter to express this culture's character and meanings. A concurrent modification of the word-image of man is the behaviorist confection which B. F. Skinner first produced as "Walden II" and now diversifies as "Beyond Freedom and Dignity".

Precision, Certainty,
and the Rhetoric Art

PERHAPS BECAUSE Plato had himself such a propensity for metaphor and myth that he shared more of the insights of Protagoras and Gorgias than he knew, so that he held those to be "artists" who bring to birth some new reality. He could not have been unaware how such reality is shut out by the logic which urges that reality must be a hierarchy of eternal and universal essences, each always and everywhere self-identical. His dialectic excluded from reality the Becoming it could not exclude from experience. For Becoming is metaphor; it commingles and interfuses all which it is the survival-function of logic to arrest, segregate, distinguish and reorder. That this function is of paramount importance in our struggles to live on does not, however, render the non-logical comminglings of our figures of speech less so, nor does it give any variety of "logical atomism" a more vital role in our struggles to keep on struggling than any other variety of atomism or than the alogical commingling of events which the word Becoming names. For experience, the Schoolmen's maxim, *nomina mutantur, permanent numina* is less than a half-truth. After recognizing that consequentially *numina* signifies meanings, Homo sapiens has found the maxim's converse far more trustworthy. We need only examine our dictionaries to realize that they are mausoleums where *nomina permanent, numina mutantur.*

Whatever be the medium which presents phonations as sights—clay, stone, wood, papyrus, metal, paper: whether molded, carved, incised, painted, penned, photographed or printed—the visible word, however briefly, outlast the spoken one. It, too, soon or late perishes. Outside the caves of Altamira, paleographers have mostly fragments of a few of the works of the artists and thinkers of prehistory, the oldest presumed less than two millennia old; but the speech they imaged perished in speaking. The visible word endows the spoken one with such immortality as it can— but as the phonation once heard, not as the meaning which enlivened it. Other meanings have followed, and still others will follow. For meaning, the spoken word becomes, changing with the speaking; the written word perdures; its formations, however diverse, seem if only by comparison, unchanging, each an image somehow repeating the others and with them together compounding into the configurations of language whereof the rhetor is first merely the speaker, thus Everyman. Then he diversifies into the specialist, the professional individual who works speech over into the art of speaking to others which we know as rhetoric. This art, as Sophist Gorgias might have conceived it, would be the method of transvaluing the sheer noises of which language is one formation, into the interhuman communication of images and attitudes and meanings. The formation would at first be an instrument, not a delightful iteration of an action satisfying by and in and for itself. It would be employed to change the scene around, commonly to change its inhabitants, their words, and their ways with things and one another.

Examining how this is done Aristotle, *en philosophe*, segregated the orchestral sequences into four parts and, not unparadoxically, argued that logic is the functionally nuclear part. For he also observed that "the greatest thing by far is to be master of metaphor," (that) "it is the one thing that cannot be learned from others, (that) "it is the mark of genius". Yet his *Rhetoric* advises that the master of logic is the master of rhetoric. It advises that working the changes aims at correcting injustice, at clearing away errors, at teaching (or informing) the uninformed, at defending the personal or public interest with words as the weapons of reason even as we defend both with bodily armaments; and at reinforcing reason with other words which both persuade and please, so that, as one Dale Carnegie observed some millennia later, they both "win friends and influence people". How and why they make enemies and influence people is disregarded. Of course Rhetoric, like all other arts, can be absurd, it can be practiced for evil ends. In fact, there were cognoscenti who held that the esthetic over-elaboration of rhetoric celled "Asiatic" was such an abuse; they preferred, the simpler and clearer "Attic" that Socrates taught and that at the end of the first Christian century, Quintillian practically established as *the* way in his *de Institutione Oratoria*. Quintillian made rhetoric the synonym for education consummated; indeed, eclectic Cicero had done this a generation before him. To Cicero, the perfect orator would be the perfection of Homo sapiens.

Rhetoric continued to be taken for the apex of learning through the Middle Ages. Among the lettered, the clerics, Rhetoric stood at the peak of a "Trivium" including grammar and logic; it was preferred over the music, arithmetic, geometry and astronomy of the "Quadrivium" which, together with the "Trivium" made up the "seven liberal arts". The seven were taken for the disputations of its handmaiden, philosophy. When, with the Renaissance, those took a turn toward upheaval, rhetoric, especially as Cicero had preached and practiced it, became a prized

r

discipline among the men and women of that Renewal; even its Asiatic variety can be said to have come to rebirth in Euphuism and Congorism.

But its concern for the spoken word and for the written one as first of all a reproduceable tool of the spoken one became recessive. The printer's art made the written word cheap to reproduce and swiftly and easily accessible to more people than any speech could ever be, before phonograph (speech-writing), radio and television came into general use. Nowadays tapes and recordings free the spoken word from the limitations of time and place cultivated by the communications industry: only inability to pay keeps a would-be listener from hearing what he wants to hear when he wants to hear it. With these new conditions comes a new turn in the rhetoric art. They are the occasions of a new rhetoric not likely much to affect the art of the written word, which is by way of being renamed. The word *rhetoric* seems to have fallen out of grace. To call a speech or an essay "rhetoric" is to belittle it; to call it "mere rhetoric" is to condemn it. Nevertheless the old prescriptions and taboos continue to prevail in the churches, the law courts, the laboratories, the counting-houses, and the editorial offices of public relations firms, journals and publishers. In the schools and colleges the theory and practice of them are taught modestly as "composition" and pretentiously as "creative writing."

The issues raised by those Heracleitan wise men whom the Platonic quest for everlasting certainty and safety degraded into "sophists" making the worse appear the better reason, keep cropping up again like weeds in a wilderness, however bad the name with which the perennial philosophy tags the epigons who harvest the crop. The issues are protean as Francis Bacon might have meant "protean." The perennialists keep aiming to finish off once and for all the non-precision and uncertainty intrinsic to the many currents in the stream of our sapiency—our senses so misleading our logic so fallacious, our systematic world-pictures so conflicting, our relations with one another so combative, nothing consummated, everything stopped without being finished, everything dissipating in the nothingness of death. Reality, the perennialists diversely repeat, is in truth as the heart desires, infallibly one unaltering, unalterable, all-satisfying identity, which however defectively, Homo sapiens images; the imprecision and uncertainty of our experience can be only illusions due to our defects. They mask the real, while faith, hope and charity unmask it with logic, our all-powerful tool of unmasking. With logic we establish the foregone conclusion that the immortal Godhead is at once the original and the consummation of the human that images it; that Being is a process of instant emergence, a becoming of self-explication of the self-implicated original, only apparently the descent of man, really man's foregone ascent—all undistributed middles, metaphors mixed and unmixed.

For modern times, Karl Marx has said this in his way, Henri Bergson in his, Alfred Whitehead in his, Teilhardt de Chardin in his, Paul Tillich in his, and Mohandas Gandhi in his. Perhaps even Sigmund Freud said it, with his Oceanic Emotion, his *Id*, his image of man's existence as a confrontation of Eros and Thanatos, and his urge by means of "analysis" to bring Homo sapiens to the peace beyond logic which passeth understanding. Freud the psychoanalyst took nature's unity for granted, in spite of its implications for "nature's infinite variety." "I rarely feel the need for synthesis" he wrote in mid-career to his friend Groddek. "The unity of the world seems to me something self-understood, something unworthy of emphasis. What interests me is the separation and breaking-up of what would otherwise flow together in a primeval pulp." (Could *plasma* be a synonym for *pulp?*) But he opposed the diversification of his revealed creed like any other Pope.

Each soothsayer has his disciples and apostles, every one of them giving his own new turn to the master's transvaluation of man's experience as struggle to keep on struggling into a precise and certain picture of a world wherein, once he has died, he abides forever, having nothing yet possessing all he can want. Regardless of how unreliable the survival-value of the precise and certain may turn out to be, the feelings of ease and security they evoke render the diversification of their images and how errant Homo sapiens searches and seeks for them, perhaps the most persuasive evidence of his sapiency. On the record, searchers and seekers whom Francis Bacon might identify as Proteans discard both the *what* and the *how* of the perennialists, and have their own words for the naming of both. Their grammar is more largely a grammar of dissent than of assent, and their logic, although few can or do forego the relief of drawing conclusions to rest on, does not altogether assuage their curiosity. They busy themselves more about means and methods than matter and meanings. They are apt, like the aficionados of Ernst Mach, like the post-Russell practitioners of "Analysis", to busy themselves with words and with peoples' ways with words, intent to lay bare the sense they make through our senses or to defend it against belittlement on behalf of the Word of non-sense which the perennial philosophies make into an idol with their eikonic systems of metaphysics and theology. No less philanthropists than the perennialists, the Proteans of analysis work at producing a philosophy with words that shall not, like other opiates inducing precision and certainty, deprive the very senses of their sense; their sense must make sense.

The questions which metaphysics and theology purport to answer precisely and beyond all doubt are, according to analyzing Proteans of practically every denomination, questions to which all answers can be only "meaningless"—that is, answers which the Proteans deny "meaning" to. True, the questions get repeated, generation after generation; the answers do not. They come and go with life's wind and weather. However great the vogue of a "transcendent" *terminus ad quem* which a metaphysic or theology concludes to be the ultimate of precision and certainty, the answer passes, the questions keep on. This might suggest that the questions are their own answers, that, on the record, the ultimates of metaphysics and theology turn out to be images, or as the movie men say, stills, of the "transcendent" Heracleitan flux. Or it might suggest that the perduration of the questions and the transiency of the answers evince simply a sisyphean failure of the agonists of those disciplines to invent a reliable method for seeking the answers. Proteans of analysis believe with a firm faith that the perennialists do not really know or understand what they are seeking, while they, the Proteans, do. Curiously, they work in the belief—their works keep challenging it—that the simpler, the image of nature the more like the original it must be; from Galileo to Einstein, they keep shaving experience with Occam's Razor, endeavoring to smooth it into the thinness of mathematical equations—an economy utterly parsimonious and simple: as Newton wrote—"Nature is pleased with simplicity and affects not the pomp of superfluous causes".

If Our Proteans, whether by the methods of science or the logic of analysis, do get ever closer to that so prized utter precision, that invincible certainty of knowledge—that true image of the eternal and universal laws of infinite nature which, they say, our sense-experience samples, our sciences learn and teach and our mechanic arts harness up to work for us, world without end. But on the record, this could be no less a transfiguration of the nature we experience into the patterns we prefer, no less a pathetic fallacy, a Buberlike envisionment of Nature's *It* as our *Thou*, than the systems of the Perennialists. For the Nature we experience is not rational but reasonless, not simple but complexifying, not parsimonious but abundant; it ever exceeds. Simplicity, economy, rationality are survival-values which ever keep failing us and which we ever strive to sustain and renew. They are what precision and certainty are made of. The event is that the closer we thus come to the imaged objects of our searching and seeking, the smaller, the more changeable, the more ambiguous and elusive we image it as—the more like an infinitely pluralized Heracleitan flux we think it: particles of particles of particles appearing out of nothing, happening to meet, to join together, in an infinitude of formations and soon or late to pull apart and disappear leaving not a rack behind.

The Rhetoric of Science

EXCEPT BY metaphysicians and theologians whose goal is to account for these appearances and disappearances, they are accepted, not accounted for, and used to accounting for more lasting existences. The occasions of their happenings are noted, sometimes interpreted, hardly ever provided with explanations. The happenings might be called transcendences which the methods of science bring us to. We impinge upon but cannot penetrate the multitudinous singularities of changing identities without number. It is the word-images, the mathematical symbolizations, wherewith we endeavor to contain their indeterminatenesses in our determinations, it is these formations we create with our images and symbols which we compound into the body of knowledge of their originals. It is these which, so long as we rely on them to serve as tools and weapons of our struggle to keep on struggling, we appreciate as "precise" and "certain".

And how otherwise do we rely on metaphysics and theology? Homo sapiens is not merely Homo scientificus. As has been noted, many things make sense for his sapience which do not make sense for his scientism. He may be as wrong and self-defeating in trusting them as the scientist says. But he has as much right to be what the scientist calls wrong as the scientist has to be what he calls right; and this right must needs be acknowledged and respected and protected, even as the scientist's, without penalty and without privilege. To the true believers, metaphysics and theology and the multitude of other ways of talking as well, make sense and embody meanings that also the protean who is sure that they are meaningless nonsense which betrays those who trust in them must needs appreciate and respect.

As if science, perhaps willy nilly, does not produce its own measures of betrayal; as if its history were not also a history of truths transvalued into errors, errors into truths, nonsense into meanings, meanings into nonsense, vanity into wisdom, wisdom into folly, and vice versa!

As if metaphysics and theology can not, do not and should not be taken to make the sense they do make for and by the perennialists and the multitudes of true believers who do so take them! As if, for meaning, all non-Proteans must agree with the Proteans!

These "as ifs" emerge, more or less, from observations and discussions of science which take it for a body of knowledge made and in the making, available as books and essays in book stores and libraries, private and public, with more to be added world without end. For the most part, we forget that knowing is an activity of a living person struggling to continue alive and that the body of knowledge is a dead body capable only of being burned to ashes unless it is known by such a person and worked as a tool or weapon of his struggle. When all is said and done, science exists, like journalists' news, as the product of a consuming curiosity, of a recurrent hunger for news never quite satisfied even by news which, as is not seldom the case, shows itself to be but a later way of learning that thete wasn't any, save as a new viewing of an old image, a new reading of an old book, a rediscovery of what had been ignored or forgotten. By and large, the activity of scientists tends toward repetition, confirmation, not innovation. Changes are less upsetting, more peaceably imaged, as diversified repetitions of unchanging laws; the body of knowledge continues an identical formation, however much the size and movements of parts undergo alteration in the laboratories, the studies and the model rooms. Somehow repetition produces security; safety is habitual danger, variation short of mutation is not so likely to challenge homeostasis as new knowledge does when it indicates reformations of the body of knowledge with their import for the publishers, classrooms, libraries and laboratories of the scientific establishment. Pursuit of the discontinuities of innovation, although mostly under the guise of seeking the continuities of modification, is nevertheless an unmentioned thrust of the scientist's enterprise. Whatever be his field or direction, it will engage him in a rivalry which brings into action all the competitive stratagems of the struggle to keep on struggling—its concealments and hypocrisies, its ambushments and foul plays with persons, procedures and possessions. We recall again that Max Planck observed in his *Autobiography*, "A new scientific truth does not triumph by convincing the opponents and making them see the light, but rather because its opponents eventually die and a new generation grows up that is familiar with it."

If the unusually candid "scientific autobiography" called "the Double Helix" is a true sample—and who can honestly say it is not?—"scientific fair play" is like the Ten Commandments or the Golden Rule, far more a creed to pretend to than a principle to practice.

However, our image of "science" figures it a model configuration of men of science, with their rites and rotes ,their creeds, their codes, their plants and places, their works and ways, engaged in the quest for "truth" regardless of who finds it, whom it helps or whom it hurts, what other truth it renders false, what error is renders true. Because, until recently, it was reliable knowledge, that is, the truth, that truths of science have been serving so much more successfully than their alternatives in our struggles to live on and live better, we imagine science as the unique embodiment of "fair play" or "sportsmanship"; we have made a slogan; "scientific fair play".

Alternative words for this are "objectivity", "impartiality". They image a spectator at a fight or a play, cold to the persons and skills of the fighters, unmoved by the appeal and the art of the actors, simply mirroring the rounds or the acts as they advance to their climax of victory and defeat. If "The Double Helix" is a true sample—and again who can honestly claim that it is not?—such detached onlooking is an article of faith, a compensatory ideal of the scientist's role, not an image of how he plays it. Like all our other strivings, scientific enterprises, whether operations on things with machines or solely reflections with words on other word-images, are transaction in which the whole of the scientist functions. The role of scientist, like any other role a person may take for a living or a life or both, is not an independent variable; it is enacted by the all of him. Its diversities figure in his wholeness as his organs figure in his body, whatever his field of inquiry and manipulation, whatever his pretensions. Functionally, a scientist performs as a member of what might be called the Fifth Estate, even as our newsgatherers and news interpreters are said to be members of a Fourth Estate. "Science"—like the Humanites and the Liberal Arts, like the military professions, like the financing, making, advertising and selling of goods and services to people whose diverse groupings shape up the national economy—signifies an establishment with its differential goals, needs and wants, its quest for more money, more power and more freedom to use both for the sake of "doing its thing". Its identity defines and maintains itself as this doing. It is the "self" which "science" struggles to preserve and enhance alike by teaming up with and competing against the liberal arts, the military and civilian economies which channel the people's energies, set directions and provide roles and goals for individuals to choose from and for governments to bet the national welfare on. In terms of creativity, "science" is the nuclear figure of the complicated military-industrial configuration which, during more than a generation, has been reshaping the American way and is, perhaps only half aware, scheming to dominate the way, of course for the way's own good.

As "pure", science works by the invention and use of machines with which it segregates aggregations of all degrees into apparently no further segregable ultimates, then fits some together in new formations mathematically designed and called the true image of nature. With these it creates the human novelties which serve to convert nature into civilization. Our usual word for the invention and use of our machines is "engineering." It is science "applied." That the two are functions of one another needs no argument. Can the proclaimed ruling passion "to do its own thing" be said to have worked since Francis Bacon noted, in his *Advancement of Learning*, "But the greatest error of all the rest is the mistaking or misplacing of the last or furthest end of knowledge. For men have entered into a desire of learning and knowledge, sometimes upon a natural curiosity and inquisitive appetite; sometimes to entertain their minds with variety and delight; sometimes for ornament and reputation; and sometimes to enable them to victory of wit and contradiction; and most times for lucre and profession; and seldom sincerely to give a true account of their gift of reason, to the benefit and use of men; as if there were sought in knowledge a couch, whereupon to rest a searching and restless spirit; or a terrace for a wandering and variable mind to walk up and down with a fair prospect; or a tower of state, for a proud mind to raise itself upon; or a fort or commanding ground, for strife and contention; or a shop for profit or sale; and not a rich storehouse, for the glory of the Creator and the relief of mans estate."

Regarding any of these truth-seekers of Bacon's cannot we all say, "There but for the grace of God (or if it suits you better, Lady Luck) go I?"

Insofar as "science" can or does maintain itself as an independent variable within a national or international economy, protagonists of its diversifying varieties endeavor to arrest if not reverse this mounting domination, like the fiddler of the proverb calling his own tune, regardless of what those who pay him want. The scientist claims that doing his own fiddling is his unalienable right, not an alienable privilege; that nourishing and encouraging his solely authentic quest for truth for its own sake, let it help or hurt whom it may, is a paramount requisite for a nation's survival as a free society. To the like claims of churchmen the scientists retort that religions do not seek truth but fight for error; nor do the scientists give as much heed to the domination of their scientific establishments by totalitarian oligarchies like those of Russia or China as they give to the policed procedure and products of their Russian and Chinese opposite numbers doing "their own thing". By serving their masters, those scientists are able to serve themselves as well. But they do it *qua* subjects, with neither voice nor choice. The scientists of freer lands can at least choose between doing their own thing, accepting that of the masters for their own, or foregoing the first by refusing the second. They may choose to be faithful to the image of science as the unconditional quest for truth, not for the sake of what ensues from the quest, but for the sake of whatever questing is, as it is. One recalls Vannever Bush's image of science as an endless frontier. As such, its conclusions should be way-stations, not terminals; like the poet Thomas McGrath, writing a letter to an imaginary friend, scientists of the endless frontier might tell the world:

> I do not know what end the journey is toward
>> But I am its end. I am where I have been and where
> I am going. The journeying destination—
>>>> at least that . . .
> But far from the laughter

The "truth" is the art of the quest itself, not the "completeness, consistency and independence", in which hope and hunger image its successful conclusion: This art, however, is a creed professed, not a code observed. First and last scientists, alike in totalitarian societies and freer ones, are brothers under the skin, accepting bondage as the price of doing "their thing" rather than not "doing their thing" and struggling as free men in freedom. By and large, both play the tune the paymaster calls for; playing the tune is their survival as scientists and the pay is the gargantuan cost of the science-imaged tools without which today the scientific "thing" cannot be done. The machines with names of Greek gods in which men are sent to the moon bear their cancerous witness.

F*

BOOK II

Reprise

Creativity, Imagination, Logic
and the Free Society of Free Men

The Time of Our Lives
as We Live Them Out

To CONVEY our meanings, our languages both become logical and persistenly deviate from what they become. Usage is at once a process of repeating identicals and an ongoing succession of spontaneous-variation-like innovations within the repetitions. Much, very much, of reliable communication consists of the logical fallacies of division and composition. We name aggregations, assemblages, organizations and organisms by one or another of the singulars composing them; we name parts by the wholes they are parts of. Language develops as arrangements of metonomies and synecdoches, similes and metaphors which repeated use dulls into short-hand-like soundings. Prose might be called fossil poetry. We are not misled when we hear a reporter referred to as "the press," a policeman as "the law," a judge as "the bench," a trades-union as "labor," a business as "capital," a churchman as "the church" or "religion" a mayor as "the city"—any head of government, any leader with political authority whether elective or hereditary, as "the state," and vice versa. Our images compenetrate the forces and focus the forms of societies in the individuals we believe command their powers. *L'état c'est moi* signalizes the overt dynamic of every human group, whatever its size. For meaning, there comes no *this* we do not interpret into some *that*, no *that* we do not transvalue into some *this*. By and large, communication becomes communion as it keeps the middle undistributed, as it succeeds in including the excluded middle.

That which turns one person's sense into another's nonsense is the break-up of the comminglings of that sense into separate and centrifugal elements of paradox and contradiction of which logical "meaninglessness" is the dead end. The fragmentation is, on the record, the unique mode of our struggle for survival. We call it "analysis," and some of us have come to qualify the experiences we can thus break up with a new name, "analyticity." Prompting this name-giving is the fragmentation which "analysis" repeatedly works on our sense of time. As we live it, time is events passing, a flow and ebb of individual waves, or coming and going of individual drops, catching up with others and commingling; time is *now*

into which *soon* merges while *now* submerges in *then*. The field is topo-
logical; the direction, into a space of which the self is the center, so that
past is *behind* us, future *before* us; and *present*, where we are at and where
future and past commingle, is *within us*. We endeavor to segregate and
contain the commingling by means of clocks and ever-multiplying varieties
of the other timepieces—in smaller and smaller passing events, each with
its own singularity of irreversible *now, soon, then; present, future, past.*

Yet, that which one person experiences as present may be of another's
past and a third's future, while none can experience it as the *instancy* of all
three together. For each, time is a stretch, a present transit of whatever is
to come into what had already come, is going, and gone, a transit of future
into past, singular to himself. The time he lives is the growth of his
memory and the creation of his personal history. Challenged to give it
definition by "analysis", he can do little else than quote St. Augustine
who in the tenth chapter of his *Confessions*, discloses that he knows what
time is if no one asks him, but that if he wished to tell another what it is
—"I know not". What the Saint experienced, what we each and all of us
experience and name "time", is a unique fusion of sequences which
Homo sapiens strives to orchestrate to others such by locating and
measuring their eventuations in units of space traversed—seconds,
minutes, hours, to seasons and light-years. The collocation of many clocks
beating many times in the waiting-room of some airport is an analytical
configuration of this fitting-together, this orchestrating, of unique eventuations, a compenetrating futures, pasts and presents into a single, a
monolinear, pattern of growing time.

Since these eventuations are sequent happenings commingling, since in
them pasts and futures figure as "paradoxically" present and contemporary,
it is sometimes argued that all are inwardly such, that the diversifications
we experience are illusion, that time cannot be real, that it must needs be
but "the moving (therefore the confused and distorted) image of Eternity"
—of that infallibly clear and distinct Being forever now and one and the
same. Time, we are told to our comfort, is but the reflection of eternity
by our senses which cannot do otherwise than falsify it into the present
flow of Future into the Past which feeds and grows on it. As Josiah Royce
wrote to a friend in August, 1914, regarding the role of the "triadic
relation" (which so intrigued him he gave it a practical import with his
interpretation of the dynamics of insurance) in philosophical "interpretation": it enables us to acknowledge "an endless variety of individual
interpretations and endless change, growth and fluency" while "absolute-
ness is nevertheless chronosynoptic and universal, above all and in all the
flow of tragedy of this world whose unity means that it contains its own

interpreter". With the Absolute, infallibly "l'état c'est moi"; the Universe, portrayed as absolute, transcending yet containing all division and relation, is a life which mirrors the life of mankind, bringing existence to value and evil to good.

Power, Authority
and the Price of Peace

THERE IS in this as in every tried orchestration of the World and the Individual, of Time and Eternity, of the Many and the One, the characteristic alogical leap of faith of the true believers who create or espouse some perennial philosophy. Not by "analysis", alone by such a leap can the eventuation of experience be harmonized with the ineffable "Beyond" which "Absolute" would name. Biography and history image experience as struggles in the course of which eaches do join and permeate. The formations they thus create do shape up into unions which their creators somehow serve and nourish. Let their togetherness be as little and local as a family, let it be a global aggregation such as the United Nations or an imperial organization like a conglomerate of economic monopolies, or like the Roman Church, or like the colonial powers of history—Spanish, British, French, German, Russian, Japanese, Chinese or American. Let it be a military government, like the imperial Athenian, the Roman, the Arab, the Turkish. Regardless of what creeds such powers purport to profess and actually impose, regardless of what codes they pretend to regulate the lives of their subjects by, their peace is the permanent menace of preponderant force; their security is the pervasive exercise of police power, secret and overt.

Their ways and works can all be accounted for by Thomas Hobbes' image of the life of mankind as brutish misery tempered by authority. He portrayed this life as a war of all against all; its peace, a condition imposed, not chosen, but imposed and enforced by a power of some one or two or three to which the many must jointly and severally surrender their inborn urges of defense and attack finally and irrevocably.

For the sake of peace at last, free men must needs alienate their unalienable right of freedom in return for a security which only their bondage can insure; they mold themselves into obedient subjects of their kings, unquestioning followers of their leaders—call those popes, kings, emperors, duces, führers, commisars, presidents, or what have you. *Le roi le veut* more than suffices to justify obedience. Indeed, long before the voice of the people, the voice of the King, anointed by God's priests to be also God's agent and messenger, was heard as the voice of God. He rules by divine right, likewise when, as sardonic Alexander Pope observed, he rules wrongly. To live peacefully and safely, and to fight the wars of God's anointed in order to win a peace that suits him better must need be worth to the bondsmen the liberty with which they pay for these benefits. Especially if the sovereign is fatherlike, as Machiavelli recommended. Blaise Pascal's challenge: "Art thou the less a slave because thy master loves and caresses thee?" could hardly have meant anything to the common man of this intellectual's world. Kings have fallen out of power and out of fashion. They have been replaced by presidents, bosses, duces, führers, commisars. But the odor of sanctity has been breathed upon the replacements, white, brown, yellow, black. It suffuses their sovereignty and reinforces their authority with another than natural grace, be it a Washington's, a Mussolini's, a Hitler's, a Lenin's, a Gandhi's a Franco's or a Mao's. The peoples, whatever their circumstances and expectations, soon find themselves conforming their ways and works to the prescription of Mussolini's oracle: *credere, obedire, combattere.*

On the record, mankind has yet to devise a pattern of association without one or another nucleus of authority holding all the rest more or less to fixed roles and orbits. Two types are observable sometimes compenetrating as in the "mixed economies" which have lately become visible enough to occasion public discussion. One is as old as history—the one which Thomas Hobbes (perhaps remembering Thucydides' Athenians) portrayed and interpreted in order to revindicate a God-given royal sovereignty against the post-Lutheran theologico-political justifications of new believers *not* to believe and obey and do as of yore. They had mobilized their self-liberated powers against the divine right of kings, and had told the world that rebellion against tyrants is obedience to God. They had come to see that the royal prerogative over the arms and tools of power was the sole evidence that the power was God-granted and not vice versa. What else but this monopoly rendered the King's right to it divine? Or, for the matter, very God's? It was very God's that John Milton challenged in *Paradise Lost* with the speech he wrote for that "Lost Archangel", Satan the rebel, defeated in Heaven and with his faithful legions banished to mournful gloom from celestial light. "He" (God), Milton has Satan tell his Peers:

> He who now is sovereign can dispose and bid
> What shall be right: farthest from Him is best
> Whom reason hath equalled, force hath made supreme
> Above his equals. Farewell, happy fields
> Where joy forever dwells! Hail, horrors, hail
> Infernal world, and thou profoundest Hell

Receive thy new possessor—one who brings
A mind not to be changed by place or time.
The mind is its own place, and in itself
Can make a Heaven of Hell, a Hell of Heaven.
What matter where, if I be still the same,
And what I should be, all but less than he
Whom thunder hath made greater? Here at least
We shall be free: the Almighty hath not built
Here for his envy, will not drive us hence:
Here we may reign secure: and, in my choice
To reign is worth ambition, though in hell:
Better to reign in Hell than to serve in Heaven.

Then, somehow, the divinity which doth hedge a King is transformed
into the charisma of godless natural leaders who overthrow kingship for
its tyranny and make of God and his churches agents of their usurpations.
The might they mobilize, the weapons they seize, disclose to their active
communicants and passive followers their not-to-be denied right to overcome, suppress, enslave or kill all deniers. Like the might of the defeated,
their might makes right, sanctions and imposes their authority, which in
its turn can do no wrong.

The other configuration of power and authority is occasionally celebrated in the writings on the subject. From time to time we come upon this
configuration in letters, in the graphic and plastic arts and in the sciences.
It does not depend upon the overt or covert menace of preponderant force;
it does not threaten violence, unless. . . . It is not the power which is
carried in the barrel of Chairman Mao's gun. The power which serves this
second kind of authority consists of the consensus flowing from the self-
orchestrating consent of the power-holder's peers and rivals who are each
striving to perform a like task more excellently than he. His authority
impatterns their recognition of the achieved knowledge and perfected skill
which renders him primus inter pares. They believe, they obey, and might
even fight because they want to, not because they have to, and they might
even fight him. His authority is their consent. It lasts only so long as the
excellence and usefulness of his achievement last. It is like a championship,
always under challenge, and always, as Abraham Lincoln noted, under
the moral and intellectual requirement that it prove itself. Perhaps some
sports provide the most reliable instances of leadership so achieved and
authority so established. Hellas distinguished such excellence with a crown
of laurels and successors and emulators have since devised and employed
other awards for a leadership and authority freely, if unevenly, remembered
and acknowledged not by one age only, but through many; some even

through all recorded time, giving the originals of the images of, say Socrates or Leonardo or Shakespeare or Galileo or Milton or Spinoza or Newton or Darwin or Einstein the only immortality mankind can ever achieve. Even more so with political leaders and political authority whose immortality may so often become an immortality of immorality. The immortality of praise and reverence is that with which his peers invest the mortal when they freely take him for their leader and hold and can exercise the power as freely to reject him for another. His peers are all the humans in the field of his activity. His power and authority thereon are alienable and subject to the rules which test and govern alienation.

Now power granted and authority instituted in this second mode live in and from the freedom of the free men who institute and celebrate them. They are secondary, not primary forces, alienable, not unalienable. The grantors are free in at least two of the meanings which we use the word "freedom" to impart. The commoner one takes "freedom" and "liberty" interchangeably, and assimilates "liberty" to "right". The American Declaration of Independence, for instance, proclaims that all human beings are created equal and endowed by their Creator with certain *unalienable* rights, among them "life, *liberty* and the pursuit of happiness". The critical force of this ever-revolutionary article of faith is the word *unalienable*. It segregates rights so identified from all others. It implies that there arise also *alienable* rights and that humans are ever striving to alienate each other's rights, whether or not alienable. Yet no one, not God, not Satan can alienate unalienable rights. An individual or a group can survive an alienation of alienable rights, but not of unalienable ones: the latter can be alienated only by killing those whose rights they are. Humans, so long as they live and wherever they may dwell, will struggle to live on, to choose and refuse, to pursue happiness. Their choices, their actions may kill them but only their deaths, which end their lives, will end their liberty. From birth to death these rights are the dynamic of their selfhoods. They are the ends to which the diversifying human associations are means— more critically, more conspicuously, the political associations. "To secure these rights" the Declaration of Independence avers, "governments are instituted among men, and derive their just powers from the consent of the governed". But governments can, and often do, betray the ends they are instituted to serve. So can any teaming-up and the team members of many soon find that they can then serve their own ends more abundantly by together exploiting, robbing, enslaving or killing others, outsiders, while the stronger and cleverer work like aggressions against the weaker, simpler and timider members inside their own group. So it comes about that societies cut down their scope and diminish their members' fields.

They may condemn some to solitary confinement in a coffinlike prison cell; they may handcuff a prisoner's hands, chain balls to his feet and enclose his body in an iron band; they may shut his face into an iron mask. They may thus slowly put him to death. But his heart will beat until it can no longer beat, his lungs will breathe until he can no longer breathe; he will desire, resist, move, however minutely, until he can no longer desire, nor resist, nor move. Alienation of the unalienable is murder, is execution, and may be suicide. It is what the Nazis name the "final solution" of the Jews' struggle to keep on struggling whose synonyms are the self-preservation and survival of the inseparably compenetrated undistributed and undistributable middle which is a man's or a society's existence.

If we signify a person's past by "life", his present by "liberty" and his future by "pursuit of happiness", we may become aware why and how liberty is the perduring élan of which life and pursuit-of-happiness are compenetrating phases. This awareness if of the brute presence of an event eventuating—self-evident but ineffable. Somehow when it happens it frees us from the perplexities, the puzzles, the games which become the logistic of Logos when we idolize logic as an end-in-itself, its own sufficient reason. Somehow we then no longer require to be persuaded that freedom the unalienable right is no illusion, no deception; we learn—shall I say, emphatically?—how and why an individual's first and last concern is the liberty that his living-on, his growing up and growing old is a function of. We recognize that humans are free only as they can be ends-in-themselves and not mere means to other's ends, not God's, not Satan's. This freedom is what Immanuel Kant in effect chose to ground his ethic on, "categorical imperative" notwithstanding. It is what Hellenic humanism assumed for the premise and outcome of the struggle to outdo, to excel, the rival which it honored so reverently. It is what Aristotle postulated for his paramount vocation when he wrote (Met. A2) ". . . as we call a man free who exists for the sake of himself and not another, so too, this (metaphysics) alone among the sciences is free, for it exists only for the sake of itself."

Nowadays prevailing winds of philosophical doctrine blow scorn, even contempt, on metaphysics. On this "science" only, Aristotle, reverenced by the scorners for so much else, was lyrical. Indeed, in my youth I had my own doubts about the lyric philosophers who made metaphysics a science transcending the sciences. I had to grow old before I could concede their authenticity and sympathize with the aspirations they express.[1] I am as far from perennialism as ever, but I feel with it and for it as I do for the creations of a painter or a playwright or a writer of poems and stories. Their works may be intended for images, but they do not so exist; they exist as originals exist, by themselves no less actual than any originals they may have been designed to signify. Like our children, each has an individuality, and each acquires a history singular to itself, save that they cannot convincingly be shown "to contain" their own "interpreters". They exist but have no value to themselves; in them entropy conquers inertia. Not so their creators' existence, or any human's. The latter's existence is perduring resistance to entropy, each one's existence is his value. Currently a great deal of philosophizing polarizes the two for reasons that like Bertrand Russell's, do not so much look to the spontaneous dynamic of the divergence of the one from the other as to a roadblock set up by our quest for certainty and the consequent idolization of science and scientific method. In the transactions of any human life, I do not apologize for repeating, existence figures as value, value as existence. This means, more than anything else, that willy nilly our existence is the end which is its own means, the means which has iteslf for end; is what Leibnitz might have called, if freed of his prejudice in favor of "God", its own "sufficient reason".

Creativity, Imagination and Logic are, like Life, Liberty and the Pursuit of Happiness, constituents of this "sufficient reason". Their role in a man's ongoing transactions with his circumambience is the living of his life, the shaping of his personal history and the creation—not the search for—of his identity. That is, as he lives on he makes himself over by repeated trans-actions which diversify as they repeat; he changes himself struggling to preserve himself. If identity were the event which consummates search, identity would be the body of death. It would not be existence but the non-existence against which life is the struggle and freedom the force.

This freedom, in its human singularity, is as individual and unique in each human as are the "declinations" of Democritus' atoms in each atom's *élan*, and are like them occasions of the diverse togethernesses for which "society" is the cover-all or umbrella term. When we signalize this freedom as a "right" we do not signalize its "nature"; we do not intend its "identity" but its relation to other identities. "Right" is a moral term with which we command and forbid. It does not name the *what* of freedom; it names a *how* of freedom's existence. And the *how* is the insurance of the *haecceitas* of freedom from the aggressions of other authorities and powers, individual and collective. "Right" signifies defending the unalien-able from multitudinous ever-diversifying human drives to alienate it on behalf of their own unalienable *haecceitas* as free men. The Universal Declaration of Human Rights voted by the Assembly of the United Nations affirms rights *and* freedoms, while the American way has been to signify freedom, the unalienable right, by the word liberty and to place it in terms of right as "civil liberty", "political liberty", "economic liberty", "religious liberty" and so on. The different placings designate regions where alienation threatens, where the unalienable must be protected by both custom and law. Alienation is a threat wherever it is forbidden [Congress shall make no laws]. It must be continually guarded against. Liberty can be secure only through the eternal vigilance declared to be its price, through the prevention known to be more reliable than cure. Hence, a person's unalienable right of freedom is above all, as Mr. Justice Brandeis pointed out, his "right to be let alone—the most comprehensive of rights and the right most valued by civilized man" (I would omit "civilized"), "the right to the genius of his own independence"—the right, that is, to function without let or hindrance, to win or lose, survive or perish on his own powers, unhampered by penalties and unhandicapped by privileges.

This freedom is freedom *from* the social control which hampers and handicaps instead of facilitating the genius of a man's own independence. It is "social freedom" as a means to this independence; it requires abolition of "the law's delay, the insolence of office and the spurns that patient merit of the unworthy takes" which press so hard in every culture. This integrity of self and sovereignty of conscience which express freedom as unalienable right is what free men in free societies endeavor voluntarily to render secure by reinforcing with their own skills and knowledge the powers of the State when it is insuring their unalienable rights from the forces of alienation. It is the cooperation they must needs curtail or withdraw when, whether innocently or maliciously, these powers are subverted to serve the ends of alienation. Our various volunteer civic bodies—outstandingly the American Civil Liberties Union—have been such volunatry unions of citizens. That, in their concern for the unalienable right of liberty, they may themselves become would-be alienators of the unalienable, is a contingency against which in recent years little vigilance has been manifest.

Our tradition tends to attribute our unalienable rights to the "laws of nature and of nature's God," thus distinguishing them from the alienable rights which men institute, legislate and enforce for their peace and well-being with one another. They can and do survive violations of their alienable rights but perish from violations of the laws of nature and of nature's God. The belief that there are such laws and that unalienable rights are due to them has been variously challenged, and the multiplying disputations get diversely repeated. Perhaps the disputants could be reconciled if once they explored the meanings of *unalienable* and *natural*, or *right* and *law* as those figure in men's personal and collective struggles for survival.

NOTE

1. I do not doubt that the spokesman for "analyticity" will read this revaluation as a phase of senescence and deterioration of intellect. But, continually intrigued by the appearance of so many new *metas* that breathe strongly of the ostensibly outlawed metaphysics—*meta*-psychology, *meta*-linguistics, *meta*-science, *meta*-humanities, I recall Schopenhauer's crediting to "the consciousness that the non-existence of the world is just as possible as its existence", "the uneasiness which keeps the never-resting clock of metaphysics in motion". For 'consciousness' and 'uneasiness' read freedom; for "the never-resting clock of metaphysics" read struggle for survival and the survival which metaphysics purports to consummate.

How Intelligence and Intellect
Serve Survival, and Fail To

IN THE struggles to survive are struggles to become a past by "having" a future which feeds the past and by feeding, alters it. "Having" is obviously wishful and very imprecise. In a personal history, the future is not. We cannot "have" it until it happens. We "have" wants which are voids, hungers that we fill with images anticipating what we hope may satisfy them. The filling images are items from our past. They are memories coming up to awareness from within—and how specify the singularity of "within"?—as against originals coming into awareness from without. A person whose existence is not an actual modification, but only a repetition of his past, aware or unaware, is deprived, whether by chance or necessity or his own choice, of the future. Without it he can achieve, i.e. "have" no personal history, no human growth, no maturation, no aging unto death. He can only die what he was born as—in sum, he cannot become a person. The struggle for survival of Homo sapiens which changes from, perhaps, that of some variety of hairy ape, maybe began with a curisoity impelling the creature to seek, to taste and savor experiences not organically pre-determined, but as they came, and to accept or reject them for their immediate impact. These choices may over the ages have diversified into the functions of distinguishing, analyzing, appraising, recalling, imaging and commingling variations. Thinking[1] might indeed be interpreted as a turn of tasting in new directions by way of our other senses, especially sight, sound and smell. These continue to make our mouths water, for "good taste". We may even see a certain analogy between tasting and at least the beginnings of intelligence if we recall the opinion of certain philologists that an early phonation signifying intelligence was the expression *inter-legere* [English "to choose" (*legere*) "between" or "among' (*inter*)] used to name the art of picking things out and putting them together, and thence in time applied to the act of reading a collect as *legend* or hearing it as *lecture*—in due course, any skill with words. The events experienced get remembered; the memory-image gets, whatever perception it echoes, reinforced and reproduced finally as a word. The process gets consummated into a new, "organic" instrument of survival.

174

Unlike our other organs, this one appears to work more like an independent variable. We have named it intellect, reason. Its survival-function seems to be to subdue the circumambience we are born into to our service, to tame it, to conform it to our needs and desires, thus to free ourselves from its demands and coercions. In this self-liberation no other animal can compare with Homo sapiens.

Any wonder, then, that valuing intellect for what it achieves is first supplemented and then displaced by valuing it for what it is: an activity good by itself and in itself, its own "sufficient reason". That we—far from all of us—thus transvalue an instrument of survival into a fetish of would-be survivors is taken for a glory, not a handicap. To know, to dare to know regardless of the consequences of knowing, is like taking drugs, exalted into the revealing be-all and end-all of growing up and growing older. Ends and means change their roles. Man's life gets transvalued into the pursuit of knowledge. Knowledge gets manumitted from service to life. As Robert Browning wrote of his grammarian: "This man decided not to live but know." The *ne plus ultra* of this uttermost excellence is, of course, the divine Narcissus of Aristotle's metaphysics—pure thought, thinking itself, the unaware unmoved mover of all existences.

"This man" of Browning's cannot be, however, the Homo sapiens whose numbers crowd all other life off the earth or make it over, however unsuccessfully, to suit themselves. The latter may more or less admire, even reverence, "this man" but they rarely emulate him, rarely takes him for the Jones they strive and strain to keep up with. Whatever be "this man's" métier—preacher, poet, scientist or teacher, and however much admired for his excellence in it, he is regarded as a distortion rather than a perfection of Homo sapiens. The Self he struggles to preserve is not imaged as the living, by logic excluded and undistributed middle that strives toward the life more abundant. It is imaged rather as the Self whom the Preacher and his epigons deplore, the Self whose most precious and intimate world is the Word, yet who as Wordman is "Master of the Name" and thereby lawgiver to the law-breaking world of Homo sapiens.

For the world of Homo Sapiens is the world of words; it is the substance of the perennialist's transcendent "noosphere". Words are at once this sapient's creations and monuments. The countless generations of him are as anonymous as the animals he has not named, and like them he is first and last dust of the earth, prisoner of it and bound to its magnetism and gravity. The personal histories of the best remembered and most celebrated can be imagined as impersonal sequences of intake and output; and what remains of any is depersonalized residue, the less perishable excrementa of living and working which survive him. If the epigons care for them, learn and teach them, they are his immortality far more reliably than his living descendants. Unheeded by the living, they are as dead as he. Heeded, they are transvalued into signs and symbols, some without words, all requiring words for human meaning, words written on parchment, printed on paper, carved on stone, cast in bronze, formed into images that survive their original, but like him happenings which soon or late disappear in the anonymity of nothingness. Call them original, call his man-made immortality design or a caprice of Providence, call them a chance eventuation or a stroke of luck. Limn them in any figure of speech that language enables. Compose your portrait with all the art and rules of its logic you command, render it a self-contained and self-containing formation no one can challenge for its self-confirming consistency. Declare its divergence from the remembered image and the imaged original as the truth "transcending" both to which both must be conformed. You and your works are still figures of earth. The word-images you create do alter the originals and one another, and do immediately so transvalue whatever you apply them to as to fit that to the loves and hates of your struggle to keep on struggling. With sound and look they do identify and judge it.[2] Such words as *Yank, gook, pig, sheeney, Hunkey, Bum, bread, luv, peace, carnival, Mardi Gras, "Man"* are value-images. Russell's fantastic theory of descriptions accounts even less for their identities than it does for the identity of Hamlet, or Mr. Pickwick, or the present King of France. It cannot be over-stressed that those are originals which figure in experience like all other originals and, as the history of literature and the arts and sciences evidences, are as much objects of analysis and subjects of portraits as any. Indeed, their role in a person's struggle to keep on struggling is likely to be much more consequential than that of non-images of our experience as experience comes. The identity of their existence with their value is likely to be more telling. Their configurations make up the culture in which humans, however primitive or sophisticated, live and move and strain and strive for their being. To many moderns, this circumambience of culture has, on occasion by travel and participation as well as by words and other imagings, become global in a commingling of selves and settings of which each self is ineffably a seat of value, and all else, its content.

The achievement of such globality is conditioned by the unalienability of freedom. On the record, the achievement is the dynamic consequence of choice after choice, decision after decision. It is not a *terminus ad quem* chosen but a happening in which a sequence of works got consummated in a faith. The faith itself comes to be as the formation of an image brought to existence by the works. The American Declaration of Independence is such an image; the Universal Declaration of Human Rights is such an image. Each is the creation of a long travail of works of which only the latest came to postulate a free society of equally free men. Neither purports to be a disclosure of universal truth belied by our actual experience, nor is either an otiose utopian creed. Both are designed for working hypotheses of a common endeavor to secure men's unalienable rights—most of all, their liberty—from the alienation which keeps ever threatening them. The designs do not postulate transcendence. They assume that man's freedom is earthly and that the survival he struggles for is earth-born and earth-bounded. Of its circumambience he is part happening and part consequence. He can live on only as it sustains his transactions with it. The wordman is indefeasibly earthman. He cannot leave the land and waters of the earth for the moon or the spaces beyond save within an earth-based environment in vessels earth-guided and earth-controlled, and with earth-derived sustenance in measures believed sufficient to outlast his needs. What he excretes of his intake of them is the prototype of all pollutions, which poison to death if the earth be not purged of them.

Metaphorically, creativity identified as catharsis is excretion: our products of art and science are excrementa, residues of a process of intake and output the digestive organs of which are our laboratories, our studios, our schools, our factories, and our stores and shops. At the spring of them all are our personal urges, the creativity that our struggles to keep on struggling spend and restore, spend and restore, until no more can be restored to spend—that is, until we die. The residue, the output, which survives us is then our past in presence, and a fragment only of the multitudinous and growing aggregation of the cultures of mankind which the generations, by learning, take into themselves and transvalue into events in their personal histories and parts of their own remembrances. Facilitating such intake and digestion we call education, be its means metaphor, myth, legend, story, history or science. As these come to the generations who learn, they are arrangements in image of happenings capable of other relations than those chosen to present them in, but identifiable by none. Our sapiency, our intelligence, is their reciprocal impact, their fitting to one another in such wise that they together bring our quest for certainty to a satisfactory close, produce an infallible exactitude, a completely consistent set of axioms, provide us with norms wherewith we may measure all things—those that are and those that are not. Our measures are our containers, not the stuff contained.

The record indicates that the exactness, the consistency, the norm, the infallibility are qualities which man the measurer endows his measures with; but not the qualities of the measured. To that, an indeterminancy pertains which becomes more evident the more refined and particular the measures become. We make, we do not find, infallible norms; papal infallibility is only a notorious instance of the infallibilities we assume for other configurations of our struggles to keep on struggling. As Canning Schiller long ago pointed out, we make our struggles with postulates on which we dare to act; they get set as articles of faith that atrophy into axioms if they survive the trials and errors of experience. An axiom is a postulate which has made good so often that we rely on it without further ado. Should it repeatedly fail to make good, we would cease to trust it as an axiom, perhaps demote it first into an article of faith, then into a postulate, then into an error. The critical factor is the trust; it is the will to believe in and bet on a becoming, on an eventuation which cannot be a sure thing.

If freedom be both the aware and unaware give-and-take of the struggle to keep on struggling we call self-preservation, if the struggle is existence and existence is value, the philosophic joke of this orchestration is on those who contend that the truth of existence is peace and security assured by a providence or a scientific determinism that shapes our ends, rough-hew them how we may. So long as we exist in the world where Earth is our habitation, what else can life be if not a sequence of choice after choice, each a gamble whose outcome is not guaranteed in advance, and the whole stake likely to be lost on any bet, first to last, the losing one, because losing, being the last. That these observations fit with any of our traditional images of the free man may well be doubted. In recent years it has become fashionable to image life as a game of chance, to make elaborate analyses of the steps of choosing and deciding. Numbers of recipes for "decision-making" have come into circulation and are being plentifully bought. Like systems which career gamblers employ because they believe them sure to break the bank in Monte Carlo, such recipes for decision-making fail the faith which bets on their invincible certainty. Decisions do not come as sure effects of ineluctable causes. They come as acts of closure wherewith we shut out competing alternatives and launch ourselves on one course of action to the exclusion of all others. Decisions are literally cuttings off. They are events in an ongoing determination of the indeterminate future, postulated on hope and trust in the value of an imaged determination for survival. Whatever image they pick up, hope and trust signalize freedom *for*.

Images of determination range from the theological to the naturalistic, from the naturalistic to the humanist. All become objects of firm belief ever challenged, if not beset, by doubt. Functionally, they are value-systems on which the believers bet as means toward ways of living that other systems have failed to achieve. Name such images God, Nature, the

Beyond, Communism, Anarchism, Socialism, National Socialism, Democracy, Americanism, Zionism, Black Power, Humanism. Insofar as the futures they intend are such as our pure sciences do not forecast and our practical ones cannot produce, those forces and forms, even of nature, are *super*natural. We look to them for whatever the nature we know, appraise and with our transactions humanize, does not yield us. We thus render them "religious"; we count on them for salvation from present danger, provision of future safety. We pray, we give thanks as our American moonmen have been heard to. We are sure that these value-systems, godly or godless, are the Word and the Way out of present danger into future safety and well-being. As that unhappy, ironical supernaturalist, Blaise Pascal set down in the thirty-fourth of his *Pensées*: "We need not fear the truth that law is but usurpation: it was introduced without reason, it has become reasonable; it is necessary to cause it to be regarded as authentic, eternal, and to conceal, the beginning if we do not wish it to come soon to an end." And in the forty-second: "But what is nature? Why is custom not natural? I greatly fear that this nature is itself only a first custom, as custom is second nature". Page Charles Peirce.

If we are willing to bet on the implied contingency of law, custom and nature without holding them contingent on the will or whim of a Creator who might as soon as not have started them off, then we can postulate that the three are happenings of an evolutionary—that is, compenetrating —sequence among which free society is one formation. For "nature" names but comings and goings of events in all sorts of patterns and in no pattern, and "law" and "custom" name patterns we believe serve our survival. They name patterns of human association, ways that people come and hold together in, and that the gathered require newcomers or deviants to enter upon and to repeat. For the most part, these ways are local and diverse; each configuration of them is an individual society which cannot be reduced to, although it may be taken for, a repetition of a "universal" form or of some individual Other. On the record, each is singular, independent and autonomous, a one of many, *e pluribus unum*, working and fighting to nourish itself and grow. Its behavior toward other configurations near and far is shaped by this struggle to keep its structure and functions "identical" and secure. Servile societies act more aggressively than free ones toward other societies, whether servile or free. It is commonplace knowledge that foreign wars are customarily helps to domestic peace and that the domestic peace of servile societies seems in description to figure as cold wars with hot flashes between companies of humans who are "free" because they hold preponderant power over multitudes enslaved because they lack sufficient will to overcome, if not to resist, the pressure of the powerholders to alienate their unalienable rights. Instances are diverse; they range, shall we say, from the Helots of Sparta to the weaker "sovereign" states of the United Nations Organization.

That global society of nations was instituted to prevent war, maintain peace, secure justice and liberty among the world's nations. Its code and creed were embodied in the Organization's charter and its Universal Declaration of Human Rights. Together those postulate equal liberty, and equal safety for each of the member states from the aggression of any other; they in fact postulate sovereignty and independence as the unalienable right which all together have undertaken to insure for each separately.

By the Universal Declaration this assurance of unalienable rights is extended to all the peoples of each member state. An unexpected, though not unnatural consequence has been the blurring of the critical difference between unalienable and alienable rights. Wants and demands without whose gratification societies and individuals could live on, perhaps live on more freely and abundantly, were projected as "unalienable rights". Incidentals were transvalued into necessities. The rhetoric of the national delegations to the United Nations became largely a rhetoric demanding privileges as rights, and denouncing refusals to concede them as betrayals of the Charter and the Declaration.

The image of the World Society of Nations thus formed seems to have shaped itself naturally enough, for as Pascal reminds us, wishes and demands come with their occasions and like other happenings develop into customs which, left to themselves, tend to harden into second nature. That this should be the sequence among the nationals of the Society of Nations seems to many observers not only a happening, but a happening planfully transvalued into a design to render the Society of Nations an instrument of national aggression and personal gain. How, indeed, could any one with a commitment to equal liberty and equal safety for all people everywhere and the peace which this equality would ground, not judge the record of the United Nations the record of subversion of its Charter and Declaration; the record of a paralysis of the power of the Society, whose creed and code the latter are, to give them effect? The record shames its Security Council and its Assembly before the enlightened opinion of mankind. Their maneuvers were critical factors in the disillusion, and the untimely death, of Dag Hammerskjöld, for nearly a decade Secretary General of our global "union" of nations. This saintly, sensitive, conscientious humanist strove with valiant patience to persuade the nationals of the United Nations to honor their international commitments, to keep the faith of the Charter and the Declaration in a world-wide free society of free men.

Those commitments acknowledge that the sovereignty and independence of free societies rest on the unalienable rights of all their members alike, and first and last on their equality in these rights, primarily the right of liberty. Powerholders in servile societies made these commitments as well as representatives of free ones. The consent of the people founds and sustains the societies' institutions; by delegating, it invests them with power and authority, gives force to their laws and makes firm the order believed to assure each member his unalienable rights. A free society survives as free only as it keeps its sovereignty and independence secure from alienation by alien might and justly reinforces the struggles of its members, whether individual or joint, to defend, nourish and enhance their unalienable rights among one another.

In sum, societies are free societies of free men only when and as the latters' powers of creativity, imagination, and logic, with their trials and their errors, function together, and with good luck, unhindered. Mankind's struggles to keep on struggling are, indeed, its exercise of these powers for which "life, liberty and the pursuit of happiness" are equivalent expressions. Servile societies differ from free ones in that their institutions are so patterned that the people's ineluctable urge to exercise their unalienable rights is hindered, denied, policed, and punished as a necessity of law, order, and social security. In freer societies like the American, minorities such, say, as the women, Indians, Negroes are denied this exercise but soon or late demand it by law; policing is for the most part selective, occasional or incidental. As current exposures of J. Edgar Hoover and his F.B.I. warn us, although illegal, it happens; it is not at first designed. Servile societies from the first hinder, deny, and police everybody by design, "constitutionally."

Obviously, the powerholders of servile and free societies will image the free man by his relation to their own survival, and he by the relation of his freedom to theirs. His unalienable rights in a servile society are valuations of *freedom from*; in a free society of *freedom for, freedom to*. His security in a free society is government, instituted "to secure these (unalienable) rights", to be their guardian and guarantee. In a servile society these rights have no security. They must be their own guardians and guarantees. Against them, as the Germans under Hitler well knew, government is geared to direct all the persuasion and force at its command. Save where it wants or needs to harness them to its own service, as the government of Soviet Russia is known to harness Russian scientists and artists, these must pay for a certain freedom in their own métiers with all their other rights. The relationship is not confined to Russia, nor to the diversity of totalitarian establishments. It obtains wherever authority is a manifestation of preponderant power. Him who would free himself from this power it portrays as an infidel, a criminal, a traitor, a rebel, a revolutionary, a madman, an enemy of society—be the society a family, a club, a gang, a church, a business, an army or navy, a school, a tradesunion (like, say, the Teamsters or Miners); and be the authority named father, boss, chief, priest, prophet, general or admiral, führer, duce or chairman, manager, president or principal. In all, the individual is portrayed as surviving on sufferance; his existence as a privilege, not a right, and its value is the price he pays for the privilege.

As history records them, no society is purely free or purely servile. All figure as comminglings of freedom and servility, with one or the other dominant in each, and shaping its form of government. Neither entirely nullifies the other. Any society's struggle to go on struggling for its survival as this-society-and-no-other is signalized by the preponderance of freedom or servility in the relations of its multitudes and it is imaged accordingly: Patriarchy, Matriarchy, Monarchy, Tyranny, Dictatorship, Oligarchy, Republic, Democracy, name the whole by the dominant party. And of course, in the servile society the would-be alienators of the people's unalienable rights are able to work at this because their might keeps their own unalienable rights immune to alienation. They are the free men of the servile society, the sufficient cause of its existence.

NOTES

1. Sapiens is said to derive from *sapere*, to taste.

2. Would a rose by any other name smell as sweet? Call Carnival "goodbye, to meat", Mardi Gras "fat Tuesday" and what happens to the look and value of the events they name?

Some Philosophic Images
of the Free Man

PHILOSOPHIC IMAGINATION works the imaged singularities of experience over into new formations. Largely, the experiences of freedom are experiences of strain and stress, of change and resistance to change. They are events in a personal history which convention names "free will". They begin as a complex of confrontations that becomes a struggle [of which deliberation is one phase] and end up in a closure of the open action. We name the closure choice or decision. There is a tradition of identifying such closures with the act of creation. There is another which identifies it with the rare untrammelled emergence or emanation or repetition of the always-one-and-the-same as the multitudinous, diverse and diversifying renovations of experience. For this tradition the act of creation is a flux of emergents without separation, of diversification without fragmentation, of activity going on without stress or strain, without choice, without decisions. It happens in experience as a configuration of partings which nevertheless are without parts, and hence devoid of any determined structure that logicians may analyze, painters portray, musicians compose or wordmen depict. It is an excluded middle and neither order nor disorder can be attributed to it. Whatever it follows, it does not follow *from* that. It happens a *this* and or a *that* but not an *either this or that*. *Either* is subsequent. *Avant garde* artists and thinkers do purport to take such happenings as they happen. To the tradition which cherishes their like they are free events eventuating; ultimately, they are freedom itself, the One, *causa sui*, becoming Many without ceasing to be one, but not the Many thus tending toward Oneity.

This sequence of emergence or emanation or repetition is not existential but logical and as *causa sui* must be symmetrical. Josiah Royce, Henri Bergson, Teilhardt de Chardin can be taken for recent authorities in this tradition. Their Free Man is that one among the many who, realizing the hazards of the struggle which is his separate existence, chooses to free himself from them. By reversing the process of emanation and making himself one with the One, yet continuing to be the fragmented drop of his age and place, he makes himself truly free. His liberation is consummated in mystical intuition such as Brahmans, Taoists and Buddhists choose to undergo the stresses and strains of Yoga for; such as near-Easterners and Westerners take drugs to reach.

Or, as did Baruch Spinoza, a man pursuing freedom might create an image of all Being *more geometrico*—definition to axiom, to theorem, with corollaries and scholia in a sequence of explications of the implications of his ineffable premise *causa sui*. Spinoza thus composes his true portrait of his original self-contained and self-containing "eternal and infinite essence" of God-or-Nature which our necessarily fragmented experience distorts and falsifies. For our experience is events coming and going one after the other, present, future, past; their succession is our mortal struggle to live on, each a fragmentation of the selves we immortally are as unstruggling parts of the unstruggling infinitude of God-Nature. Separately, we are battlers in the Hobbesian war of all against all; each of us strives to prevent all others from nullifying the defense and aggrression which are our self-preservation. Separately, we are not effects which have themselves for causes, not causes which have themselves for effects, and we can become such only as we abolish our separateness without destroying our true identities. Separately we are other-determined, not self-determined, and determination is negation; it shuts out and cuts off. Only God-Nature, the eternal and infinite One-and-All, is self-determined—that is, *causa sui*, and in some degree we can as mortals become such by mastering the passions which keep us separate and struggling and thus make slaves of us. We are not only creatures of passion, separate and separating, we are also creatures of understanding. Separate as we may be, we can realize the essence of the infinitude of causes one of whose effects we are; we can see ourselves and our personal histories under the aspect of eternity and thus take in what passion cuts off and shuts out; we can thus, without forfeiting our identities realize them as in and of the eternal and infinite One-and-All and therein *causa sui*. Our understanding rejoins what our passions separate. It enables us to achieve the blessedness which signalizes our liberation from our bondage. This achievement is "the intellectual love of God" and part of the infinite love wherewith God loves himself. It is the very substance of virtue, the joy of strength, the strength of joy, our freedom as men of flesh and blood. For by understanding we abolish fortune and transvalue fate into freedom. By the power of our understanding we so free ourselves to be ourselves unshaken by fate or fortune. We have attained wisdom.

But not many of us. "The wise man", Spinoza concludes his *Ethics* with, "the wise man in so far as he is regarded as such, is scarcely at all disturbed in spirit, but being conscious of himself and of God, and of things, by a certain eternal necessity, never ceases to be, but always possesses true acquiescence of his spirit. If the way which I have pointed out as leading to this result seems exceedingly hard, nevertheless it may be discovered. Needs must it be hard, since it is so seldom found. How would it be possible, if salvation were ready to our hand, and could without great labor be found, that it should be by all men neglected? But all things excellent are as difficult as they are rare."

Spinoza's image of the free man has been called mystical, it seems to me despite the geometric method with its deductive configuration of clear and distinct ideas to portray—i.e. understand—an original *causa sui*. The act of portrayal Spinoza calls "the intellectual love of God" and imagines it as part of the "infinite and perfect love" with which God, being *causa sui*, necessarily loves himself. If this be mysticism, it is not the mysticism of the Yogins, the neo-Platonists, or Bergson's or Royce's. It is a logical topography which those are not. An event in Spinoza's personal history, a consummation of his too brief ascetic, suffering yet cheerful, one might even say joyful, life, it seems the creation of a decision to transvalue *freedom from* into *freedom for*. He did it by modulating his personal "negations" into the depersonalized naturalistic, pantheist "true acquiescence of the spirit" which is to him salvation. We might well say he "accepted" the universe, but neither what he accepted nor his way of identifying this *what* was like the Stoics' or Margaret Fuller's. His philosophy of freedom and his image of the free man render Spinoza the first of the moderns. The universe he accepted is not incongruous with the universe which science has been portraying, nor is his logic, which in conclusion but repeats and elaborates his premise. The true believers in that which he freed himself from, hated and denounced him not only for this, but even more for the image he created to challenge and displace their idols, and to proffer valid salvation to mankind self-endangered by their passions, yet able, by freeing themselves from their subjection by means of the logic of their understanding, to attain a secure blessedness—if only they dared.

That so few of us, whatever our vocations, dare to choose Spinoza's hard way, or for the matter any other—say the Jesuit arduous discipline of self-liberation from the evils of our passionate struggles to keep on struggling; and that salvation in and through "the intellectual love of God" should be so rare and difficult, need not imply studipity, cowardice and indolence. The failure to choose can be that of the intellect's supreme industriousness, its highest courage. It can be—Existentialists argue that it is—the *haecceitas* of the human condition, for which "the intellectual love of God" is the imagination's compensation, but no practical way out.

The human condition is not a problem for which daring and persistent research can discover or create final, life-enhacning, life-perduring solutions; immortality is only a compensation in longer-lasting images for the experience of mortality: aging, dying and death are nullifications we would prevent, not problems whose solutions we seek. Our sciences of man indicate that every solution becomes in its turn a problem. In sum, the human condition is a predicament, is an ongoing commingling of dilemmas, quandaries, jams, pickles, fixes and the like. Our struggles to keep on struggling consist in detail of a succession of transactions in which we have to choose between alternatives of action none of which we can be sure will satisfy; so very often we choose to go on being puzzled or perplexed; or we choose even to mess up our situation still more, increasing its pain and confusion; or we choose to subside into a passivity so inert that our give-and-take with the circumambience lapses into take without give, stimulus without corrective response, and we become carriers of the anxiety which existentialists celebrate.

These consequences are however what our struggles to keep on struggling strive to avert or alter. Freedom both *from* and *for* is success in this striving. Our choices select and our decisions determine the tools and weapons of our struggles and how we use them; their *whatfor* can be only the struggle itself in all its diverse formations. Its intent, its direction, is irreversibly "beyond", as space is not but time is. Being born, growing up, growing older embody them. So, discerning and imaging a past requires a future which, as lived, brings something new and different and alters the remembered image—even though desire projects it in hope (who was it said hope is the bread of the poor?)—and the project is utopian. As Shakespeare's Prospero reminds us, "the past is prologue" entirely unaware that it becomes epilogue. Anticipation, looking "behind" to see "ahead" whatever it hopes for or fears, selects a memory and reshapes it into an image of the future which, becoming past, shall banish fear and fulfil hope. Neither is certain. Anticipation, however intense, is "iffy". Its logic is the imaginative speculation "if-then" without asking *when* is "then". Hope and fear could not occur in a world of inevitables. They can be native only to an open-ended, an indeterminate world where determinations thus-and-so-and-not-otherwise image the future desired and hoped for. But the future as such is faceless; it is the void that creativity gives a face to.

Its coming brings, also with the least possible of "iffyness," feelings of wonder and release as well as satisfaction. Experience is suffused with them, but they hold the foreground in our games; not inconspicuously, our word-games—acrostics, cards, ciphers, mathematics, metaphysics.

The problems they present express the urges of this unalienable freedom. They are artifacts which already contain their answers, which figure at once as premise and conclusion. Their conclusions are believed foregone and sure to be reached. Each game consists of the search for them. Each is a gamble, whether played alone or in company, because it is the searching which occasions hazards and stresses, which demands choosings and decidings that must meet the challenges of the play. Although the solo player cannot be prevented from reaching the foreknown solution of his problem, reaching it nevertheless brings him feelings of wonder and release. Where the conclusion is not foregone, players must end up some winners, others losers, as in competitive sports, on the stock-exchanges or in the gambling palaces—hells, if you prefer. The players bet, and if the games are not rigged the bets cannot be on sure things for the honest player. Their conclusion is not foregone, and who can guess what side Lady Luck will back? "Gambling" is a more authentic instance of the human predicament than prostitution, addiction to alcohol, tobacco and other drugs. Nevertheless, there is the like widespread disposition to deprecate the practice, to deny it any survival value, to brand it anti-social and immoral.

The disposition advises of the primacy of freedom. Freedom is the *sine qua non* of both morality and immorality and the validation of their survival-values. Both name appraisals of the diverse, ever-colliding methods and means of survival by which strugglers identify each other. That the valuations get reversed as time, place and circumstance occasion is not news. The valuers decide their values in fear that they may not, in hope that they may, live on more freely, more safely, more abundantly than before. And to live on thus is to be able, if only for the next moment, to live solo, so that consciousness flows in ongoing reverie, action is unhampered spontaneity, existence a sequent compenetration of events which, looking back to the past, we call means and looking forward to future we call ends of the urges which propel our lives until we die. Both names identify free eventuations that, as they succeed each other, orchestrate into a personal history which has no meaning save as it becomes its own meaning, and no responsibility save as this meaning can be rendered a responsibility. Tradition, however, construes meaning and responsibility otherwise, and fruitfully when the meaning construed is commingled with this primal one. Traditionally, meaning and responsibility are social images, they relate to others, especially to God. But by himself struggling to live on and not die, the free man, although a figure in an aggregation, or organization, or an organic union with others, means himself and is responsible for himself to himself. He is not an egg that must be hatched in order to consummate his nature as egg. His meaning is not the cockerel he might be transformed into. Unless the egg is self-hatching, hatching does not fulfill, it only nullifies the egg. The egg is not fulfilled by the action of external forces which destroy its identity; it is fulfilled by rendering itself with or without their help an ever healthier, more excellent Egg-o. The Butterfly is the extinction, not the survival-value nor the meaning of the chrysalis. Egg and chrysalis, as existences, are ends in themselves, not matter nor means to other ends.

The Free Man's Free Society

REFLECTION ON the eventuation of chickens from eggs, butterflies from chrysalises, or on the other repeating sequences in which the circumambience infinitely abounds, leads to the belief that every existence has an immortal identity. This, ever by itself and for itself, is held to shape and guide its mortal formations into instances of its immortal selfhood or Thisness. Currently the preferred name for this power is "Transcendence". Its earlier alternatives were the Platonic Idea, the Aristotelian Form. Darwinism dispensed with the transcendent identity and endeavored to account for the changing formations of nature by means of give-and-take between observable sequences within, and selective influences without, the life-forms or species. It had to postulate "spontaneous variation" as an indispensable force in its account; if not its precise and certain account, still one more consonant with the facts observed and analyzed, of "the origin species." The word nowadays is "mutation" and the study of biological innovation has shifted its focus from the readily observable "form" to the molecular gene and its cellular environment. Those image currently the scenes of spontaneous variation or mutation and of natural selection. They permit a more acceptable version than hitherto of "the inheritance of acquired characteristics" and enable a certain commingling of the biological repetition of identicals or heredity, and its alteration going on. For the new biology, the past repeats while the future keeps joining and changing it; the immemorial practice of pronouncing a changing event self-same even as it changes without imaging an unchanging identity, is now philosophical and scientific sense as well as commonsense.

And so with Homo sapiens. In his *haecceitas* he is the extinction and not the fulfillment of the Hairy Ape, and such likewise is Nietzsche's Superman to Homo sapiens, who must be to Superman, Nietzsche says, what the Hairy Ape is to man—"a reproach and a burning shame". In our struggles to preserve ourselves, to survive all that we struggle against, and with all the changes which the transactions of our struggles occasion, we are each, ends-in-ourselves; our existence is our value, our value our existence. From birth we rely particularly on others of our species to reinforce and enlarge this identity of ours and they rely on us. The reciprocal reliance, its varying degrees of togetherness, from accidental nextness to compulsive massing, from familial linkings through every range of contrapuntal union and teaming-up, is either hopefully or fearfully imaged in the world's Utopias, its charters and constitutions from say, Plato's *Republic* to George Orwell's *1984*, from the Constitution of the United States to the Charter of the United Nations, from the laws of Moses or the Confucian Analects to the American Declaration of Independence or the United Nations' Universal Declaration of Human Rights. Hopefully, the images designing the future are patterned presently to alter the past; fearfully, they are patterned to secure the ongoing stretch of the present from hazards and ills to come. The union and teaming-up which we keep renewing against our ever-pressing centrifugal inward urges is the social meaning of responsibility and the social responsibility for meaning. Our reliance on this mutuality would be a feature in a fully rounded image of the free man as an end in himself in the free society.

The free society! The free society is a society of hazard, of insecurity, struggling to maintain and enlarge the union of the diverse which it constitutes by enabling unlike and like freely to come and go yet hold together amid a circumambience of configurations—such as the sciences of nature and man image as a commingling of comings-together and pullings-apart, alike among the infinitely small and the infinitely great, in sequences of unions, separations, fights, flights, and reunions. Those happenings the sciences portray and measure with their words, equations and graphs. Other members of the society feel impelled to apply their images and measurements to imputed originals in such wise as to turn the latter into means for human ends. To create them and to use them as weapons and tools and playthings are differentiae of Homo sapiens. They signalize him a mutation among animals. These weapons and tools and toys of his extend his arms and legs and diversify their roles in his struggle for survival; they add eyes to his eyes and ears to his ears, so that he can behold what by themselves his bodily eyes cannot see, hear what his bodily ears cannot hear. They bring the far near; they make the small large; they extend his horizons indefinitely. They break to *bits* and remold earth and water and air. They harness sunlight. They compact space. They compenetrate time. They heighten and diversify the sensitivities of his tongue, his palate and teeth, his hands and skin, the power of his nerves and brain[1]—in sum, of his entire body, to reach beyond the penetrable boundary he knows as his skin.

By means of the tools and toys and weapons of his invention, man's business ranges from his place and times, forward, backward and around in devious turns toward the oneness which he imagines all existences together turn toward, in one turning: the uni—verse. He is enabled to portray his own body as the compenetration of the total past of his stock, from its protozoic beginnings in a primeval slime, through its fishy, reptilic, mammalian mutations that the embryo recapitulates in the mother's womb; through the hairy ape whose residues, as he alters into the hairless one, our cultural anthropologists hunt for, sometimes come upon, and use as motifs in creating a present image of an imagined long-vanished living original struggling to preserve itself. From such creations our hunters extrapolate images shaped to still other finds that should consummate in Homo sapiens, the base and organ of whose sapiency is a new brain formation, a formation which diverges signally from the heritage of brain he believes he has from the now cousin, the ape. It is in virtue of this divergence that he is sapiens, the name-giver, the wordman, the knower whose knowledge is power.

How he comes, or is brought and held together with others of his kind—his ways of teaming up in, or fighting or fleeing from, this together-ness—are transactions. They make up the interpersonal give-and-take of which consists the interior dynamic of his group's struggle for its survival as a this-and-no-other, via its trials and errors to adapt its environment to itself or itself to its environment, hopefully without altering itself. We call the commingled transactions and their products the group's culture, its "way of life," more recently, "life style". It is what our cultural anthro-pologists seek to describe, to account for and to interpret. Not a few have even joined the simpler of such cohesive groupings with this in view, believing, perhaps often unaware, that they could understand, appraise and measure their dynamic by the works and ways of the culture they themselves were born into and grew up in—that is, the culture of that variety of Homo sapiens who in their own group knowingly struggle to keep it the final and peak consummation of the unceasing process of change, to hold it the self-sustaining *terminus ad quem* of change.

Currently there has been in evidence an active aversion from this peak consummation which our culture's established prophets and seers envision. During a generation now, strivings and strainings have recurred to turn from the engineered extensions of our sensibilities to the extended func-tioning of the sensibilities themselves, to next-to-next contacts with neighbors or strangers via all the senses, not alone via seeing and hearing and written, spoken and painted images of them, but also via touching them hand to hand, naked skin to skin, and with lips and tongue and teeth. Especially naked skin to skin. For our skins are organs whose role in our struggles to live on is unappreciated. We think of them as containers, enclosing us and cutting us off from the communication with the world

G*

around of which they are ever media, but media with functions more and more blunted and obstructed as we grow up and grow older. It is not an accident that the meanings of "feeling" and "touching" so compenetrate or that in the blind to touch and feel becomes the precise, the reliable, surrogate for seeing and understanding, so that the education of the blind is the intellectualization of touch, with an alphabet and grammar singular to itself. By means of the education of "sensitivity", humans' awareness of one another is thus to be deepened and broadened in direct perception with its full gamut of feeling. Among the troubled captains and subalteras of our military-industrial-complex the new turns have shaped up into configurations of "sensitivity training" and even "participative democracy". Less vocationally oriented persons have entered *ad hoc* gatherings or clubs or communities of which 'Esalen' may be a true or half-true sample.

Among their younger peers or their offspring the new turn is signified by "generation gap" or by "Woodstock nation" or by "Weathermen" and by "counter-culture". Negroes of their age group choose other designations for themselves, such as "Black Panthers", "Black Nation" or "Black Muslims," although they attribute their own aversions and aggressions to different causes. Puerto Ricans and Indians, even some Jews as Jews, profit from their example. All form their own companies of fight or flight. Aficionados of the counter-cultures tend to supplement the alcohol and tobacco of their elders with miscalled "consciousness-expanding" drugs such as marijuana, peyote, psylocybin, lysergic acid, in addition to the traditional opium, hemp, cocaine, heroin, or the amphetamines. Some take them as sacraments of a ritual of their counter-culture, to the rhythms of a sacred music known as "rock", the faith in which some old churches have adopted. The faith and hope of all would seem to be set upon an indeterminate image of a future all beauty, love and peace, and their aim seems to be to bring it to existence by means of an implacable war of words and deeds in the cities, in the schools and colleges; to raze the past and to build, upon a bombed, bulldozed and bloodied void they would thus restore, a new Jersualem of liberty, love, peace and plenty. The faith and works of their counter-cultures has been welcomed as "the greening of America", a greening which the alienated young of other lands, such as West Germany have emulated and even of Russia, even of Maoinated China, and of other Iron Curtain countries might well emulate.

To the knowing and sympathetic of all generations this imagery must needs seem a self-deceiving utopianism which adds one more compensatory value-system to the perennialist demonstrations that the dead live on, that the good, the right, the beautiful and the true are eternal and universal manifestations of a transcendent Necessity (to some inexorable, unaware and unconcerned, to others a divine providence knowingly shaping creation's destiny, each always and everywhere the same).

In the course of human events these current additions to history's value-systems figure like variations upon the eighteenth century image of the naked child of nature with its Edenic innocence and spontaneity, such as Rousseau glorified and Voltaire measured his contemporaries by. Its original was a European image of the American Indian and his ways and works upon his land. Christopher Columbus had been the first to claim man and land for a European monarch to be disposed of as the latter chose: the people could be enslaved, the land could be apportioned as favors or for cash or services. And Britain, France, Holland almost instantly emulated and rivalled Spain. While refugees as well as conquistadores from all those countries tended to take the natives of the Americas for likely chattels to be exploited and enslaved, the refugees took their lands for places where Europeans could at last freely and safely worship their gods as they were sure their gods commanded them to; places where rebellion against tyrants could be true obedience to the true God. Self-defined servants of God who fled enslavement of conscience by man imagined the land as like the Bibleland of Jehovah God's promise, the hopeful land of liberty and abundance. Some even believed its natives to be the lost ten tribes of the Hebrew Scriptures, while the unregenerate misbelievers were sure that somewhere in the land they would find the Fountain of Youth, and everywhere else treasure in goods and in man-power with souls they could save by making obedient Christians of them, and whose bodies they could use up by making frightened serfs or slaves of them.

By and large, in this part of the history of imperialist Christianism, the beliefs of the regenerated prevailed over those of the unregenerate. Libertarians of Europe came to take such figures as Roger Williams, as William Penn, as Benjamin Franklin for avatars and prophets of that new freedom and its power to regenerate the European breed. As the *Gazette de France* wrote of the land in 1744: "an innate taste for liberty is inseparable from the soil, the sky, the forests, the lakes which keep the new country from resembling other parts of the earth. Our seamen are persuaded that any European brought to those scenes will contract this particular characteristic". We may read into this observation an early recognition of changes in Europeans due to the land that were later identified as rendering them frontiersmen. We may imagine the land's influence reaching an apex in the profession of faith and its authors' utter commitment to it which we know as the Declaration of Independence of 1776, and in the 1787 design for embodying the faith in ways and works of living together we know as the Constitution of the United States.

The image of a free people in a free land was so different, although imputed to historical precedents, ancient and recent, as to win approval and sympathy from all sorts and conditions of Europeans, from poets like Scottish Robert Burns and English William Blake, German Wolfgang Goethe (he, in Wilhelm Meister, yearned over Robert Owens' *New Harmony*, and is reported to have remarked: "America you are better off than Europe. If I were twenty years younger I should emigrate to America"); to aristocrats like the French Marquis de LaFayette, the German Baron von Steuben, the Polish Count Pulaski. Thoughtful politicians like Edmund Burke, who believed that political liberty, free enterprise and free trade were interdependent, held that in America both could at last get a fair trial (perhaps like Siamese twins, neither could survive without the other, nor live in peace with the other). German Baron von Steuben was sure that in America any person who worked hard would prosper, for he would be free to achieve success if he had it in him.

In sum, Europeans kept in subjection and poverty under the police-power of Church and State imaged the actuality of America as opportunity for liberty, safety, plenty, much as their descendants in Europe and America together imaged the Russia of the Bolshevik,[2] and a generation later the China of the Maoist, revolutions. It is no news that disillusion followed the libertarian wishful thinking about all three. Within a generation after the American Revolution many friends of freedom came to fear that its victory in America but raised barricades to the ways of freedom. Prosperity confined and choked off liberty. Freedom of conscience, freedom of thought, of expression and communications, freedom of assembly, of protest, of demand for change, were first invoked, then misused, then contained by the freedom of enterprise with its ruthless competition practiced by the diversity of humans who came to be named capitalists. The latter were sort of biting the hand that fed it. That new man, the American, grown rich and strong, was seen as the enemy of the child of nature whom the European was believed to have been reborn as in the new land. In the course of the years, Americanization got taken to mean deterioration, not improvement; imprisonment, not liberation, "the American way," the ugly, the vulgar way which does not fulfil but kill the European's dream of America. In Charles Dickens' judgment, the works of American man only polluted the American land: "the earth", he wrote, "the air, the vegetation, and the water they drink, all teemed with deadly properties". Had not Jonathan Swift written with characteristic gusto a generation or two earlier: "I have been assured, by a very knowing American that a young healthy child, well nursed, is at a year old, the most delicious, nourishing and wholesome food"? Not much later Heinrich

Heine called America "a gigantic prison where one is chained to liberty". And in the land of freedom and opportunity itself, authentic libertarians mourned, like Ralph Waldo Emerson that "things are in the saddle and ride mankind," or like William James denounced "the bitch goddess, Success"; on the other hand, their companion in the faith, Theodore Parker, invoked loyalty to the articles of the Declaration of Independence, which he named the American Idea, the Idea of Freedom, and enmity to its opposite, the Idea of Slavery.

Of course, none of the disillusioned Europeans, not even Dickens "the uncommercial traveller" had, like LaFayette or Steuben, encountered the original they were condemning, nor had any made the circumstantial and perceptive study for which de Tocqueville's observations of Americans and their ways are celebrated. Sigmund Freud's: "America is a miscarriage", antedates his single, brief, and very confined visit. Franz Kafka's "America" is only a foreign mask of his own visage which he shaped from a succession of happenings without rhyme or reason in the experience of a young person whom his parents send across the Atlantic to rescue him from the clutches of a, to them, "unacceptable female". America, the scene of the youth's salvation, is portrayed a commingling of changes and confusions. And our *now* philosophical Jeremiah, J.P. Sartre, writes of Americans *en existentialiste*. He imagined them a people and land lacking 'any tragic element' and needing badly to suffer. Maybe he has since been gratified by the patent suffering of their bizarre imperialist criminal war to defend equal liberty in Southeast Asia from the totalitarian Communist aggression for which he and self-proclaimed Cassandra-like Bertrand Russell have tried them and infallibly found them guilty. Maybe, too, some notion of their reformation may have come to east the Existentialist conscience in the sufferings of the "average American" inflicted by youth's "counter-culture" with its paranoid violence of word and deed against "the establishment's" faith and works.

Optimally, the counter-culture's value-systems would seem to be new images of the variety devised by one or more of the religious philosophies which console true believers for the hazards and hurts of experience with ikons of a creating power and a creation that guarantee them the safety, the freedom, the health and the happiness all mankind are said to keep pursuing and never quite overtake. The sages and seers of the counter-cultures, teaching its images, prescribing its ways, strive to establish those as lasting institutions which shall be at last that which all should always have been and none ever was—shall be for Homo sapiens the *terminus ad quem*, the satisfying peak and consummation of the unceasing process of change of which his birth is but one happening and his death another.

Indeed, they might look to it as Nietzsche looked to his *Übermensch*, not the fulfillment but the extinction of Homo sapiens as he is: "What is nihilism" that sufferer cried, "but this, that we are tired, that we are tired of Man"? Or, if they prefer to sound like deterministic behaviorists instead of romantic idealists, they might echo Utopian B. F. Skinner's (is he in his own way their echo?) "to man *qua* man we readily say 'good riddance'." Unto each New Sinistral, in his manner, a Heavenly City, a non-theological Heavenly City, such as the Enlightenment challenged the theological one with!

NOTES

1. In the poem he titled *The Thinker*, Berton Braley paid a modern's tribute to the new role of the brain. The poem is one of a collection, "Songs of the Workday World" and published by Doran in 1915. Here it is:

> Back of the beating hammer
>   By which the steel is wrought,
> Back of the workshop's clamor
>   The seeker may find the thought,
> The Thought that is ever master
>   Of iron and steam and steel,
> That rises above disaster
>   And tramples it under heel!
>
> The drudge may fret and tinker
>   Or labor with dusty blows,
> But back of him stands the Thinker
>   The clear-eyed man who Knows:
> For into each plough or sabre,
>   Each piece and part and whole,
> Must go to the Brains of Labor
>   Which gives the work a soul!
>
> Back of the motors' humming,
>   Back of the belts that sing,
> Back of the hammer's drumming,
>   Back of the cranes that swing,
> There is the Eye that scans them
>   Watching through stress and strain
> There is the Mind which plans them,
>   Back of the brawn, the Brain!

Thought, thinker, brain, mind, soul—what does Homo sapiens experience them *as*, and record his experience with, if not words which outlast sequences of meanings whose multitude he compenetrates into a One—the Logos which, he keeps arguing, was in the beginning and perdures without end, so transvaluing his most efficacious organ of survival into its Alpha and Omega?

2. "I have seen Utopia and it works" (Lincoln Steffens in his *Autobiography*).

Survival as Immortality, Immortality as Experience

For, at a closer look, the true believers of the counter-culture are as impelled as their forbears whose ancestry they reject by an urge which renders the divergence of Homo sapiens from other mammals so conspicuous. Humans are aware of death, of extinction, as other animals are not. Those whose drives end in death, such as lemmings or some species of whales, are aware only of the drive, not of its exhaustion into nothing. Mankind becomes aware of the exhaustion, although none can experience it himself for himself and live to tell it. To be thus aware of his own extinction a human would need to be conscious of being unconscious, aware of being unaware, aware of existing without becoming, of existing but without a future or a past, which is the same as not existing at all.

On the other hand, every one can and does experience death as another's body become unmoving and rigidly immovable, irresponsive to any and every stimulus, impossible to help or hurt, a thing for the dissecting table, the funeral pyre, the birds and beasts of prey. Not every one any longer tends to image this cadaver, sometime the body of a person, the soma of a psyche now extinct, the work of a gaunt and bearded ancient with a scythe and hourglass, or of a jostling old hag who extinguishes the soul of every one she touches. Even William Hogarth's *Bathos* signalizing the end of the world, or the draped skeleton with the scythe, whom the medievals limned as the choreographer of the dance of death they dreaded, no longer carry the import which had inspired them. That had been the intense fear, the repulsion, which the experience of death aroused. It continues to call forth these responses however the religious serve to mitigate them; and modernly, the embalmers' art has become more and more the art of giving the corpses they prepare for the last rites, the most lifelike look possible. Perceiving the dead stark and unmasked is an experience that repels the senses and the imagination, of which feeling is the drive. The deadness it presents hits us as the terminal alienation of the unalienable.

This is what our struggles to keep on struggling aim not alone to post-

197

pone, to prevent, but above all to defeat, to nullify—not ever to be diminished to a cipher empty of meaning, empty of élan. Aiming thus, we tend to treat death's happening as if, with all our schemes and stratagems, we had *not* failed to prevent it. So far as I can remember, no culture has been described which does not image its dead as somehow living on, be it joyously in a heaven or anguished in a hell, but living on. Each has its own way of both imaging its dead and proving that they continue alive. Each mobilizes a creative Word to annul death with. And where the image, whether as written or spoken or as some other surrogate, has at last failed to hold and nourish belief, the misbelieving Wordmen—the poets, the philosophers, perhaps also the wizards and the priests—speak and write to dissipate mankind's fear of death and to provide consolations for the extinction of life.

If, however, we have been bound to our dead in friendship, or love or hate, or the togetherness and teamplay of shared causes, no consolation quite consoles. In the topology of our lives a place has been emptied where this one, no one else, could fit; and our future must needs continue this emptiness and the hurt of it, strive as we may to fill it. We live on, perhaps even more abundantly than before our loss, nevertheless with that singularity missed, a note in the orchestration of our selfhood silenced, and the silence not a rest but a break. Indeed, it may happen that the silence turns intolerable, however it be compenetrated with the ongoing validities of survival. We need our dead alive, somehow; at least we need that death should be a name for but a longer sleep—sleep, the necessary gap into which we nightly or daily lapse from waking to waking. Life, even as recollection of things past, is future eventuation, its images are not yet, but become, present perceptions, while death is simply an instant nothingness between falling asleep and waking, between living on where we are now and living on hereafter in an Afterworld.[1]

The common human need to have their dead somehow alive comes to sympathetic utterance in even the quite disillusioned and skeptical among us. I recall William James's letter to his father, when he feared the old man might die before he could see him again. At the time William was in England, his father in New England. It was a goodbye letter, in which the son also assured his father that he need have no anxieties about certain matters which had been presently troubling him. Regarding an Afterlife, in which the elder James firmly believed, William wrote: "As for the other side, and Mother, and our possibly meeting, I *can't* say anything. More than ever at this moment I feel that if that *were* true, all would be solved and justified. And it comes strangely over me in bidding you goodbye how a life is but a day and expresses mainly but a single note. It is so much like the act of bidding an ordinary Goodnight. Goodnight my sacred old Father! If I don't see you again—Farewell! a blessed farewell."

A generation later, speaking in Concord at the celebration of Ralph Emerson's centenary, James commented on the, to him, ghostlike—one might even say, ghastly—character of our remembrance of our dead. "The pathos of death is this," he said, "that when the days of one's life are ended, those days that were so crowded with business and felt so heavy in their passing, what remains of one in memory should usually be so slight a thing. The phantom of an attitude, the echo of a certain mode of thought, a few pages of print, some invention, or some victory we gained in a brief critical hour are all that can survive the best of us. It is as if the whole of man's significance had now shrunk into the phantom of an attitude, into a mere musical note or phrase suggestive of his singularity— happy are those whose singularity gives a note so clear as to be victorious over the inevitable pity of such a diminution and abridgement".

Yet to an empathic student of the record of the transactions between William James and his father, the latter, his beliefs and his ways were a much more dynamic present in William's personal history than the so piteous residues that William, in his tribute to Emerson, listed as surviving their originator and than the more durable stuffs the latter worked into things and printed words and emotional resonances which a few of the multitudes who outlived him held in mind. On the record, within the psychosomatic configuration that was Henry the Elder's eldest son, the father's diversified image perdured as when he was alive, in the orchestration of vision and action which constituted the genius of William James.[2] Diminution and abridgement of the father's image may have occurred, but the more, for all this, was the image the father's immortality, as indeed such images are the immortality also of the most celebrated of humans, whether for good or ill, whether posterity be glad that they have lived or glad that they have died. The unremembered anonymous multitudes of the dead beyond number are so utterly; for not only their personal histories but their genes have fallen apart and scattered into nothingness. The past of the remembered dead lives imaged as memory in those who remember and as their residues of thoughts and things for still others to image. Indeed, the conservation of the past even as its recreation in images may be a survival-function of memory. Insofar as remembering is nuclear to civilization, and our sciences and arts are veritably formations of its increase and its progress, they are such because they develop as memorials which exercise a survival-function in the measure that the unprecedented future penetrates their pastness and by suffusing, both changes and conserves it. Our prevailing images of immortality have been our reach toward an imaged future whose imputed original we can never grasp.

However, grasp can and does consummate reach for any who can be said to have understood and mastered the human predicament. Such a one shapes the succession of his experiences of happenings and images into an ongoing orchestration singular to himself. The orchestration constitutes his personal history and identity. Struggling in his own mode to keep on struggling, he shapes and reshapes an order which renders his life for him a life of reason, however absurd others might hold it. The shaping advances by way of his selecting images from the multitudes that come as he struggles with the world around to keep on struggling. It advances in a succession of orchestrations, inward and outward. What first and last we may intend by "creative imagination", "creative intelligence" would be the new-come images, the person's choosings between them, his orchestration of the chosen in a sequence of compenetrating acts. If, as I believe, human creativity is the species' paramount means of survival, then it works as an ongoing compenetration of image-finding, image-making, image-arranging: works, that is, as imagination and logic inseparably together, each absurd, when on its own alone. Also those who are sure this can't be so bet their lives on such workings. They identify the future which the bettors can grasp that renders reach successful.

What is grasped is not imaged as an After-life in an Otherworld. It is a future designed in images that can and do outlast their designers: in portraits, in landscapes, in buildings, in personal and interpersonal records and in their variously adequate picturings of the ways of the miscellany of mankind with one another which we name history, social science, philosophy, poetry, literature. They are the images we undertake to collect, to preserve, even to treasure, in archives, in libraries and museums, in churches and schools and other shelters where a few or multitudes—more and more, multitudes—may gather to behold, to admire, to revere, to copy, to study and to use in fields and mines and factories, in banks and arsenals, upon and within the seas and in the air. In them, the absent is somehow present and we are gladdened and grateful that their makers have lived, readier to celebrate their births than to recall their deaths. In them, the future of any culture would seem to have its perduring prologue. and not only in its imaged past. Cultures live on in that the artifacts which start them off survive their makers and become pervasive forces in a struggler's transactions with the obstructive surroundings of his own struggle to exist. All the varied configurations of a society's total economy —its creeds and codes, its weapons and tools and toys, and its styles of work and play, of war and trade and worship—are histories compacted into institutions. They began as events of a future entering a present. They changed into a presence ever passing yet never quite past, although the oncoming future kept repatterning them. Civilization as of the here-and-now is made up of such compactions and repatternings. It might be named the living past—the past ingesting the new images of its now spent and diversified once future formations, or of formations still to come, imaged spontaneously or by the repetitive art of extrapolation. Such images serve for working hypotheses, utopias or science-fiction.

Immortality as experience is civilization thus imaged. Civilization thus imaged, it is, which gives experience the original of the compensating Afterlife imagined and cherished by theologians and philosophers, rendered radiant by poets such as Dante and Blake. The image would seem to be the creation of an image-maker whose images—whatever his medium—are immediate presences, surrogates for an original, formations that othernesses keep passing into and prompting changes of the formation as they come. As such experience, immortality neither diminishes the reality of death nor translates existence out of the here-and-now we are born into, and die out of, to render it the transcendent Other Elsewhere where death is not and cannot be. Immortality as experience is the future we actually live until we die, not the future we hope to live in an Other-world after dying in this one. So perceived, immortality is our present learning of the past while the future keeps changing it; immortality is education, and education is the lifelong acquisition by one generation after another of remembrances wherewith Homo sapiens can and does overcome the oncoming hazards of the struggle to keep on struggling which is his existence. The now banal way of saying this is that living is learning, that learning is the wrestle by trial and error whereby we come to make the different into the same and the same into the different and thus to alter the past which installs the future. So imaged, immortality cannot be simply, as Aristotle thought, sons repeating in themselves the features and the figures of their fathers; it must needs be the knowledge and the knowhow of the fathers, their works and their ways, reshaped and advanced by the sons. So imaged, immortality is progress—not, that is, a life's possession of an already existing future but the life becoming of itself a new enlargement of the evergrowing past, or becoming this by way of its sanguine or anxious designs to have it so; by way of its prophetic imaginings or its scientific postulates and extrapolations from the past. With those we endeavor to route and pace the contingencies of the future's coming. We use them to institute immortality as a determination of the indeterminate that might render it a tool or a weapon of our struggle to survive. Neither postulate nor extrapolation transvalues immortality into a nullification of death. They simply pattern it to be our serene recognition of death's ongoing imminence and a bold creation of ways to avoid the nothingness we know is our unsought but unavoidable *terminus ad quem*, until at last it engulfs us in its ineluctable peace.

And not alone us humans. What price a philosophy for which all that is, was, and will be is a commingling of futures that come out of nothing, become presents that strive not to but do, become pasts soon or late to vanish as they came? In the give-and-take between quanta which we image as conservation and entropy, entropy is destiny; creation is consummated in destruction, existence begins as a struggle against extinction ending with defeat. Ultimately there is no future, no "real" immortality, no eternity other than the eternity of the nothingness which creation populates without rhyme or reason, and as laughably depopulates. If, then, Homo sapiens is merely a blind happening that begins and ends, his successes must needs, through the years of his life, turn out to have been, over and over again, variations upon his old struggles, and his entire personal history rendered a vanity of vanities, because its consummation is death. What worth can his existence have for him, what meaning can he bring it to, in a universe where only nothing lasts? What else can it amount to, save "a tale told by an idiot, full of sound and fury, signifying nothing"?

The tradition could not pay this price.

The wish for a meaning that shall survive all transient meanings has prompted Socrates' feeling that "the unexamined life" is not worth living. It has prompted the many assertions and defenses of the belief that death is transition and not termination; the perennial crusade that has been called "the quest for certainty", and the current "searches for an identity" to come to rest in, an identity that shall be always and everywhere the same and that only immortality can in fact establish. Examination, quest, search, and the imaged originals they hunt could even be appraised as diversifications of the creative élan which "wish" might be taken to signify. First and last, they could be Homo sapiens in transactions with the world of inescapable predicament which are his existence; they could, over the ages, start and continue as changing embodiments of Protagoras' observation that man is the measure of all things, of those that are that they are and those that are not, that they are not. They might be said, each in its own way to signalize the inseparability of existence from value, value from existence—a theme which has dominated the philosophies of every age we know to have produced them, and which has shaped the images of man, of nature and of their relations produced by the philosophical perennialists.

NOTES

1. Or as so many peoples of Asia believe with a firm faith, death is only the trans-migration, in the same world, of the living spirit from the body it leaves to the body it merits, and one's immortality is his living many lives and dying many deaths until, if ever, he merits body-lessness and dies a last one.

2. The need and doubt it might have been that kept James's mind open to alternatives. Wrong, remote, and improbable as they might have seemed amid the prevailing winds of doctrine of his times, they were entitled to proof or disproof by the most reliable methods of inquiry within reach. It was this openness that led James, among other things, to join the British Society for Psychical Research, to participate in a variety of seances and to judge the records with respect.

Philosophic Images
of Value and Existence
as Optimism, Pessimism, Meliorism

THE ENDEAVORS of mankind to ease the human predicament by querying the value of existence, the existence of value, have produced world-wide pictures for whose diversities three words might serve as short-hand symbols. They are Optimism, Pessimism, Meliorism. Perhaps it should go without saying that Optimism continues the most favored of the three. The various images which divergently bespeak the relations of existence and value that Optimism signifies transvalue the changes and chances of experience which we name its challenges, its hazards, its hungers, its lusts, its anxieties and fears and rages at its cruelties and sufferings—into multitudes of distorting, diluted appearances of one, unique, ineffable Reality that is the Value of Values, that is Goodness, Truth and Beauty, identically one and the same, overflowing without change or diminution into the nothingness which multiplies, distorts and dilutes its single and singular identity. The evils of experience are appearance due wholly to this nothingness, and nothing in and of themselves. They signify only in the light of the ineffable effulgence of the emanations whence comes to existence our experience of the positive values we pursue. As a whole, as the self-containing yet self-giving system of values the world, whether ready-made or ever in the making, is the best of all possible worlds.

Such is the image of existence, value and their relations which recurs with many variations from Plato's *Dialogues* to Teilhardt de Chardin's theological epic. We may even recognize a resonance of it, perhaps via Teilhardt, in the "scientific humanism" of such an authentic humanist as Sir Julian Huxley. It is a point of departure for religious philosophies, notably the *now* ones, but hardly less for any of those concerned to save mankind from the death brought into existence by its progenitor's freely choosing to sin in disobedience to the command of the ineffably good God.

This Optimist image of the dynamic of value and existence cannot be referred to an Original which it portrays, and by comparison with which its reliability as a design for human existence can be tested. It must needs be taken as itself the Original. The consequences, the meanings, of its presentation of value and existence and their configurations is to be sought first in other words interpreting those of the presentation, and in words interpreting the interpretations, until interpreters give out, and obbligato, in the deeds which the words direct or suggest or which simply flow from them. First and last the reliability of the Optimist image, as indeed of any other, can be only a measure of his faith who relies on it, and what of his life he bets on it. How Optimists practice is more convincing than what they preach. And truly convincing would be that they refrain from practice and do nothing. For nothing they could say or do could improve or spoil the best of all possible worlds. A true believer could only look with satisfaction on the course of events as they came along and like Voltaire's Dr. Pangloss confirm their perfect goodness with his logic.

The Pessimist is committed to like passivity. The Optimist's best possible world is the Pessimist's worst possible. Nothing that the latter could do or say can render it any worse or better. Transvaluing the tragic course of experience into the illusory appearances of an imagined Transcendence can in no way alter, can only confirm the evil which is the substance of experience. As I think Arthur Schopenhauer suggested, putting oneself to death, collapsing into extinction, might be a liberation from the pangs and penalties of the struggle to keep on struggling. But what can freedom mean to sheer nothingness which is utterly incapable of meaning? Not only Homo sapiens, all the infinitude of existences are in struggle to keep on struggling. Schopenhauer imaged them as Will ever unsuccessfully striving for its own nullification into the unstruggling Idea. Brahmins call the struggle Maya—its extinction Brahma, Buddhists call its extinction Nirvana, Chinese sectarians call it Tao, Europeans and Americans call it the Absolute, call it Transcendence.

But how do these namings or their alternates, magically segregating existence from value, nullifying the evil of Evil and transvaluing it into transcendent Good, free true believers from the insistent routines of the daily life, from the repeated pursuit of the commonplace assuagements of food and drink, of love and play, of labor and rest, to say nothing of the world-wide assents, submissions and obediences demanded by others to the believers' chosen rules and ways? Platonizers and true blievers in any other variety of Transcendence may give their struggles to keep on struggling an ascetic turn; they may emulate anchorites; they may form celibate companies of silence who consume their days in work and prayer, their nights in meditation upon, with perhaps an occasional image of, the transcending Value of Values which saves existence from itself. Some may freeze or starve themselves into envisioning their transcendence, others may even beat their bodies in bloody stripes, to bring on the ecstacy of the saving image. Nevertheless, the daily lives of all, although their chosen existence of deprivation and hardship and suffering continues—when compared with the existence which they, like Francis of Assisi or Ignatius Loyola, abandoned—an existence of struggle to keep on struggling, of strivings to satisfy needs which keep ever repeating, of filling voids which never stay filled, of battles which, however often victorious, must ever be resumed. They have their peers in the Yogins and Bodhisatras of India and China and Thibet and Japan; Mohandas Gandhi was one, giving his role a secular intention.

Neither the personal histories of such Optimists nor of true-believing Pessimists can be read as the explication of an innate propulsion toward a Transcendence wherein their struggles are consummated, whether as immortality or as extinction. Neither the Pessimist's despair of the future nor the Optimist's confidence, segregating existence from value as they do, much affect the event that in the struggle to live on from day to day, both act as Meliorists. They do not stop to question that human existence is a predicament of which both Tantalus in his pool and Sisyphus at the bottom of his hill might be taken for symbols or parables. In our experience not the most commonplace satisfaction we achieve endures; for our survival all our doings must be variously repeated. Unless we acquiesce in the repetitions as their own consummations, and in our struggles as their own goal. Indeed, Optimists and Pessimists, in simply living their daily lives do, like the rest of us, so take existence, meeting each fresh problem as it happens, solving it as they can, solving it with a difference as it recurs, in the matter-of-fact hope without illusion which cultural anthropologists like Levi Strauss interpret to be the survival-values for the unsophisticated miscellany of mankind.

For the philosophically sophisticated, those attitudes and actions, their imagings in words and other signs and symbols, and their manipulations with rites and rotes that range from the magic of primitive wizardry to the "science" of sending humans to the moon and beyond and bringing them back to the earth becomes the staging ground for a philosophy of Meliorism.

This philosophy sees little than can profit mankind, little that Homo sapiens can rely on in the Pessimist's despair of the future or in the Optimist's confidence. On the record of the give-and-take in the human struggle to keep on struggling, both mislead. Each presents the future as a foregone conclusion from an eternal present of which both it and the past are inalterable parts. Only, the Pessimist's eternal is an immanent impersonal necessity which nothing we may do can modify for our salvation from death and the Optimist's is a benevolent Transcendence which destines us all somehow to live on eternally unstruggling in eternal bliss. But neither system of existence and value intends a future, present and past as we actually live them, as the times which compose our personal histories and compenetrate into our identities. For both Optimism and Pessimism the lives we live out in our struggles to live on can be only self-deceptions which their eternities predestine us to make of ourselves.

In the perspectives of Meliorism, per contra, the future we experience is no preexisting part of an eternal present, nor is the past we remember such a part. In this perspective the future is not a foregone conclusion from anything. Before we experience it, we can assign it no exclusive identity; it is an undetermined event, and living it is determining it. Before we live it, we can not know whether it will be good or bad, we can not be sure of its value or existence. We can prefigure it with images which our wishing, hoping, fearing draw from our remembered past, and we can shape these anticipations as our wishing, our hoping or our fearing impel us, we can ongoingly elaborate and check their coming with images—*models* is the *now* word—shaped for cumputerization, and use them as instruments of determination, as working hypotheses. We may hopefully bet that the oncoming future will confirm our prophetic projections; or if it does not, that we may apply them to reshape it closer to fulfilling our wishes or allaying our fears. Their role in our survival is to conserve and better the *now* if it satisfies, to change it if not. Living our lives, this is the best that our most inclusive "systems" can do for us. Their vital meanings for each of us are the specific *haecceitas* of their consequences from day to day, whether in the household, on the fields, on the waters, in the mines and factories, in the shops and banks, on the battlefields, in the submarines, in the spaceships or wherever a human struggles to keep on struggling. *Solvitur ambulando*, piecemeal, problem by problem as the problems come. The vital significances of our most imposing "systems" and "systems analyses" are functions of the concrete and individual consequences of their application, not of their logical consistency or esthetic elegance. The consequences are events within the human predicament and cannot take Homo sapiens out of it. As solutions they are quite likely to engender new problems no "system" could imply, that require solutions in their turn, with none the last. Optimisms and Pessimisms imagine a last which is also and always a first: Meliorism but takes experience as it happens; aware of the survival-value of the Aristotelian precept, *ananké steinai*, it chooses for firsts and lasts what might the better serve survival than its alternatives and measures the service by its consequences, making the best of the human predicament instead of vainly purporting to transvalue it. Thus for

Meliorism, immortality is not a nullification of death but a day-to-day achievemt and celebration of life and its own sufficient reason.

As a meaningful word in the languages of philosophy, Meliorism came into use with the formation of the pragmatist interpretation of man, his world and his luck—destiny, if you prefer. The first to use Meliorism as a seminal term in philosophical discourse was, so far as I know, William James. I doubt that it has since been used as fruitfully as it might in the philosophic configurations of images of value and existence. I think this is a pity, for I believe that it orchestrates less discordantly than Optimism and Pessimism with the role of Creativity, Imagination and Logic in mankind's struggle to live on as Homo sapiens; orchestrates less discordantly than either of the others even when each is taken for itself alone. Meliorism fits at once with the common sapience of Homo sapiens that anthropologists infer, and the sophisticated knowledge and knowhow of our perhaps ominously ongoing age of the industrial-military complex. Recognizing the human predicament as a sort of Siamese twin of the human sapiency, Meliorism seeks not how to escape from it, but how so to humanize it therein as to render the value of human existence and the existence of its value bit by bit surer, freer, more satisfying. In any Meliorist context value and existence are but two perspectives of an identical orchestration. The divergence of the perspectives does not diminish, it creates, the singularity of the orchestration. But each perspective is an image which in due course develops an existence and value which characterizes itself, but not the Original it had purported to portray. Optimism and Pessimism are inferences from the portraits; Meliorism turns on the original. In the way singular to his genius, dying William James made this point in a letter (*The Letters of William James*, Vol II, pp. 344-347) he exchanged with Pessimist Henry Adams concerning the latter's measuring the value of human history by applying thereto the Second Law of Thermodynamics, the Law of Entropy, and the inescapable death of the world. I have quoted from one of them in discussing existence as value. My Melioristic last word at the eleventh hour can well be: Read all the letters. But I can't resist adding some words of my own which the singularities of our current cultural situation impel me to write. . . .

*   *   *

Optimism, Pessimism and Meliorism are valuations of existence. As formulated, Optimism and Pessimism are irreconcilable absolutes. Each images our struggles to live on, their unending succession of changes and chances, as but transient appearances of a reality eternally one and the

same utter Good or utter Evil. For the Optimist, the Good keeps transforming our hopes into infallible promises of perfect fulfillment, the Evil
keeps transforming our fears into false affirmations of inevitable defeat,
but the Good transforms them into hopeful thinking and courageous doing
bound to reshape the defeat we fear into victory at last. For the Pessimist,
the Good is the Evil which keeps embodying our fears in plangent or
resigned suffering until the suffering kills us or we kill ourselves. Optimist
and Pessimist alike image their Good and Evil as the reality at once ground
and goal of the appearances which arouse our hopes and fears. They image
each as Being which is what it is as it is without struggle, without hope,
without fear, and all Everything or all Nothing. Creations of Homo
sapiens, their images are verbal portrayals of the consummations that,
struggling for self-preservation, he hopes for or fears as the *terminus ad
quem* of his strivings to live on, in whatever place, his ever-identical Self.

It is not our lot to come to either consummation while we live, wherever
we may live. Yet most of us hold them for the struggle-free termini and
foreordained conclusions of our day-to-day strivings to preserve ourselves.
In our thinking and imaging, we take termini and conclusions for premise
of the historic proofs that we live on after we die. We argue immortality.
And the immortality we argue is personal, not collective; the Otherworld
is the individual's, not the state's, not the church's, not the family's.
Indeed, the City of God is the inversion of the City of the World: If it
is a society, it is an anarchist society where each socius lives a sovereign
soul free in its associations with other souls and unchanged by them.
Somewhere in his wisdom Homo sapiens may have argued and proved the
immortality of a society, but it has not been my luck to come upon it. For
groups—that is, for gatherings of individuals into diverse configurations
of different shapes and sizes—extinction is always in prospect, whether as
a scattering or an annihilation of their members: even paranoic Hitler
allowed his precious Reich a life-span of only a thousand years. A society's
immortality consists of the stretch of time between some legendary or
historical beginning and extinction, or of the theologian's combination
of the two, such as St. Augustine's *City of God*.

Just now all varieties of Homo sapiens are being alerted to several newer
images of collective extinction. The images overlap. They are creations out
of perceptions and experiences recorded as the new physics, the new
chemistry, the new biology, the new calculators, tools, vehicles and
weapons which the creators and developers of this new knowledge were
called upon to devise so that World War II might end in victory, whether
for authoritarian Nazism or the freer societies. That both Optimist and
Pessimist of the embattled powers each claims the end although it is only

a stoppage and not the finish, adds yet one more item to the ongoing history of experience and the Meliorist efficacy of faith and reason in mankind's struggles to live on as Homo sapiens and no other. In this struggle the form of togetherness is an experience which has changed into a memory being used as a weapon or tool. Not in use, it is a working hypothesis about which Homo sapiens the Wordman may argue or speculate.

Today, argument and speculation have their critical occasions in the challenge to human survival not only, but to all earthly life from the exponential increase of humanity and from what is believed to be its correlative economy, the military-industrial complex. Pursuing power and profits as the paramount forces of self-preservation, the leaders with authority within this complex work over the land, the water, the air of the earth, regardless of what else happens as they alter them. Their end-in-view is the greatest possible profit and power in the shortest possible time at the least possible cost.

This working over is one variety of the circle of homeostasis which each of the institutions of civilization endeavors to keep turning. Making its turns, each seeks not only to restore but to enlarge the pattern which inner processes and outer pushes and pulls tend to distort and to break up. Its homeostasis is its own way of overcoming entropy, of keeping itself the same against the forces that would render it different; of not changing, of becoming stationary without ceasing to be active. In terms of the military-industrial ecomomy however, stationary as the form of an identity growing ever larger, regardless of other consequences than this end-in-view. Such homeostasis is Cain Adamson getting fatter and fatter yet still the same Cain Adamson. Here, for instance, is Mr. M. P. Venema, the chairman of the National Association of Manufacturers declaring, so the press reported, that it "would be unthinkable" for the nation's business to forego higher profits by undertaking to prevent its poisoning of the environment and thus rendering survival ever more insecure because of ways of securing profits. It seems not to have occurred to his kind that the rival economies work from like assumptions and that the globally joint effect of their several rivalries to get the most for the least could be their own committing suicide while committing others to sickness and death. This business leader has peers in every one of the ongoing organizations and of the rivals and opponents all of which we lump together as "society", while each segregates itself and calls the others alone "society". Not merely is their homeostatic goal an image of the future which can never become a present fact; more, it is like any obsessive drug a present sinking of the realizable future toward nothingness. Aware or unaware, globally the military-industrial economy is a *now* configuration mindless of any consequence other than that immediately in view. If a creed and code were nakedly to express it, they would be: "However we despoil the land and pollute the waters, let us make money and eat and drink and breed and fight and make merry roday, for tomorrow we die. Let the people of tomorrow care for tomorrow; our care is for today."

Measured by Francis Bacon's conception that knowledge is power over nature and man in the service of an ever freer and safer survival of mankind, this theory and practice of self-preservation is as ignorant and false as any that Bacon condemned, or that the sciences reject. Its perspective of the human predicament postulates a present with little past and no future. By ignoring the consequences which their ends-in-view shut out, they keep their total economy one of scarcity, although a bona fide abundance can be made practicable. The concurrence of an exponiential growth of population with the like scientific and technological alteration of the environment from a supporting force into an ominous hazard to all life, no less than man's, cuts short the imaginable future of the terrestrial life we have come to know. Since World War II, alarms have been sounded in almost every land regarding the menace. And an intellectual here and there has been ringing his own from Malthus' day on. Currently warnings resound; programs multiply for securing Homo sapiens from the self-destruction which the power-holders of his societies—however differently they call the rationalizations of their power: democracy, communism, fascism, anarchism, capitalism, socialism—install by making power and profit the paramount motives of their cultures, and by teaching knowledge and knowhow to this end above all other ends.

The salvational counter-culture postulates a perduring equation between the number of humans struggling to preserve themselves and the goods and services they need to live on growing up without growing fat. They assume arrival, "with all deliberate speed", at a numerical boundary within which mankind may live on generation after generation without limit. They assume that by means of education and wise policing this boundary will be kept fixed. They assume a lifestyle which inverts the current rivalry in high living and fancy thinking. They assume a "stable" society whose members, John Stuart Mill said somewhere, "may be content to have it stationary before necessity compels them to it." The projectors of this *Nowhere* seem to have in mind, perhaps unaware, a true homeostatic organization of want and satisfaction that reproduces the quality and quantity of all values as they are consumed—no better and no worse, no more and no less. They imagine the world's "underdeveloped" peoples no longer taking the "developed" ones for their Joneses to keep up with—

and surpass. The news from this *Nowhere* would be that the ponderables are maintained in a "steady state", while the imponderables, the ways and works of the arts and sports and sciences engage mankind's creative powers, not circularly but spirally. Thus the historic dead-end of modern man's perversion of homeostasis, is reopened to life. His transactions with his environment cease to be the blind pursuit of profit and power heedless of the menace to survival which their attainment generates. By undertaking to prevent pollution and overpopulation by making the transactions ongoingly an end-in-view, the self's existence becomes the homeostatic constant its survival sustains, and homeostasis the perduring method of self-preservation, of not-changing in changing. This could be signalized as an immortality, not the Otherworldly immortality which theologians assert and philosophers prove, but the experiential one of living on as Homo sapiens lives on in a circumambience where he is a happening, not a goal; a transient configuration, not a consummatory figure. The image could be put to work as a Meliorist hypothesis of survival. It is more likely, however, to serve as an Optimist hypostasis into a compensatory Utopia.

Individuals, as they live out their lives from the day they are born to the day they die, live them out, even though they believe themselves Optimists or Pessimists, as Meliorists. Their strategy of survival is, aware or unaware, tantamount to George Santayana's revision of the biblical Preacher's counsel:—"The only cure for birth and death is to enjoy the interval". First and last, this is the hypothesis with which mankind work and strive, the rule for their valuations of each other and of the world which philosophers hypostatize as Good and Evil.

So what then?